MONOGRAPH PUBLISHING ON DEMAND
IMPRINT SERIES

ILLINOIS LANGUAGE AND CULTURE SERIES

A SERIES OF SCHOLARLY MONOGRAPHS
AND TRANSLATIONS ON A WIDE VARIETY
OF SUBJECTS IN THE HUMANITIES

Volume 4

EDITOR

David J. Parent, Illinois State University

Applied Literature Press
1422 Hanson Drive
Normal, Illinois 61761

ASSOCIATE EDITORS

Robert C. Conard, University of Dayton
Charles B. Harris, Illinois State University
Joseph L. Laurenti, Illinois State University
Ralph Ley, Rutgers College
Richard O. Whitcomb, Illinois State University

PHILOSOPHY

Its Mission and Its Disciplines

MICHAEL LANDMANN

Translated by David J. Parent

with a foreword by
Richard Schacht

APPLIED LITERATURE PRESS
1977

Published through the Imprint Series,
Monograph Publishing on Demand.
Produced and distributed by
University Microfilms International
Ann Arbor, Michigan 48106

A second German edition of this book has appeared
under the title *Was ist Philosophie?* (Bouvier
Verlag Herbert Grundmann, GmbH, Bonn,
Germany, 1977).

Library of Congress Cataloging in Publication Data

Landmann, Michael, 1913-
 Philosophy, its mission and its disciplines.

 (Illinois language and culture series ; v. 4)
 (Monograph publishing on demand, imprint series)
 Translation of Was ist Philosophie?
 Includes bibliographical references and index.
 1. Philosophy—Introductions. I. Title. II. Series.

BD21.L2813   100   77-23671
ISBN 0-8357-0275-8

TABLE OF CONTENTS

FOREWORD

by Richard Schacht

Recent European philosophy is known in the English-speaking world primarily in terms of the thought of leading representatives of several of the more spectacular and novel developments to have emerged in it (and against the current of the mainstreams of both the classical tradition and twentieth-century Anglo-American philosophy) since the turn of the century. Thus up until a few years ago it was commonly believed to consist primarily (setting aside the Vienna Circle) in a variety of different developments within the phenomenological movement, beginning with Husserl and culminating in a variety of diverse existential and neo-ontological phenomenologies of such figures as Sartre, Merleau-Ponty and Marcel in France, and Heidegger and Jaspers in Germany. This simplistic and narrow conception of the situation has been modified subsequently, but little more than to the extent of acknowledging the strong revival of Thomist and Marxist philosophy, and the emergence of "structuralist" philosophy in France and of "hermeneutic" philosophy and the "critical" philosophy of the Frankfurt school in Germany.

The supposition that these additions complete the picture is understandable, since few works of European philosophers not identified with one or another of these developments have found their way into English translation. In point of fact, however, this revised picture is still far from complete. It conveys the impression that what is new in recent European philosophy is exclusively a matter of one or another of the novelties indicated; that a radical break with virtually the entire classical tradition has indeed been made, the opposition of Marx, Kierkegaard and Nietzsche to it thus having carried the day as was always supposed; and that the predominant concerns of contemporary European philosophers since Husserl likewise remain no less remote from the main body of their Anglo-American counterparts than they were formerly thought to have been. This impression, however, is wrong, on all three counts. And one of the larger merits of the appearance of the present volume in English translation is that it should serve to help correct this impression.

Michael Landmann is one of a considerable number of German philosophers of stature who have remained very much within the classical tradition of philosophy from Plato and Aristotle to Kant and Hegel, even while being both sensitive to the importance of subsequent developments on the Continent and also

conversant with those on this side of the English Channel --
and who moreover have kept their distance from the above-
mentioned European philosophical fads and fashions of the
present century. They and he have had to pay a certain price
in consequence of this latter circumstance, at home as well
as abroad. But it is to their credit that they have held to
this course despite that fact. And it is our misfortune, as
well as theirs, that they have not received more attention in
the English-speaking world.

Landmann's primary interest lies in a branch of philosophical inquiry that has been the focus of yet another movement
in recent European philosophy. While not allowed to predomi-
nate in this book, his concluding chapter, entitled "Philosophical Anthropology," is devoted to it. He has much broader
concerns as well, however; and in his approach to them, he has
remained steadfastly faithful to a conception of the tasks and
procedures appropriate to philosophy that is at once more
traditional and also closer to our own than those associated
with the various more spectacular developments to which reference has been made. As the title of this book suggests, he
has here undertaken to express and elaborate this conception,
affirming and defending it in the face of old and newer doubts
concerning it and attacks upon it. And beyond this, he has
attempted to give an account of what he takes to be the major
philosophical disciplines, and to sketch in a broad and general
way his understanding of what has been and is to be said with
respect to their subjects. The book is not meant to constitute a complete and rigorously argued presentation of a system;
rather, it is intended and should be read as a concise and
general statement of Landmann's views with respect to philosophy and its central disciplines. And where objections on
specific points suggest themselves, the contentions at issue
for the most part are well within the compass of serious and
legitimate philosophical and scholarly controversy.

In any event, this book is a significant document for
anyone concerned to achieve an understanding of the condition
of philosophy in Germany at the present time. It is more than
this as well; but its publication in English could easily be
justified on these grounds alone. In Landmann's concerns --
his conception of the philosophical enterprise, his identification of the kinds of problems and issues which are central
to it, and his view of the manner in which they may most
suitably be dealt with -- his book should be a source of
encouragement to English-speaking philosophers who may previously have doubted whether sufficient common ground existed
to make possible a meaningful and fruitful philosophical dialogue between them and philosophers on the Continent.

That such common ground is discernable here is not simply

a circumstance owing to Landmann's exposure to English-
language philosophers and philosophical literature. Indeed,
readers of this book may be struck by the fact that, except
in his chapter on the philosophy of language, he neither
relies upon nor even makes more than occasional passing mention of those figures who have dominated the Anglo-American
philosophical scene since the turn of the century. The recent
philosophers to whom he refers most frequently and upon whom
he draws most extensively are primarily Central European. But
they are not, for the most part, those identified most strongly
with reaction against and radical departures from the classical tradition. Rather, they are generally those who, in one
way or another, have continued it; and it is perhaps in this
way that the common ground referred to is established.

On this common ground, however, Landmann proceeds to trace
developments and elaborate positions which differ markedly in
many particular respects from those one encounters in books
of this sort written by contemporary Anglo-American philosophers. This is only to be expected, of course, since the
recent figures taken account of in each case are largely different. But precisely for this reason, Landmann's book is of
considerable interest in yet another respect, especially in
his treatment of the various main philosophical disciplines
and their subjects. Readers who have come to have certain
rather definite expectations concerning the philosophers,
issues and approaches to them to be dealt with in such discussions, in the light of the character of the comparable recent Anglo-American philosophical literature, will undoubtedly
be rather surprised to find very little conforming to these
expectations here. Subjects broadly familiar to us are
examined, but are seen through other eyes and from perspectives different from our own.

Thus in place of a chapter on the philosophy of mind and
of action, for example, Landmann has a chapter on philosophical anthropology, in which he develops a framework for the
consideration of matters pertaining to this general domain of
philosophical inquiry diverging significantly from that to
which most English-speaking philosophers will be accustomed.
And while his chapters on such disciplines as ethics, aesthetics and metaphysics do not present one with further instances
of differing nomenclature, one does encounter in them comparable departures from the preoccupations in these areas characteristic of our own philosophical community.

Landmann thereby affords one a glimpse into a different
recent philosophical tradition that is neither linguistic-
analytical nor existential-phenomenological in orientation,
but nonetheless clearly and firmly rooted (perhaps even more
deeply than either of these others) in the history of philos-

ophy, ancient and modern. While he attempts to provide no
comprehensive and complete historical account of developments
from the Greeks onward in each such discipline, he does give
considerable attention to them, appropriating many of them
even as he subjects them to criticism and proceeds to take
account of the thought of certain more recent writers. And
the latter include numerous figures whose philosophical
importance is largely underestimated or unknown outside of
Europe, such as Georg Simmel and Wilhelm Dilthey, Nicolai
Hartmann and Ernst Bloch, and the philosophical anthropologists Max Scheler, Helmuth Plessner, Arnold Gehlen, and Erich
Rothacker.

It may strike one as not only odd but also unfortunate
that, while such men as these figure prominently in Landmann's
discussion, few recent Anglo-American philosophers are even
mentioned. But his book serves to help correct the much more
common imbalance in the opposite direction characteristic of
comparable efforts in the English-language literature. And
it also is of considerable interest because of the different
light shed on the various philosophical disciplines when they
are viewed from the perspective of a philosopher for whom such
writers, rather than those with whom we in our own provincial-
ism tend largely to be concerned, are of central importance.

In undertaking to discuss each of seven basic philosophical disciplines in a series of relatively brief chapters,
Landmann attempts something which few philosophers are willing
to try, because of the difficulty of doing anything of the
kind at all well. In the eyes of historians of philosophy
and specialists in these areas alike, as has already been
suggested, the results may leave something to be desired,
even in ways which are not inevitable. Yet it is not primarily for them that he here writes; he is aiming at a larger
audience, though one to which philosophy is no complete novelty.
And an undertaking of this sort has some merit even for members
of the former narrower audience. Without occasionally step-
ping back from involvements in the finer points of specific
problems and reflecting in a general way upon the topics to
which the three main divisions of the book are devoted, the
larger perspective required in order fruitfully to pursue
narrower lines of inquiry is easily lost. Landmann's discussion of these topics may not be definitive; but it should
prove helpful to both sorts of audience, in their attempts
on different levels to come to terms with the issues they
pose.

That this is so, despite the availability of many other
efforts along these lines, is above all owing to the fact
that he does not here simply give expression to the viewpoint
of some established and familiar orthodoxy in this matter.

His extended consideration of the relation of philosophy to
religion, science history and practical action -- stressing
both areas of contact and interdependence and also points of
difference and irreducibility -- is a most useful contribution
to the discussion of this fundamental problem in which sensible
voices are currently to be heard only too infrequently. And
his brief discussions of the various philosophical disciplines
take on a significance which transcends their considerable
intrinsic value, when they are seen as attempts to show concretely (rather than simple statements proclaiming abstractly)
that philosophy can and should be conceived as a form of
inquiry going well beyond both arid analyses of minutiae
devoid of genuine substance and human relevance, and also
cognitively problematical flights of speculation and articulations of outlooks and feelings.

The procedure Landmann generally follows in these chapters
is rather unorthodox. For the most part, he neither approaches
their subject-matters systematically by neatly identifying
sub-topics, issues, and positions which may be taken concerning them, nor resorts to straight historical exposition. He
does not simply describe and explicate, but rather identifies
certain large problems -- usually in something like the form
in which they were initially or are most naturally posed --
and then works his way through various treatments and refine-
ments of them, adopting such approaches temporarily and pro-
visionally only to move beyond them to others when their
inadequacies come to light. In this respect, his procedure
is somewhat reminiscent of Hegel's in his Phenomenology of
Spirit, rather than characteristic of historical surveys or
"problems" textbooks. And it is at least arguably a more
illuminating and rewarding one than those usually taken in
works of the latter sorts, which render an appreciation of
the development of thought in the various disciplines difficult precisely in their externally cataloging manner. Landmann attempts to draw the reader into this development, so
that it may be grasped in its internal unfolding; and his
ability to do this effectively will undoubtedly be found by
many readers to be quite impressive.

In his last chapter, however, on "philosophical anthropology," he departs from this course, and proceeds rather
more systematically. In a sense this is unfortunate; for
he might have better served the cause of enabling English-
speaking readers to comprehend the nature of this discipline
and its re tion to more familiar traditional and contemporary
lines of inquiry, had he taken the same tack in dealing with
it. However, he has in a sense already done this, at considerable length, in his Philosophical Anthropology (Philadelphia:
Westminster Press, 1974). And it would seem that he has

chosen the present occasion to set forth the outlines of the
comprehensive philosophical anthropology which it has been
his central concern over the years to develop.

In his most important earlier contribution to the literature of this discipline, Der Mensch als Schöpfer und Geschöpf
der Kultur (Man as Creator and Creature of Culture, Munich:
Reinhardt, 1961), he had already made a major effort in this
direction. In that book, however, as its title suggests, he
had been concerned primarily with the nature of human cultural
life, and thus with but one aspect of human reality -- albeit
a very large and extremely important one. Here, on the other
hand, he attempts to do justice to the whole of our distinc-
tively human nature, giving equal prominence to a large number
of traits (which he terms "anthropina") to which attention
has been drawn by a variety of philosophical anthropologists
over the past half-century.

It is his conviction that conceptions of our human nature
cast in terms of only one or a few of those "anthropina," or
attempting to construe most of them as merely derivative in
relation to one or two of them, are invariably inadequate. A
satisfactory philosophical anthropology, in his view, must
avoid any such narrowness of focus or reductive tendency. It
must acknowledge the distinctness of these traits and the
consequent complexity of human reality, even while seeking
to discern their interrelations and the larger gestalt to
which they all contribute. Indeed, he is quite prepared to
admit that even his substantial list of anthropina is only
provisional, and may eventually prove to require further
supplementation. But he is persuaded that all of the traits
identified in it must be taken into consideration, and that
there is no sound alternative to accepting the resulting
complexity of the account of human reality which emerges when
one does so.

As it stands, his list has a somewhat ad hoc air about
it, seeming to be little more than a compilation of traits
which certain other writers have hit upon or which he himself
has noticed. He recognizes this, but maintains that the
inventory he sets forth here in fact is by no means arbitrary.
Indeed, in a discussion I had with him while visiting him in
Berlin in the summer of 1975, he expressed his confidence
that he would be able to dispel this air in a future work.
The way in which he proposes to do this is to attempt to
provide something along the lines of a transcendental deduc-
tion of the various items which are only enumerated here.
Whether any such undertaking will or can prove successful
remains to be seen; but it is to be hoped that we soon will
be able to see the results of further efforts on his part
along these or related lines, for they are certain to be of

major interest [cf. Organism, Medicine and Metaphysics: Essays
in Honor of Hans Jonas on his 75th Birthday, Ed. Stuart F.
Spicker, D.Reidel: Dordrecht/ Boston, forthcoming in 1978,
which will contain Michael Landmann's "The System of Anthropina"].

In Landmann's most recent books, however, he has been
temporarily diverted from work in this area by the need he has
felt to address himself to certain tendencies in contemporary
philosophical and intellectual life -- in Europe especially,
though by no means exclusively -- which seem to threaten the
very continuation of the philosophical enterprise as we know
it and he understands it. These tendencies are associated in
Europe with "the extreme left" or radical Marxism in particular, whose adherents have recently achieved great influence
in European universities, and have made life very difficult
for traditionally-oriented scholars like Landmann.

Landmann is no reactionary thinker by any reasonable
criterion; he not only is something like a "classical liberal"
by disposition and philosophical persuasion, but also has long
had the deepest personal and intellectual attachment to the
Marxist philosopher Ernst Bloch. Yet the philosophical orientation to which he is committed has in recent years come under
strong ideological attack by the far left as a manifestation
of a form of social consciousness which is to be utterly
repudiated in the name of the revolutionary transformation of
Western society.

This experience has been deeply disconcerting to him, as
to many others like him in European academic circles; and
readers of this book will find a number of passages in the
first parts of it in which his anxieties and even pessimism
with respect to the future of responsible rational inquiry
find expression. In the atmosphere which has thus arisen, he
has found it both impossible and irresponsible simply to try
to carry on as before, with his work on his main philosophical
interests. In the first part of this book, therefore, and at
greater length in Entfremdende Vernunft (Alienatory Reason,
Stuttgart: Klett, 1975) and Anklage gegen die Vernunft (Accusa-
tions against Reason, Stuttgart: Klett, 1976), Landmann
attempts to meet and counter the dangerous challenge to non-
ideological, rational intellectual inquiry which, if triumphant,
could well mean the end of philosophy itself. It may be dis-
maying that such a task should have to be undertaken at all.
But the outcome of this fateful contest is very much in doubt;
and no efforts Landmann might make in the area of philosophical
anthropology would be to any avail, if neither he nor anyone
else stood ready to defend the larger enterprise of which this
discipline is a part in the face of the forces ranged against
it.

Viewed in this light, the present book would stand as much more than a mere reiteration of commonplaces, even if one were (wrongly, in my view) so to regard what is said about philosophy in it. Rather, it is a courageous statement of (in Jaspers' phrase) "philosophical faith." And even Landmann's discussion of the various philosophical disciplines takes on a particular significance in this setting. For it thus re-affirms them <u>as</u> central disciplines of philosophy, rather than mere relics of its outmoded past. And furthermore, together with the more general reflections preceding it, it constitutes a stock-taking of what is most significant about and in philos-ophy, which Landmann has been moved to make under the pressure of very trying circumstances.

As such, it is deserving of special notice and close attention. Stock-takings of enterprises are seldom made when their legitimacy is unchallenged and their future seems secure. And when they are made under such tranquil conditions, one's sense for the distinction between what is of major and what of lesser significance easily becomes dulled or distorted. But when an enterprise is seen to be in dire peril, one committed to it may well be moved to take stock of it in earnest, and be stimulated to acquire a sharper and more judicious eye for what matters much and what little in it.

In this book, we are confronted with a case in point. Landmann here sets forth his perception of the mission of philosophy and its disciplines, as the ordeal of his time has led him to discern and comprehend them. His perception of them may not be without gaps and defects; but it is a valuable one nonetheless. We can learn from it, and should -- not least because we would be blind to fail to recognize a kinship between his philosophical spirit and ours, and because we would be deceiving ourselves were we to suppose that no such ordeal as his could ever become our own.

University of Illinois
at Urbana-Champaign

PART I

THE PLACE OF PHILOSOPHY IN MAN'S INTELLECTUAL WORLD

CHAPTER 1

OPPONENTS OF PHILOSOPHY

There are forms of opposition to philosophy within philosophy itself.

Feuerbach, Kierkegaard and Marx believed they were opposing philosophy as such when in fact they opposed the Hegelian system, which was regarded as the culmination of all previous philosophy, both in its own estimation and in the eyes of others. In reality what they opposed was only a particular kind of philosophy. In their critique, which combined with criticism presented by the non-philosophical camp, they articulated alternate forms of philosophy. Dialectical materialism is based on Marx, existentialism on Kierkegaard.

In antiquity the Sceptics, in respectively different ways Bacon and Kant, and in our century Mauthner and Wittgenstein (by proving the dependence of our thought on natural language), as well as the sociologically colored "critique of ideology," contest not only particular theses or schools, but philosophy's claim in general. Our knowledge, according to them, is not as powerful and efficient, nor does it have as long a range as especially metaphysics had believed. Its limits must be defined much more narrowly. But all these critics are philosophers who simply no longer believe in traditional philosophy. They become the originators of new, more modest, more reflective philosophies.

The present book will first deal not with such intra-philosophical polemics but only with polemics directed against philosophy or against "the principle of philosophy" from standpoints located -- supposedly or actually -- outside philosophy.

Philosophy, though it has since ancient times ranked high in the intellectual world, is today in a state of crisis and retreat. "Uneasiness about philosophy" is widespread. In the disputes of the twenties it was still a voice to be reckoned with, but today it seems unable to provide the insights that were formerly expected of it. The sciences have developed highly refined methodologies, and the various disciplines -- mathematics and the natural sciences, psychology, sociology, political science, etc. -- theorize on their own respective foundations and investigate the bases of their specific methods and principles. Linguistics, for example, can no longer be satisfied with the old philology, nor the study of literature and art with general aesthetics. The sciences themselves have become philosophical, but by this very fact they have become

emancipated from a separate philosophy. Even general
theories are today based on individual sciences: dialectical
materialism on economics, cybernetics on physics, structuralism
on linguistics and ethnology. Enlightenment, which first
borrowed its language from philosophy, is today being more
effectively continued in practical areas of life.

But philosophy was impugned in earlier times too, indeed
from its very beginning. For it arose relatively
late in human history. And no place was, as it were, reserved
for it until its arrival. The place it claims was already
occupied by prior interpretations of the world. From its very
first appearance, therefore, philosophy appeared as a rival.
It opposed something that already existed, and its hostility
was returned in kind. Opponents of philosophy are both those
it takes up positions against (subjective genitive), and
those who, in turn, take up arms against it (objective genitive).

The Revolution of Reason and Conservatism

Philosophy replaced the magical and mythical world-view
with a less imaginative, less concrete one. It replaced the
so-called natural world-view of everyday life with one deeper,
more systematic and abstract, and better founded. By a second
effort of reason it then dethroned the ancien régime of the
earlier Enlightenment. It did this not merely by adding new
content to the already existing stock of knowledge, but by
discovering causes and backgrounds, and so opening up new
horizons and instigating a "revolution in the mode of thought"
(Kant). It thereby came into conflict with the existing
intellectual structure -- both with the truth it contained
and with its errors, which were still emotionally satisfying.
Even within philosophy itself, the Romantics, Dilthey, Bergson,
and phenomenology advocated a world-view not exclusively
rational and conceptual.

The conflict is further aggravated by the fact that philosophy is not only an interpretation of the world, but -- as
ethics -- also gives instructions on how to live. Based on
rational principles, it seeks the Utopian transformation of
society and government. Thus it finds itself opposed by the
entire older way of life, by the natural inertia of customs
and institutions and by the vested interests of the privileged
classes.

Autonomy and Heteronomy

Philosophy appeals to our own reason. It urges upon
reason the right and duty to reject traditional errors on

the basis of truth self-acquired and corroborated with the
facts. Philosophy's confidence in the individual's independent knowledge is contradicted by the community's reliance on
the "old truth," the higher truth of tradition and, in religious matters, by superior, divine wisdom, to which our feeble
reason must submit. Compared with those hallowed authorities
of truth, independent reason and the individual who relies on
it seem to be Promethean and hybrid. Especially when they
seek not only to know, but also to change conditions: by this
they disregard the "boundaries of humanity" and challenge the
powers that govern and protect us.

Thought and Action

From another perspective, philosophy seems to be purely
neutral and inoffensive: all it seeks is knowledge. But
knowledge is, by nature, often controversial, and its exclusive
quest calls forth an opposite standpoint: pragmatic interest
primarily in action. All action must, of course, be preceded
by knowledge, to plan its objectives and select its means.
But philosophy transforms this type of pragmatic, action-
related knowledge into autonomous knowledge for its own sake.
Knowledge, previously incorporated as a factor in the totality
of active life, now becomes independent. The strictly practical man considers such independence of thought a superfluous,
indeed disturbing, luxury. "Coal and iron" was a slogan used
in the nineteenth century against the aesthetic and philosophical culture of the Age of Goethe (1749-1832). Bismarck
mocked "the professors." But Marx too wanted to "abolish"
philosophy.

Practice is not limited to technology or politics.
Kierkegaard too opposed the contemplative attitude (which he
called "aesthetic") since he saw man as intended not for
contemplation but for decision, for mastering his existence.
Existentialism adopted this view: philosophy, by having us
observe ourself from the outside as an object of knowledge
and by subsuming the self under general truths and laws,
causes us to completely bypass our own full truth, the
distinctive, real individuality which nothing can take away.
"Against the philosophers" is the motto of Franz Rosenzweig's
Stern der Erlösung (Star of Salvation, 1921), mainly because
philosophy cheats man of his fear of death. In the twenties
the desire for political change as well as a revival of
Kierkegaard in dialectical theology and existentialism, i.e.,
revolution and inwardness, converged -- in common opposition
-- into what Margarete Susman has called "the exodus from
philosophy."

Speculation and Empiricism

Philosophy is seldom free of speculative or ideological factors, for its legitimate function is to penetrate beyond the observable data and its object of study is the system of categories that gives a formal framework to observation. It both can and should fill in the gaps in our knowledge and come to an overall interpretation of the world. It must weigh possibilities and prognosticate the future. But philosophy is inherently subject to decadence: it misuses its freedom, disavows its own claims, calls its hypotheses intuitions, transcends the facts not toward objective probability, but instead allows itself to be harnassed to human, all-too-human, and social interests, such as the doctrine of immortality, thus degenerating into uncontrolled wishful thinking. Therefore it is attacked by empirical and exact science, which develops a more precise, more modest style of thought. For positivism, philosophy is just an archaic preliminary stage of science and the only part of it still legitimate today is restricted to the theory of scientific principles and methods. However, many apparent opponents of philosophy are really opposed only to speculative excesses. They are scandalized by Hegel and unfamiliar with Nicolai Hartmann.

Abstraction and Concreteness

Since Plato philosophy has been seeking knowledge of the universal essence, viewing the real and particular object as only a weak reflection of the essence and therefore not worth separate attention. Thought goes further than perception. Many sciences, on the contrary, study precisely the concrete particular thing. They are based on empiricism, which we meet for the second time, here as the opponent of abstraction rather than of speculation in general. Science too rises to the universal; but its universal is not the qualitative concept but a structure involving mathematical quantity and law. The historical sciences, especially, are dedicated to insight into and contemplation of the singular and particular, which is, for them, more than something merely material and accidental. Precisely in the particular they perceive an inextricable meaning that can never be captured by generalized rational formulations and in fact volatilizes immediately on contact with them. In this they are akin to aesthetic experience, for which the particular points symbolically beyond itself. On a religious plane, Christianity opposes the universal and therefore "timeless idea" with the "unique historical event" of the life and death of Christ. Individual real life, as seen above, also struggles internally against non-discovery

of itself in the form of mistaking an idea of itself for the
real self.

The antagonism of intellectual principles can also be
traced back to the different intellectual styles of entire
nations (just as they are behind Jakob Burckhardt's "three
powers": culture, state and religion). To see the world
philosophically, to shape life and society rationally was a
discovery and achievement of the Greeks. Compared with them
the Romans lived not by theory but by tradition and for
practical political tasks. Likewise, among the Jews, traditions handed down since the patriarchs prevented independent
individual reason from gaining ascendency because these traditions were considered a divine revelation and to transmit them
was the highest commandment. In contrast with the Greeks, who
saw reality as recurrent, unhistorical and universal, the
Jews discovered the uniqueness of the historical process and
of every event in it, though for them each event is not "only"
real but also contains a message. This Biblical heritage of
the West erupts again in nominalism and leads to open conflict
with the Platonic-Aristotelian tradition in the sciences of
the modern nations, which are based on it. The particular is
the object of study of the natural sciences, for they connect
the facts no longer in a philosophical but in a mathematical
universality. Since the Age of Goethe, the human and social
sciences (Geisteswissenschaften) also have been interested
in the particular, because they see it no longer as directly
divine in a pantheistic sense. Just as philosophical reasoning deindividualizes objectivity, it also, as the bearer of
reason, which is common to all, deindividualizes its own
subject. Since the Renaissance, the modern age too has opposed
this tendency and effect of philosophy by its qualitative
individualism, its cultivation of the personality, its emphasis
on subjectivity and historicalness, and its discovery of
"existence."

Philosophy is a world power. But this world power now
stands isolated and at war with a whole phalanx of anti-
philosophical styles of life and modes of thought.

Philosophy, as can be seen, attacks and is attacked by
numerous opponents. These opponents are in part interrelated:
for instance, in the insistence on the uniqueness of history,
in research into the concrete, and in modern personal ethics,
the same principle of particularity again and again in different ways opposes philosophy's tendency to generalize. Other
opponents stand isolated; separated from the phalanx, they
frequently engage in single combat. These opponents are
unaware of their common enmity. They can gain this awareness
only -- through philosophy.

In fact, the opponents of philosophy are drawn into its

orbit by their very opposition. They declare themselves
opposed to philosophy and prove it philosophically. Moreover,
because the contrast with philosophy makes them aware of their
own difference, because philosophy forces them to reduce themselves to a principle, it transforms their structure and
becomes a part of their own substance. When Cato tried to
defend the old Roman culture against Greek influence, he could
do this only with Greek methods; a conservative way of life
was thus transformed into intellectual conservatism. The
dispute with Greek philosophy added to Christianity, a revealed
practical religion, the dimension of theology. Nominalism, in
its counterattacks on the realism of universals, has hardly
declared the "this" (Aristotle's todeti, "this-there") to be
real, when Duns Scotus transforms it into "thisness" and thus
paradoxically back into a universal. Bakunin's glorification
of action aims to be antiphilosophical and yet as such it too
is a philosophy.

  As the opponents of philosophy gain profile and clarity
only through philosophy, so philosophy in turn learns from
them and is enriched by them. From its opponents it learns
its limits and its place in the greater totality of intellectual forms. Moreover, through them it comes to know itself;
in fact, by a dialectical articulation, it becomes itself in
a fuller sense. In the mirror of the various dogmatic theories
it duplicates and develops its own problematic nature; in the
mirror of fact-bound positivism, its power of synthesis, etc.
New oppositions -- such as that of science since the beginning
of the modern age -- help it, by antithesis, to attain new
self-definition, growth, transformation.

CHAPTER 2

PHILOSOPHY AND RELIGION

Points in Common

In the gods, or in God, all religions recognize an invisible superior being above the world, who causes it and governs it and whom the world, despite all its abundance of forms, contrasts with as a unity. All metaphysics deals with the real being behind or in things, a foundation of the world that supports them from below and of which they are all shallow superficial appearances. Thus, in both cases there is a duality of spheres and a hidden truth beyond everyday appearances. In religion the objective numinosity of the gods corresponds to the subjective numinosity of the preter-terrestrial eternal soul; philosophers, likewise, attribute freedom to the mind compared with the causality of nature and they regard it as a creative wellspring. For both religion and metaphysics, determinative action is what gives meaning to the world and to life; both therefore require of man not only knowledge but also a certain mode of behavior.

This could be interpreted as stemming from their common roots or from the fact that despite their essential differences they are closely related. At any rate, they are historically often interwoven or even indistinguishably united. The religions of the Orient are philosophical, the philosophies of the West are religious. The Pythagorean brotherhood is as much a philosophical school as a religious community. Many mystics (Plotinus, Meister Ekhart) belong to both fields. to philosophy through the mental stages of the "journey of the mind to God" (Bonaventure), to religion by experience-laden unification with Him, which is then not a mere consequence of thought but results by grace in ecstasy. Philosophers designate their world foundation, their ultimate principle, their One and their Being as God (already Xenophanes); religious men designate God with philosophical terms for metaphysical being, such as the Absolute, the Infinite or the Transcendent.

Even genetically, philosophy often develops from older religion. Renegade priests, such as the Orphic cultists, invent speculative systems. Often metaphysics seems to be merely the rationalization of religious convictions. It depersonalizes the gods, but it keeps God as the highest point of unity or as a pantheistic neutral "divinity."

Indeed it even retains contents of faith but claims to reach them independently, as when Plato for instance tries in his <u>Phaido</u> to prove the immortality of the soul.

Essentially philosophy means a new effort of the mind. It originates as much in contrast with religion as in derivation from it. But because religious impulses were also at work in it and because it often could find its own form only within the already existing, imposing form of religion, it often in history gave the impression of being merely secularized religion. Therefore, the verdict of the Enlightenment against religion also applies to metaphysics. For Comte it represents the second stage of the mind after the religious one, but it still remains so entangled in religion that both then must be overcome by the "positive" stage of science. For Marx metaphysics was only the putrefaction of decaying religion. "Crypto-theology" is what Nietzsche calls it. In Hegel it is different. For him too religion and philosophy constitute two successive stages; but since for him even religion has its own historical positiveness, philosophy (which he considers the last and highest stage) does not lose its value because it is based on this prior stage. Today the two are seen as different modes of crystalization of mind. They are related to each other not as stages on the same scale but as heterogeneous types of thought. The genetic model was suggested to the evolutionistic nineteenth century only because philosophy is more recent.

As philosophy can stem from religion, merely transposing and supporting it, so an already completely independent "secular" philosophy can revert into a religion. Comte wanted to deck positivism out as a church with his mistress as the "positivistic virgin" and a new calender of saints comprised of the great discoverers and inventors. Schopenhauer assumed that his philosophy eventually would turn out to be a religion. But the most important such radical change took place in late antiquity, especially in mystical neo-Platonism, after ethics had already gained predominance in the Hellenistic systems. For Porphyry the goal of philosophy is the salvation of the soul. Proclus even calls his philosophy "theology." Therefore it is false when many histories of philosophy first treat of pagan philosophy down to the fall of Rome, then in the next chapter or volume go back a few centuries to start again with the Christian Apologists. At that time it was not yet decided that one line would die out and the other survive into the future and be continued in the Middle Ages. Kurt Schilling was more accurate in his history of philosophy when he treated the Imperial times as a single epoch and placed them as a whole under the title, "The Age of the Transcendent God."

Just as philosophy can become more like religion, the

opposite development is also possible. When Christianity came
into existence, it entered into the late Hellenistic world
that was already stamped by philosophy. As a new religion,
"to the pagans a foolish thing," it had to justify itself --
whereas the older religions could rely more exclusively on
their living traditions -- and it could do this only by philosophical means. The formation of its own dogma first took
place in the dispute with philosophy, which thus (as disputes
always do) became enriching for its own being. In the process,
philosophy was not only the opponent, but often the guide or
even the model. Nietzsche, who had learned from his friend
Franz Oberbeck that Christianity still belongs basically to
antiquity, later called it "vulgarized Platonism." This can
be true only in the sense of an internal relationship, for
Jesus himself and his whole first community knew extremely
little of philosophy. Plato's name could hardly ever have
reached their ears. On the other hand, even the earliest
Christian writings contain concepts from Greek philosophy,
like Logos at the beginning of St. John's Gospel. Proclus,
as was mentioned above, understood philosophy as theology; so
vice versa early Christianity contains schools, such as the
Apologists of the second century, for whom Christ is only the
Divine Reason that has become man, the earthly appearance of
the Idea, the solution to the questions of philosophy (Justin
Martyr). For Minucius Felix the Christians are the true
philosophers, just as the philosophers of pagan times were
already Christians. Christian Gnosticism is based completely
on this equivalence, for both philosophy and Christianity
seek to free the soul from sensuality. Clement of Alexandria
therefore considers Gnosticism as nothing else but the tradition of the apostles elevated to knowledge: it interprets the
Holy Scriptures in a higher sense. Origen went furthest in
this synthesis. A long process of self-reflection was
necessary before patristics realized once and for all that
Christianity is not philosophy.

Historical Contrasts

The relationship between faith and intellect continued to
preoccupy Scholasticism. Although it presented the problem
systematically, it actually was achieved historically --
therefore the Greeks themselves did not yet know it -- by the
fusion of two traditions: Greek philosophy and Biblical
devotion. Fides (faith) is the translation of the Hebrew
emuna (confidence) and becomes intellectualized to the meaning
"belief" only by confrontation with intellectus (knowledge).
The Greeks had no concept of "faith" in this sense. (Thus
Wilamowitz' book The Faith of the Greeks is wrong even in its

title.) Even our reason, the conciliatory school says, reaches
God, since it stems from God. It claims to prove the existence
of God from reason. Catholicism adopted this "natural theology"
of reason as a preamble of faith. There are contents of revelation such as the Trinity which remain inaccessible to reason --
God has arranged this to make faith meritorious -- and we should
relate to even the rationally comprehensible contents not only
by reason but also by faith. Faith must therefore complement
reason. On the other hand, the sectors of dogma located beyond
the range of reason are not irrational; they merely transcend
reason. Faith and reason stand in harmony, according to the
general principle that "faith does not abolish nature, but per-
fects it." Rational theology constitutes the inescapable first
stage upon which revealed theology is built.

But the synthesis of High Scholasticism breaks apart again
in nominalism under Scotus and Occam; and Siger von Brabant
proclaims the doctrine of the "twofold truth": what is theologically true does not have to be philosophically true, and
this breaks the ground for the Reformation. Catholicism,
despite Augustine's polemics against Pelagius, always retains
an element of semi-Pelagianism: by our own power and achievement, by cooperation, we advance part way toward salvation on
our own initiative. Catholicism considers man only "wounded"
by original sin: weakened but not despoiled of his "innate
nobility." The Reformation, however, holds him to be "corrup-
ted" through and through, and his entire nature darkened and
perverted. Not through one's own effort, by good works, but
only through God -- sola gratia -- can man be redeemed. This
also applies to our knowledge: for Luther and Calvin what our
ruined reason can think never attains to revelation. Only by
faith -- sola fide, in the words of the Bible -- can we be
justified. Philosophy can only make us aware that by our own
power we can never know anything about God. It was only as a
secondary development for pedagogical reasons and contrary to
Luther's hostility to reason that Melanchthon reintroduced
philosophy into the schools and so became the founder of Protestant Scholasticism, which survived until into the eighteenth
century (except only in Holland and at the University of
Göttingen which was founded in 1735 with a non-denominational
program). But philosophy never attained such importance in
Protestantism as it had in Catholicism and this had an unforeseen result: because Protestantism banned the philosophical
drive from its own church walls, a great secular philosophy
developed precisely on Protestant soil.

The Reformation revived Tertullian, who as early as 200 A.D.
had cried out to a Church that was becoming philosophical:
"Christ against Plato! Jerusalem against Athens!" and opposed
the derivation of duty from knowledge, and to whom the slogan

"I believe because it is absurd!" has been attributed, along with his medieval renewer, Peter Demian. Ancient Judaism and Catholicism had already had to save the "living" God, who is capable of such a thing as the "wrath of God," from false spiritualizations that made God into a Stoic wiseman. In a cognate spirit Pascal wrote on a slip of paper which he then always carried on his person: "God of Abraham, God of Isaac, God of Jacob, not of the philosophers and scholars!" It was a deeply Protestant instinct that led Kant to refute the proofs for the existence of God, "abolishing reason in order to make room for faith," in opposition to the rational theology of Wolff (from which however he was unable to break away himself): faith supported by proof is less internal and warm than unassisted faith. One can pray only to the living God, not to the God of thought. After Hegel (Catholic in more ways than one) had reinstated the proofs for the existence of God, Kierkegaard, coming from the same background as Kant, vented his sarcasm on them. After World War I, Karl Barth opposed nineteenth century theology from Schleiermacher to Harnack for compromising with secular scholarship. Despite its initial anti-philosophical prudishness (because it lacks the counter-balance of a rich ritualism), precisely Protestantism is most exposed to the danger of being reduced to a pious "world-view" lacking conviction and paying only lip-service to God as not only the highest being, the most real entity, but as a person, the creator of the world, the Crucified. Just as God himself is, for Demian and Scotus, not bound by the laws of reason, which would tend to limit his omnipotence and which he himself had to create, just as for Calvin he owes us no accounting about his unfathomable predestination -- "so I will it, so I command, let my will be the reason" (Luther) -- so he remains in his transcendent majesty eternally inaccessible to reason and incomprehensible. Jesus Christ, says Karl Barth, has abolished all philosophy once and for all. Here again the wisdom of the world is seen as foolishness before God (Cor.1, 20).

But Catholicism's openness to philosophy extends only to the kind of philosophy that regards itself as the "servant of theology"and obediently fulfils its auxiliary role. Philosophy is not to be an uncommitted, inventive form of thought, but only a demonstration of dogma: what it deems to be its result is in truth already predetermined by faith. Every philosophy that deviates from its doctrine is condemned by the Church, and in extreme cases if the Church has the power, it is persecuted as heresy. Giordano Bruno died at the stake (1600), Galileo in prison. Fearing the same fate, Descartes held back his book On the World. Spinoza published his works anonymously and escaped the Inquisition, which had already initia-

ted proceedings against him, only by is early death. As late
as 1864, in an encyclopedia, the Pope expressly demanded the
subjection of knowledge to faith. The same is true of other
cultural circles. Even in antiquity, which had no religious
dogma in the Christian sense, Socrates fell victim to a trial
for atheism (though this was only a pretext). The Arabs
burned the writings of their enlightenment, of Averroes and
Avicenna.

In the Middle Ages religion's verdict is directed not only
against knowledge contradictory to the content of its doctrines,
but even against knowledge having nothing to do with religion
or pursuing a different line of thought. Like magic taboos
of touch, there are also taboos of thought. A strict "ethics
of thought" in Scholasticism regulates what fields of knowledge
can and should be studied at all. It delimits the "desire to
know," which from a certain point on becomes sinful because
it dissipates the mind with a multiplicity of worldly trivia
and distracts it from God. Thomas Aquinas contrasts this
"curiosity" or "knowledge of just any truth" with "studious-
ness" which he limits to only "knowledge of the highest truth."
Roger Bacon, a precursor of the scientific, experimental
method, was thrown into prison not because of a particular
heresy but only because of his trend of research. Only the
Renaissance finally made the point that what God has considered
worth creating is worth knowing. Contradicting the inscription
said to be inscribed on the pillars of Hercules, "nec plus
ultra" (nothing more beyond), Charles V had coins stamped with
the motto "plus ultra" (more beyond). The title illustration
to Francis Bacon's Novum Organon shows a ship crossing the
pillars: like the physical globe, the intellectual globe too
will be explored.

Philosophy defends itself against suppression by religion,
which seeks to harness it to its own purposes and to rob it
of its freedom of inquiry and research (as well as against
suppression by the state, or in a broader sense by tradition
in general). It defends its rightful autonomy and thus it is
a form of enlightenment. It is so, first and foremost,
because it renounces tradition, no matter how sacred or vested
with authority, and seeks a purely rational and factual interpretation of reality. From Myth to Reason is the title James
Nestle gave to his depiction of early Greek philosophy.

Secondly, philosophy is enlightenment as a direct
critique of religion. Xenophanes in his Silloi already mocks
at the anthropomorphism of the Homeric gods. According to
Critias, a clever swindler -- a Sophist -- first converted
the masses to belief in the gods, a belief he did not himself
share, in order to render them submissive to his rule by fear.
This theory of religion originating through priestly deceit

re-emerges in the eighteenth century; this time the means of
intimidation are not the gods but the horrors of hell. For
Marx and Nietzsche, on the contrary, it is ideas of happiness
in the other world that serve the purpose of social manipulation. According to Marx, rulers indoctrinate the oppressed
with such ideas for ideological purposes so that in the hope
of future comforts they will not rebel against their hard
earthly lot. According to Nietzsche, the oppressed seek the
comfort of religion as a compensatory illusion, but together
with it they invent a new value system to inwardly undermine
the power of the rulers. Another theory holds that it was
ignorance of the natural causes of things that led men to
imagine the gods as supernatural causes. For Epicurus, the
human significance of natural science is that by teaching us
the true causes of things, it frees us from faith in and fear
of the gods. He banishes the gods, who were born of ignorance
("fear first brought the gods to the world," Lucretius) and
who inspire fear, out to the spaces between the worlds. For
Comte, religion is still a primitive, misguided physics.
Religion, he believes, begins where natural explanations (which
he unhistorically considers to be more ancient) fail. Why
does the mountain spout fire? Because demons throw it out.
Feuerbach gives his critique of religion an anthropological
turn: man projected his own, subconscious powers and qualities
into God and became aware of them only in this projection; now
it is necessary to transfer them back to man. From this,
Nietzsche and Sartre conclude that man can achieve his full
stature and freedom only by the death of God.

Essential Contradictions

But the real conflict between religion and philosophy lies
not in their content, where they run into superficial conflicts,
but in their mode of knowledge. This conflict remains unbridge-
able even where their content is identical. We already saw
this in the Protestant stance toward the proofs for the existence of God: their deficiency is not that they are false but
that they seek to deduce by argumentation something that ought
to be experienced in the soul. Religious experience takes man
down to the most fundamental strata of his being. He shudders
and trembles before the "tremendous mystery" (Rudolf Otto).
As something handed down by tradition, religion shapes man's
innermost being, as a sudden personal event it shakes and
transforms him. It is always infinitely serious (Kierkegaard).
Philosophy is, in comparison, not so much existential emotion
and subjective experience as objective knowledge gained rather
by the mind separated and detached from the totality of life.
Philosophical truth too is sought and comprehended not only

intellectually but "with the whole soul" (Plato), but compared
with religious truth it has something cerebral and sober about
it. In Thales, the first philosopher, the world originates
from something as real and commonplace as water. This philosophical sobriety is even expressed by the fact that his
disciple Anaximander is said to have written the first book in
prose. Philosophy, like religion, is even proverbially serious; but this seriousness is indirect, for the philosopher
keeps a certain internal distance from any one of his convictions and he can reproblematize it again. Philosophy's
suspension between the adherents of a position and those who
question it is thus of its very essence. Religion perseveres,
philosophy must be renewed again and again. Dogma is no part
of philosophy. Philosophy combines the deepest engagement
with critical distance.

The difference in attitudes can well be shown by a single
concept which occurs both in the New Testament and in Plato.
When the disciples found the tomb of Jesus empty and a figure
clad in white sitting in it, the text reads:"ethambethesan"
(they were astonished). A word with the same stem in Plato
means only "to be surprised," and this is the source from
which philosophy stems. It is a sign of a common factor that
language in both cases employs a cognate word. But how differently it is modified! In religion it designates a numinous
astonishment, a perplexity that brings man to the limits of
his existence. In philosophy the perplexity has paled into the
theoretical; it is de-energized and intellectualized. The
believer is faced with a miracle and a mystery; the philosopher
faces a problem. For the believer, no matter how much he knows
of his God, the mystery of God, his impenetrability to human
understanding, always remains; for the philosopher the encounter with a problem is only the first step toward analyzing
and solving it: it contains an appeal for a solution. The
goal is Democritus' athambiae, Horace's nil admirari, freedom
from astonishment.

Philosophy can even have a sense of dissatisfaction with
its own mode of knowledge: not only because its sobriety
excludes the participation of the senses, but also because its
conceptuality excludes the imagination, but most of all because
it presupposes the subject-object division and does not speak
from an original state of unity with the world. Thus, so it
is said, precisely what is not conceptually comprehensible,
the preter-objective mystery, escapes it. The Age of Goethe
(Hamann, Herder, the young Goethe, the Romantics) sought to
revive the still naturally subconscious, pre-rational and
extra-rational forces of the soul, and maintained that not
the rational clarity of our progressive age, but ancient times
which still lived from such forces had the deeper wisdom

(Schlegel, Görres, Bachofen, Klages). Religion thrives on these forces and therefore, now as always, philosophy can cause a return to religion, or also a return to art, not for its beauty but for the more essential truth it discovers (Schelling, Heidegger).

Religious knowledge is based on tradition just as religion in general is part of communal tradition and originally was an inextricable ingredient of all tradition. Many religions appeal to revelation, which is accepted as a higher criterion of truth than, especially, the opposite possibility of rational knowledge offered by philosophy. The personal experience of God, or illumination, is also considered higher. Therefore, the pious man is sure of his truth; it must be handed on unchanged. The wellspring of philosophy, however, is -- to use Descartes' expression -- the self-reliant individual's "natural light" of reason. It does not desire merely to profess a truth, but to perceive it; it wants to see for itself and to check truth against reality by its own power. Thus truth becomes more variable. Since it proceeded from reason, reason can also reject it again and replace it by a new truth. As the religious man subjects his mind without question to old sanctioned wisdom, he also subordinates his actions to ancient traditional forms. He trusts in the guidance of a higher power. Philosophy, on the contrary, sets man free under the responsibility of reason. It enjoins him to shape his own life and change the world on his own initiative and according to principles he discovers for himself. To religion, both things, to want to know by one's own reason and to act according to it, seem presumptuous and arbitrary. To religion, the delusion of the self-redeemer, relying more on himself than on grace, seems to contradict the weakness of human wisdom (ingenii limites) and the destined boundaries of our planning and action.

Both religion and philosophy know of doubt. But doubts are a temptation for the religious man and he prays to be preserved from them. If they do molest him, God removes them by giving him renewed certainty. Descartes, however, makes a special quest of doubt. No content of knowledge from one's own experience or from tradition can be accepted unexamined; each point of knowledge must pass again and again through the turngate of doubt. It passes only by showing concepts known clearly and distinctly. In religion, however, doubt results only in a subjective "rebirth" of the believer. He is now doubly convinced of his previous knowledge. But in philosophy doubt changes the knowledge itself and raises it to a higher level.

Like the religious man's relationship with his God, which reaches deeper layers of the soul, religion was originally

never just a matter of knowledge or "faith" but it was enclosed
in action and behavior: Robertson Smith saw cult, and Friedrich Heiler prayer, as the germ-cells of religion. In part
religion is life in and with God, but it also ordains the
mores of an entire community. Philosophy too -- in ethics
and Utopian politics -- strives to shape reality, but firstly
not all philosophical disciplines do this, and secondly even
for those that do, whether their findings are applied remains
secondary. As branches of philosophy they place theory ahead
of practice. Philosophy is neutral as to practice; it is
characterized by its more exclusive emphasis on knowledge.

In an interdisciplinary Berlin lecture "Thought and Faith"
(Winter 1963/64), the theologican Gollwitzer stated that
philosophy is compatible with religion. As an expression of
the finiteness of man, it continues to exist after faith has
taken hold of man. It loses its ultimate seriousness, but it
is not necessarily eliminated. On the other hand, Weischedel,
representing the philosophical point of view, said that philosophy must radically question being, meaning, and even the
questioner's very existence. Faith transforms existence; it
re-determines it from a different basic experience of reality.
Therefore, in a believer, thought has lost its urgency; it no
longer thinks toward an answer but from an answer and is
therefore no longer genuine philosophical thought. There is
no such thing as "assured questioning." Philosophy on the
basis of religious confession is a contradiction.

The most impressive religious attack on philosophy was
made by Kierkegaard. With an immoderation which only our
century was willing to listen to, he accused Hegel, as did the
aged Schelling, whose Berlin lectures Kierkegaard had heard,
of overlooking the reality of God as reality, for God too was
for Hegel only a concept of general speculation. One can and
should know of God not as one knows theoretical contents of
thought, but in fear and trembling, in love and confidence.
It is not enough to lecture on Christ's doctrine as a system
proposed 1800 years ago, but one must become "contemporary"
to it. We discover what God is, not as subjects of knowledge
but only as concrete individuals. No one else can do this
for us. As Hegel transforms God into a concept, and so misses
him completely, he has in his "world-historical distraction"
forgotten what it means "to be a man! not man in general, but
that you and I, each one for himself, are men." Hegel reduces
man also into a representative of an idea and so fails to see
that man always exists as a specific and singular individual.
The category of singularity is not one among others, but the
characteristic determination of reality. Kierkegaard called
himself "that individual." Only the individual as such can
acquire a relationship to God and in him his own full relig-

ious existence. As soon as one speaks of this experience, however, it is transformed into a generality because all our concepts are just that: general concepts; only by "indirect communication" can we "call attention" to it and lead someone else to follow us in performing this "double reflection."

Kierkegaard seeks to remind the speculative person who understands everything, including the Christian message, as a mere object of knowledge of no direct concern to himself, who thinks as if there were "no thinker," that the genuine religious figures, Abraham and Job, did not abstract from themselves, did not consider themselves "in the light of eternity" in Spinoza's manner. They did not contemplate, they acted and suffered. They endured the divine mission, the divine test from within. Religion is akin to literature in this, for it too has no use for contemplators but only for heroes and lovers. When the scientific quest for objectivity and the concomitant stoic ethic require us to replace passion with cool indifference, each in its own way asks us to overcome subjectivity in ourselves; but, for Kierkegaard, this applies only to subjectivity in the sense of unusual self-seeking; in essentials we should, on the contrary, start from the subject we already are and become a still fuller subject; we should become, precisely, subjective. The thinker who not only speculates but also lives thinks of everything "with infinite interest" with reference to himself. So he discovers himself, while the speculator loses sight of himself and his destiny. Man must repeatedly choose between these two forms of existence.

Existentialism will later extend this line of reasoning in a still more secular way with its appeal to help one's real self make a breakthrough, to rise again and again out of the rut of the loss of self in which we wait out our existence, and to attain our true nature. Only by plunging deep into our interior can we have perceptual knowledge of being (Heidegger) or read the signals of transcendence (Jaspers).

CHAPTER 3

PHILOSOPHY AND PRACTICAL ACTION

Both philosophy and religion are interpretations of the
world as well as manifestations of life. The contest between
them draws its sharpness but also its fertility from this.
They are angry sisters who again and again have something to
say to one another because they are, after all, related. They
can go a way together and fight battles in common self-defense.
The enmity between philosophy and practical action does not
result from affinity between them, but because they are
strangers. They have nothing in common.

Theoretical and Practical Knowledge

In Herodotus' famous scene in which he has the Athenian
Solon, one of the seven wise men, on his voyages, spend some
time as a guest of the wealthy Lydian King Croesus, Croesus
says to Solon that he has heard that Solon "in search of wisdom" (philosopheon) has traveled in many lands "only for the
sake of knowledge" (theoriaes heineken). Clearly Herodotus
is here voicing the astonishment of the Oriental to whom such
a thing was unfamiliar; Herodotus himself at times probably
encountered a similar astonishment on his voyages of discovery.
Indirectly it also voices the pride of the Greek who knows
that his people excel other nations in this theoretical
attitude.
Compared with the animals, however, an extra measure of
impractical knowledge is characteristic of man even in his
natural structure. His practice never proceeds "directly."
It develops its course by way of knowledge and planning. But
the Greeks were the first to cultivate, expand and refine this
natural anthropine tendency above all else. They made it
independent as a force by itself in contrast with the merely
practical. They elevated it to a special discipline committed
only to the value of truth and assigned to it the cultural
areas of philosophy and science. It is no contradiction that
something already present from the first later turns out to
be only a seed that was to grow, that a tendency can be
intensified and become more than what it first contained.
Theoretical anthropology and theoretical history of culture
coexist and cooperate.
That the timeless seed grows to fullness in history was
Aristotle's way of thinking (though he knew only the develop-

ment of a pre-formed essence, not its historical enrichment and transformation). He says, for instance, that tragedy acquired its intrinsic telos (end, goal, completion) only late. The same is true of the power of knowledge. On the one hand, Aristotle's Metaphysics begins with the famous sentence: "All men by nature strive for knowledge." In fact, not for merely practical knowledge. All men feel pleasure, for instance, in the perceptions of the senses. Yet, as Aristotle says a little later, the first men do not yet ask such questions as "Why?" or "Of what nature?" This happens only after enough inventions that facilitate external existence have been made, i.e., after men, because of a certain ease and pleasantness of life, are no longer constantly hard-pressed by care for their basic daily needs. It first happens in the priestly class, because they have leisure. Basing himself on Democritus' naturalistic theory of culture, Aristotle distinguishes between the older technai (arts, crafts, applied sciences), which are still subject to the external purpose of making useful things and the more recent philosophy (which then included physics and mathematics) as "unnecessary" knowledge or theory with a purpose of its own, namely to comprehend being "as itself." Of all the arts, philosophy is the only "free" one, not only because it helps us to live but because it obtains for us "the good life." All sciences, so he says, are more necessary than philosophy, but none has greater dignity (necessariores omnes, nulla dignior).

A critical objection to Aristotle's statement must however be raised: in its own fashion early mankind too had answered metaphysical questions -- they are psychologically inevitable -- by the magical, mythical and traditional world-views immanent in its languages. Metaphysics appears only later in history as an independent field of investigation and knowledge and the professionional metaphysician as a specialist who dedicates his life to this field.

The two-phase model of knowledge first limited to the practical, then followed by a higher, less practical knowledge recurs in a completely changed form in Marx: as long as a class society exists, it produces only ideologists whose purpose is to defend the power position of the ruling class; religion, by its promises of an afterlife, and metaphysics, by giving first priority to an eternally static being, sanction the existing hierarchal conditions, and all other modes of thought also are subject to "ideological suspicion." Only after a classless society has been established can this knowledge-hampering prehistory give way to an age of the pure knowledge of truth. While for Aristotle the second phase has begun long ago, for Marx it still lies in the future. Schopenhauer, who also is a superstructure/substructure theoretician, makes a similar distinction, namely between intellect exclusively at the service of the will and intellect as the pure metaphysical and aesthetic "world-eye" that has broken free of servile subjection to the will; however he does not divide them into two phases of history, but has them always coexist in two different types of persons, the ordinary man and the genius.

Plato and Aristotle see the mind as a guest on earth like a stranger from higher regions. The body with its needs only draws man away from the truth. Man is by nature oriented not to the real but to the ideal (also called noetic, intelligible). Man first discovers his destiny when he finds the ideal behind and above reality. Practical knowledge is only a preliminary, lower level of real knowledge. Modern pragmatism, on the contrary, assigns a place to the mind within the context of life from the first and essentially -- in this way it is a form of naturalism. Pragmatism denies the existence of any criterion in us by which we could, for undiscoverable reasons, judge such a thing as pure truth. All our understanding of the world has, rather, the sole task of orientating our actions, of guiding and facilitating them. The data of our knowledge originate "in the molds" (Bergson) of our practical necessities. Thought is only "the dream of action." Truth is not adequation of the intellect to the object, but must be defined as something biologically useful (to which we must object with the question whether it cannot perform its service to life only if it also contains an element of adequation).

Compared with this, Schopenhauer's and Marx's analyses of practical knowledge make them precursors of pragmatism. But they are only semipragmatists, for both hold to the classical concept of truth, both distinguish between two forms of knowledge (one conditioned by practice and one remote from practice) and both expect the real and higher truth only in the latter. Only this type of truth has their approval (whereas Nietzsche, on the contrary, advocates precisely the beneficial errors, the life-preserving strong delusions and myths).

Bergson and Scheler (as contrasted later with the more radical Karl Mannheim) are also only semipragmatists, for in addition to practice-conditioned falsifications, Bergson recognizes an intuition that in the face of physical time (temps) grasps the continuum of duration (durée), and Scheler a view of essence that grasps the truth of things in the material data and stems, according to him, in its humility and love, from a completely different theoretical primary emotion than dominance-oriented knowledge. But both (following the process again of Marx and Nietzsche) now apply the theory of pragmatism, of which they leave only its metaphysics untouched, to that effort of knowledge which since the beginning of the

modern era has, in rivalry with philosophy, claimed the exclusive capacity to reveal truth, namely natural science.

Despite the great practical utility of the natural sciences,
of mathematics and physics for mechanical technology, of chemistry for agriculture and medicine -- which is why business
and government have promoted them -- the self-image of modern
science is that it too, like philosophy in the tradition of
Greco-Roman antiquity, consists of self-purposeful theory
concerned only with research into truth for its own sake. It
regards practice based on science as external to science
itself and as merely a secondary, though useful, application
of the pure knowledge of nature which is the exclusive quest
of science. To this, Bergson and Scheler answered: it is
incontestable that the individual scientist, according to his
personal conviction, is concerned only with the truth (actually
in the early modern era only Leonardo da Vinci and Leibniz
were interested in technology); yet, behind the whole trend
of knowledge of modern natural science, though the individual
scientist need not be aware of it, stands a will to power and
domination. For why does it "spacialize" (Bergson) what is
fluid, transform qualities into quantities, break down continua
and forms into elements? Because this reduces everything to a
transposable particle of mass that can be classified and manipulated. Even when its findings are true, they still are not
truth for its own sake, but for its applicability. It is only
one segment of truth among others, artificially prepared for
its usefulness, an abbreviation, a coarsening. Mechanism
falsifies nature in order to subject it to manipulation. In
opposition to the whole nineteenth century, to both positivism
and neo-Kantianism, Bergson and Scheler no longer believed in
science. Since science was born from practice, it must, so
they think, be untrue. Against the background of this mystical
romantic dream, Ernst Bloch revived the theory that a different person would perceive a different nature; the better the
person, the truer the perception. Actually one could argue
the other way around: that truth must withstand the test of
practice is a controlling factor to keep it in line with objectivity, while intuition and contemplation of essences can
far more easily fall prey to fantasy and wishful thinking.

Every form of practical action is based on knowledge. The
Greeks have the term "techne" (art, craft, applied science)
for this interlocking of knowledge and skill. Aristotle
illustrates the difference between the two forms of knowledge
by this example: a medical practitioner also has successes;
in fact the scientifically schooled physician is often
inferior to him in experience and in individual treatments.
Still he is superior to him as a type, for only he knows the
general (katholou) context and the cause (dioti). He knows

not only: "this helped once, therefore perhaps it will help
again," but he knows why he selects a certain treatment and
why it must cause a certain effect. He not only observes
from the outside whether a medicine happens to succeed or not,
but he studies the nature of the body, its laws and causality;
on this scientific basis he discovers new and better treatments.
Yet he does not study the nature of the body only as a general
theoretical biologist does, to enrich science by further insights, nor is the medical application of these insights only
an unintentional side-effect of his study. Rather he is moved
by the same interest as the practitioner has, namely to heal,
but his interest does not hope to proceed directly to action,
it goes a roundabout way and first acquires a deeper and more
general knowledge, which is, as such, really practice-neutral,
though it is sought only with future practice in mind.

     This quest for knowledge became independent for the Greeks
in a Wundtian "heterogeny of purposes," just as in cultural
history former means became autonomous purposes in themselves.
By a division of labor conditioned by temperament and effici-
ency, one man can be the theoretician, while another puts his
findings into practice. The mind can also study areas the
knowledge of which is of absolutely no relevancy, at least as
far as is currently known. Then the desire for knowledge is
no longer a clever tactic of practice in order to become
better practice -- like Hobbes' "enlightened self-interest,"
which   behaves   altruistically only in appearance -- but
an independent self-promoting force. Truth is discovered to
be an absolute value and need. Only in its service do we find
the nobility of the theoretical attitude" (Freyer), as Aristo-
totle has described it in an unforgettable chapter of the
tenth book of the Nichomachean Ethics and praised it as participation in the blessedness of the Immortals (athanatizein).
Democritus said he would be willing to give up the throne of
Persia for one single mathematical truth.

     But by the end of the fourth century B.C., the Hellenis-
tic systems had put philosophy in the service of ethics, just
as later, in the Christian era, it had to serve theology.
After the Renaissance and the Enlightenment had freed it again
from such tutelage, in this sense a repetition of the action
of the Greeks, the pendulum is now swinging back again today.
Even the three great outsiders of the nineteenth century,
Kierkegaard, Marx and Nietzsche, for various motives, no longer
represent the ethic of knowledge. Their seed has blossomed
forth in our times as existentialism, historical materialism,
and behaviorism. Even the historian today no longer seeks,
like Ranke, to extinguish his personality in order to attain
pure knowledge of the past, but he draws history into a
relevant "dialogue" with the present. Thus, for a second

time "knowledge for its own sake" is being lost to an external will. In world history, the moment of unpurposeful theory always seems to be very brief.

The historical transformations of theory are, however, based not only on misunderstanding and usurpations by its opponents; they are in part also motivated from within theory itself. Aristotle accepted only one ideal. He did not see that even behind theory which seeks to be and sees itself as just theory, other interests can nonetheless be at work within the total structure of a historical situation and constitute its unreflected preconditions that determine its direction and its theses. Oswald Spengler spoke of the dependence even of mathematics on the shifting "ideas of destiny" of great cultures, though the preliminary decisions which he held to have always been made in advance by the culture as a whole were not based primarily on interest, but were metaphysical. Aristotle, however, made the further error of overstylizing theory and practice as pure types and therefore contrasting them too sharply. He isolated pure theory, which is only a peak, from knowledge gained by and for practical action. Nietzsche and Scheler, and also Rothacker, pointed to the important heuristic function of pragmatic interest for dis- covering the very existence of an area of reality. Practical requirements have always been the stimulus for discoveries which could not have been made otherwise. Today not only scientific physics, chemistry and biology discover knowledge, which is then applied by technology, but the research labora- tories of industry, which as such have only the practical assignment of making inventions, also strike upon contexts and principles of a more general kind. Thus the two things interpenetrate and can hardly be separated anymore.

Two developments are responsible for eliminating the former radical separation of theory and practice. First, the common discovery of historical materialism and of the "bour- geois" thinkers that even apparently isolated theory can be interest-conditioned. A theory is not necessarily wrong because pragmatic interests are hidden behind it. It can still countercheck itself by the criterion of objectivity. For Marx, social reality is only a precondition, not, as for Engels, the constituent of knowledge. Scepticism as to truth, on the one hand, and the will of the party, on the other, can cause a theory to be exclusively interest-bound. The only concern then is to subordinate it to the right interests. This model, if it were not being proclaimed to a liberal world as a corrective but were implemented in its full political implica- tions and imposed by a world police force, would denature philosophy to a mere instrument in the hands of the mighty.

Secondly, theory itself has changed in the course of

history. In antiquity, philosophy was carried on in part as
reflection on the eternal principles beyond the practices of
life, and in part it merely systematized and established norms
for an already existent practice -- as Aristotle, for instance,
did in writing his poetics and rhetoric. In contrast,
modern science, and increasingly also economics, political
science and sociology, by their rational point of departure,
put practice on a new foundation and change it. Today even
the practitioner no longer acquires his knowledge as formerly
in the professions and the arts, for these too have become
scientific and are based on a mode of seeing that only science
can communicate. Therefore today theory also has to reflect
on its link with practice, which it always in fact did involve,
and to become aware of its "social mission." If it is, as
Comte established, prognosticatory knowledge (savoir pour
prévoir), then it should not pretend to be pure knowledge,
but should accept prognostication as part of its self-image.
As justified as this demand is, it contains the danger of
exaggeration, so that because of its practical or political
purpose science would lose its necessary theoretical dimension and consequently its freedom.

The same danger can be seen on the pedagogical level in
the organization of the university. Traditionally the university professor transmits his science. He is not concerned
with how his students will later apply the knowledge they have
acquired. This is true even where future practice consists
only in transmitting what was learned. Hence the frequent
complaint that science is carried on in the university in an
ivory tower, that it drags along a lot of useless ballast,
that the personal research preference of the professors is
dominant, that the gap between them and their function in
life is too great. This complaint leads, on the one hand, to
necessary reforms (e.g., Gothic has been dropped as a requirement for German studies); yet on the other hand one ought not
to believe it completely. For the university stands between
the two poles of professional training and science. Therefore
it must always allow room also for sciences that have no
practical application (Byzantine studies), and for non-pragma-
tic studies within every science. Occupational training
through science means precisely that not mere techniques, but
fundamental principles are learned (and these ought not to
be confused with programs of "general education," (cf. Scheler
and Schelsky); between these fundamental principles and one's
profession there always remains a gap which must be bridged
by each individual. If the university gives up this scientific
claim, then it not only ceases to be a university and becomes
a technical institute while research emigrates to the academies,
but it fails, as has already been recognized in the United

States, even in its specific pedagogical assignment: the mere
technicians it trains are less skilled than scholars who can
fall back at all times on their theoretical surplus knowledge,
complement it meaningfully, and apply it anew in changing
situations.

Contemplative Life and Active Life

Independently of whether theory results in practical consequences in the world, the theorist himself often displays a
certain external behavior. In the popular mind a philosopher
is not only a person who makes wise general pronouncements
about life but also anyone who displays introverted and reflective demeanor. In fact it has even been said jokingly of the
marabus (or hermit-birds) that when they stand there for hours
apparently rapt in deep contemplation, these birds remind one
of philosophers. Most men are extroverts: they observe the
world around them, are interested in it, and react appropriate-
ly to the momentary situation. The introvert, on the other
hand, clings to far-fetched ideas, is preoccupied with his
own problems and therefore pays little attention to the world
around him and has a bewildering effect on it, and that is
expressed in the word "philosopher" which connotes fear of the
person with a deeper temperament but also good-natured mockery
of the odd fellow. This mockery can become quite aggressive
when the philosopher's pensiveness and eccentricity disturb
events around him and he thus becomes a threat to himself.
Once when I was crossing a square lost in thought and not
paying attention to the traffic someone yelled from the
driver's seat of a beer-truck: "Hey you, philosopher!" The
idea is widespread that the philosopher is remote from reality
and necessarily a failure in practical matters.
   None other than Plato once said, in the so-called "Episode"
of his Theaetetus, where the philosopher's unfamiliarity with
the world as seen in caricature by the outsider is described:
the philosopher doesn't even know the way to market, he doesn't
know the prices of merchandize, he doesn't know whether they
are sold by the piece or by the weight, he doesn't know where
the courthouse or the city hall are, doesn't participate in
political life, has no idea how people relate to one another
and when someone boasts of his prominent family background and
claims that his twenty-fifth ancestor was Heracles, that makes
no impression on the philosopher, for he says to himself that
the fiftieth back from him was also just a man, whoever he may
have been. For all these reasons the philosopher is awkward
in reality and easy to deceive. The description climaxes in
the anecdote about Thales of Milet who, wandering along gazing
at the stars, fell into a well. A Thracian maid mocked him

for that: he saw what was above him, but he didn't see what
was right at his feet. "The laughter of the Thracian maiden
is immortal" (Nietzsche).

That Plato allows for such an image of the philosopher
has autobiographical reasons. While he was writing the dialogue after the death of Dionysios I, he received the invitation of Dionysios II and his friend Dion to travel for the
second time to Syracuse, where Plato hoped to turn his political ideas into fact. Then Plato asked himself: should I
accept the invitation, am I as a philosopher at all suited to
playing a direct role in politics? The "Episode" is a crystalization of his hesitancy. Plato takes the caricature of the
philosopher's image quite seriously. There is a trace of
truth in it. But at the same time he knows that to be a
stranger on earth and in the face of daily tasks is only a
superficial aspect and converse side of the philosopher's
role. The philosopher lacks knowledge of this world simply
because his thoughts are directed to the eternal world beyond,
and it is the higher and truer one.

That Plato in his Theaetetus can also see philosophy
through the eyes of his contemnors is nothing unusual or new
for him. Since his youth he had always postponed taking an
active part in Athenian politics as would have befitted the
tradition of his patrician family. His motive was that he
did not want to associate with those who had executed his
teacher Socrates. More basically: even the most famous states-
men cannot account for their activity (logon didonai), and in
this they are similar to the poets whom Plato also rejects;
they cannot, as the Socratic principle requires, trace it back
to rational principles. Socrates has ruined Plato, so his
family argued; philosophy has made him insubordinate to the
state, he must be re-educated. The exponent of this opinion
was Plato's half-brother Demos, and he is the one concealed
behind the figure of Callicles in Gorgias. Maliciously,
Socrates says of him that he and three companions of the same
age had reflected up to what point one ought to philosophize,
and they had mutually given themselves the advice not to get
too involved in philosophy lest they become excessively wise
and be plunged to their ruin. Philosophy, according to Callicles' thesis, is not only useless but harmful, for it makes
a man unsuitable for action by oversharpening his ethical
sense. It is praiseworthy to study philosophy in one's youth;
but an adult doing so makes himself ridiculous. "He ends up
spending the rest of his life whispering in a corner with
three or four cronies." Instead of philosophizing, he recom-
mends, Socrates ought to practice the beautiful art of deeds
(eumousia pragmaton). With these last words Plato is quoting
Euripides' Antiope, in which one of two brothers, Amphion,

praises the advantages of the practical and the other brother
the advantages of theoretical life. Since then this contrast.
has been a _topos_ of ancient literature. Aristotle,too, in
the passage cited above, contrasts theoretical life with the
practical one (as well as with that of pleasure): man must
make his choice between these forms of life (this had also
been a Platonic and before that a Sophistic _motif_). Among
Aristotle's students, Theophrastus defended the theoretical
life against Dikaiarch who, contrary to his teacher, gave a
higher value to life in earlier times which was completely
filled with activity. Only through Dikaiarch, who wrote a
cultural history of Greece, have many of the anecdotes which
report of the worldly awareness of the wisemen been channeled
into the bedstream of tradition.

The struggle within philosophy is, however, only a reflection of the struggle between the world and philosophy. Like
religious persecution of philosophy, there is a state persecution. Because of their traditional and practical politics the
old Romans at first opposed Greek philosophy as superfluous
brooding, meeting no real need of life (they preferred their
own rhetoric, from which the forensic and political orator
can learn). Epicureans were expelled from Rome because unlike
the Stoics who approved state office as a challenge worth
accepting they proclaimed renunciation of public life and a
retreat to private existence (_lathe biosas_ -- "he lived well
who hid well"). Thousands of years later the Enlighteners of
the eighteenth century had to contend with censorship and
often were thrown into prison. When the French Revolution
executed Lavoisier in 1794, its answer to the reproach that
he was an important chemist was: "We have no need of learned
men!" Lenin's pithy statement could be placed alongside that:
"The immediate purpose of science is to provide a slogan
suitable for the struggle."

In addition to this opposition from politicians, there is
in modern times also a Romantic animosity on behalf of "life."
In the eyes of Romanticism, the awareness, in its philosophical, conceptual and analytical late form, does not even attain
its most essential goal, namely deepest knowledge. It weakens
and cripples us, for complete understanding implies not only
complete forgiveness but also the inability to muster the
nonchalance, or more radically, the "unscrupulosity," necessary
for action. This causes us, like Hamlet, to miss the right
moment. Besides crippling action by immediately dissecting
every internal feeling and setting it off at an observable
distance, awareness robs us of the immediacy, the innocence,
the vitality of life itself, and can even drive us to our
death, as Jean Paul depicts it in his _Roquairol_. In the
special form called historicism it even relativizes our models

and values and so makes us into epigonal and unproductive late-
comers (Nietzsche therefore held science and wisdom to be engaged in a "struggle"). But even for Goethe, Faust's higher
apprenticeship begins only after he has passed beyond all
science and cast himself into the whirlpool of events. Character can be developed only creatively (and Goethe also
approves partiality to it). Formerly philosophy had to prove
itself and survive in world conditions of mere practicality.
But after the success of the Enlightenment had revealed its
dangers and limitations, the following generation rediscovered
the wisdom of the pre-Enlightenment, though now on a more
conscious plane.

Such problematizations of the philosopher's life and
activity certainly give him cause for reflection. But he
should not let them destroy his faith in himself completely.
Immediacy and proximity familiarize one with things, but they
also foreshorten perspective. In antiquity Heraclitus
expressed contempt for the many who have eyes and see not,
because the world Logos remains hidden from their sight.
Often the outsider discovers something that routine-locked
specialists have failed to see; indeed, being an outsider
can in practice be the very condition that frees the view
for fundamental principles and total contexts. The essence
of one's reality, which is still hidden as one experiences
it, is manifested only to the memory, as Hegel applies this
principle in his philosophy of history (cf. Proust and
Benjamin). Historical distance further magnifies contemplative distance.

Progress made by the contemplative man may later be of
advantage to the man of action. That awareness reduces
security and fragmentates vitality is, the philosopher will
answer, only its negative side and a symptom of its atrophy.
Every opportunity contains a danger, but one must see both
sides. The more primary form of awareness opens new goals
for man, helps him find the means for their realization and
shows remedies for evils. Even where its criticism is destructive, it is exercised for the sake of something better. Though
life apparently blooms so primevally and instinctively in
natural forms, actually it owes its existence to analytic and
order-creating mind, which produced those forms long ago,
though long tradition has finally given them the appearance
of complete naturalness.

Theory does, it is true, often distract from the most
immediate tasks. But in return it illuminates and establishes
more distant and higher goals. It is alien to petty details
of practice. But in the long run it turns out to be necessary.
It has effects on the whole. The great man of action also
knows this; he realizes that practice is never self-sufficient.

Therefore he honors the theoretician, whom only the mob mocks
because of his external clumsiness.

But even if some areas of theory should be totally devoid
of practical connection and in this sense useless, that is no
reason to reject them. The great questions about being and
meaning, about history and the good, cannot be swept under the
rug. Man, by virtue of his rational nature, must inevitably
face up to them. To occupy oneself with them has intrinsic
significance. Whoever wants to deny us this, is cheating us
of a human dimension. In Greece the reduction from objective
philosophy, open to reality, to exclusively practical or
consolatory philosophy took place only in the weaker, less
productive period of Hellenism. If today a behavioristic,
pseudo-Marxian clique either condemns theory or reinterprets
it praxologically ("hermeneutic action," "aesthetic action"!),
that is a sign of our own late-Hellenistic danger.

Practical Reason

Whether or not it affects the world, all philosophy does,
at any rate, affect its bearer, who by the very act of philosophizing assumes a certain attitude. In fact, the immediate
content and goal of philosophy can be to give form to our
actions, to shape an attitude or a life.

This is so in all ethics. Kant, following the tradition
of antiquity, calls ethics "practical reason"(which contrasts
not with "pure" but with "theoretical" reason, for in both
critiques he is concerned only with what is "pure," i.e.,
a priori). Today we know that the field of human activity
can neither be described nor normified by ethics alone. A
"general theory of human action" is being developed ever more
comprehensively in various disciplines.

The philosopher attains a certain distance from the things
around him, from the everyday matters so urgent to others.
They no longer impress him so much. Stoicism, which was the
main trend of philosophy for 800 years in antiquity and whose
influence extends down to Spinoza and Kant, elevated this
spontaneous, as it were natural, effort of philosophical
activity into an ethics and thus intensified it tremendously.
Indifference toward the surface of the here and now, with
which the philosopher's contemporaries often reproach him, now
becomes the goal in a deepened, ethicized sense.

The Cynics, with the form of life they endorsed, namely
lack of needs, were eulogizers of the harder, simpler primitive times, close to nature -- Rousseauists before Rousseau.
Especially numerous and well-known are the anecdotes of
Diogenes, who possessed nothing but a coat, a walking stick,
a bread sack and a wooden cup, and even threw away the cup

when he saw a boy drinking out of his hollow hand. The
beggarly figures of the Cynics could be seen in all the Greek
cities. The Christian sermon can be traced back to the moral
sermon they developed, the diatribe.

Softening the rigorism of the Cynics, Stoicism does not
demand complete renunciation of the goods of this world. But
we should enjoy them in constant awareness that they are
indifferent (adiaphora) and that happiness therefore does not
depend on them. Our relationship to them must not be one of
identification, of self-dissolution; it ought to be mediate
and conditional: "I possess, and am not possessed" (echo, ouk
echomai, said Aristippus). What matters is only the "internal
values of the person": moral, not material wealth, freedom
from desire, not the social status of the free man. Stoicism
frees the rational person from all bondage to the world, and
actually this entails the discovery of the person and his
higher, spiritual value, which is truly his own (oikeion);
compared with this, everything else sinks to the level of
alien, worthless, external triviality (allotrion).

Thus Stoicism becomes -- and this was its central motive --
the great consolation. Since the Stoic cannot lose reason
or virtue, which is based on it, the Stoic always remains
superior, he persists in serene apathy (apatheia) and imper-
turbability (ataraxia), even when a hostile fate takes away
from him everything commonly considered essential to happiness.
Even in poverty he is what he was, even in slavery he refuses
to become a slave interiorly, and when life becomes unbearable,
he remains its master by committing suicide. The Stoics
accepted Socrates as a model not because of the philosophical
principles he discovered, but because of the calm resignation
with which he drank the cup of poison.

As external vicissitudes cannot dislodge reason from its
dignity as the decisive determinant of man, nor can elements
in his own soul affect him or make him a passive recipient
(hence the etymology of the words "affect" and "passions").
The non-rational is not part of the true person, therefore
he holds it aloof and represses it.

Stoicism has, in part, shaped the concept of the philosopher down to our day. Even a simple craftsman is called a
philosopher if he has a higher perspective, sees individual
events in terms of a universal law, remains moderate amid the
joys of life, and does not lose his equanimity amid suffering.
Life has made him what the Stoics sought to educate through
philosophy, namely, a wise man (sophos). The Orient is also
familiar with the figure of the wise man. He embodies, and
this is reminiscent of religion, a still unseparated unity
of conviction and resultant attitude toward life. Whereas
the wise man only repeats or relies on old doctrine, the

concept philo-sophy, since Socrates first actualized its com-
poundness, denotes independent striving for a truth that does
not yet exist. Thus the theoretical factor is stronger in
philosophy. But the fact that it too involves an attitude
will always remain a factor in it. In Stoicism the philosopher again becomes a wise man.

The Stoic ethic did not go uncontested. First of all,
worldly possessions as such cause happiness; therefore they
are a part of complete happiness (Aristotle). Secondly,
values of mind or character can depend on them: for instance,
access to education, on wealth; or the strength for meaningful work, on good health. Only from the world can the personality obtain the tasks to work at and to grow by and so to
become itself in the fullest sense. Thus the external and
the internal cannot be neatly distinguished. It is therefore
but slight comfort that despite all misfortune reason and
virtue remain inalienably at the heart of the personality,
and it is not even true, for degrading living conditions and
torture can destroy even the person. Stoicism debases the
goods of the world so that we can remain indifferent as we
abstain from them, but in doing so it also narrows down the
soul. Inwardly Stoicism follows the same line of thought and
devalues the positive pole from the negative point of view:
because negative passion can draw us below the human plane
and destroy us, Stoicism seeks to deliver us from absolutely
all passions and have us live only from reason, whereas there
are in reality great and noble passions that lift us beyond
mere reason.

The Stoic, relativizing the gifts and blows of life, and
insulated against his own feelings, leads his life, according
to his own self-image, as if he had assumed a role in the
theatre, in which he must stand the test, but he remains at
heart indifferent and only an observer of his own self. From
eudemonism that seeks to remove the possible sting of misfortune in advance, life itself is no longer truly lived from
within but only play-acted and observed from the outside. But
even without eudemonistic intent all such observation entails
the danger of the de-realization of life: life is subsumed
as a particular case of a generality. Kierkegaard (and after
him existentialism) as was seen above, opposed this danger
which he found in Hegelianism by his demand that one ought not
to speculate away one's own existence in its particularity and
in its incessant earnestness, no matter how deep the despair,
and like Nietzsche he too therefore strongly affirmed passion,
subjectivity, and in short an inwardness that is not distanced
and objectified by reason, but directly experienced.

Utopia and Action

Philosophy has two roots. On the one hand, it is acceptance of being. Not of being in its infinite multiplicity
-- it leaves knowledge of this to the sciences. What it asks
about are the determining forces and laws behind reality, the
laws that affect and control it, its "origins," the principles
at the foundation of being. Philosophy thus deals with the
a priori of being, with what is (not temporally but ontologically) "prior" to all individual reality, or as is often said,
with what always was and is, with the "eternal" as contrasted
with the temporal stream of being.

If the world were perfect, then philosophical reasoning
could rest satisfied with such tasks concerning the hidden
principles. In an imperfect world, however, it must not only
determine what is, but also set up norms for what should be.
It must not merely observe reality as contemplative reason,
but it must as imaginative and creative reason also develop
possibilities, conceptual models of a political, social,
technical, and other types, "dreams of a better life." The
metaphysician becomes a Utopian. This makes him at the same
time a critic. The ideals he sees are criteria by which to
measure and condemn existing reality. They are, however, also
objective models by which it can and should be transformed.
Just as it was the innate function of reason to provide ends
and means for practical action, so even after reason has
emancipated itself for theory as a purpose in itself, it
returns to its original mission. If as ethics it affects the
individual only within pre-given institutions of life, here
on a larger scale it transforms the institutions themselves.
Philosophy becomes revolutionary activity, a world-moving
force. It becomes so all the more, when it not only depicts
an ideal condition but also communicates it together with
the given moment of history (Engels). The "concrete Utopia"
which obtains its Utopian factor from the world itself is the
"conjured Utopia" (Bloch).

Often antiquity's mode of thought, with its predominant
concern for "being," is contrasted with progress-oriented
modern thought. But as early as the fifth century B.C. there
was already an entire Utopian literature. Before the founding
of the colony Thurioi, a prize contest was held for the best
constitution to give it. Modern times, it is true, credit
reason with less power to affect events and shape the world.
This promotes both knowledge and action. German Idealism
defused the propulsive force of the Enlightenment precisely
because it totalized it. Nietzsche invented for this the
formulation of breaking old tablets and inscribing new ones.

It is also quite natural to contrast Utopianism, which

looks ahead to the future, with metaphysics, which looks back
to the past, to the origin and the a priori. But the priority
which metaphysics seeks is one not of temporal precedence but
of intrinsic reality. In fact both deal with supratemporal
principles, metaphysics with principles already realized and
Utopianism with principles yet to be. The difference between
the two arises beyond their common ground.

Still, these two fountainheads of philosophy cannot be
reduced one to the other or to a third factor. Philosophy
is both knowledge of what is and a plan for what is to come,
and it must not be restricted to either the one or the other.
Nicolai Hartmann and Ernst Bloch, ontology and the principle
of hope, are mutually interdependent and only their polarity
comprises the whole of philosophy. Therefore the Platonic
Idea serves a dual function: it is the essential basis and
structure of things, but also their paradigm and the ideal
according to which they are constructed and ought to be judged,
just as the real state is patterned after the true state in
heaven. In Hegel too the two tasks stand side by side as philosophy's two modes of self-comprehension. In the foreword to
his Philosophy of Right he says that philosophy first comes
into being when the shape of history has grown old. It con-
ceptualizes an era that is coming to an end. In this context
philosophy is not primary: the owls of Minerva take flight
only after dark. But in other passages Hegel states that the
World Spirit dictates its orders directly to the philosophers
and that if the realm of imagination is revolutionized then
reality will not be long to follow. Here philosophy is
primary. It not only finds formulations for reality as it is,
but it anticipates and causes new reality.

This dual nature of philosophy arouses enemies on two
fronts. First, as revolutionary Utopianism it comes into
conflict with the established, self-centered status quo. By
smashing the old inherited structure of opinions and institutions, it "shakes the world out of its sleep" and so provokes
the resistance of conservative forces. A conservative author
such as Sophocles opposes the Sophists, Aristophanes opposes
the Utopians. But this antithesis, as was seen above, first
makes conservatism self-aware, makes it also become philosophical and thereby transforms naive tradition into restoration
(Burke, Adam Müller, de Bonald, de Maistre, Tocqueville,
Cortez).

The counterpressure of the establishment dulls the revolutionary impulse. It not only fails externally, it conforms
internally. Thus, following directly after the Sophists, the
Cynics propagated universal equality and the abolition of
economic and social privileges: instead of wealth and freedom
in the world, what matters is whether one is rich in virtues

free of desires, etc. And precisely this internalization and
spiritualization of the concepts immediately becomes a cue for
the Stoics to abandon the program for a reorganization of
things: for if the master can internally be a slave and the
slave internally free, then obviously the external order is
totally irrelevant and can be left as it is. Everything can
remain as it always has been. A similar process of removing
reality from an original real hope of an improved world situation takes place in the transformation of the Messianic kingdom of the prophets into a merely otherworldly kingdom of God
in the late apocalypses and Christianity. Where a progressive
and a static trend contend as rivals, the static one at first
has the advantage. Augustine, for whom the City of God already
exists in the Church, wins out over Chiliasm, which hopes for
it in the future. The conciliatory Leibniz wins out over the
quasi-leftist Spinoza.

If some men find philosophy too much an accomplice of the
future, others too little so, because of its eternal aspect.
Indeed, even such philosophy as demands and prepares the new
still remains just philosophy, i.e., reflection and contemplation, which as such do not reshape existence more humanely.
There is still a huge gap between philosophy and practice.
Therefore those who press for action are existentially ill-at-
ease with philosophy; they doubt its right to exist, though
they do so paradoxically and unjustly. Philosophy shows the
way for action and demonstrates the need for it, but it only
shows and demonstrates, it does not act. Some activists also
feel the same uneasiness about art, not only classical art,
whose beauty glosses over the disharmonies of the world instead
of screaming them out and therefore lulls the awareness, but
also about Expressionism, the seismograph of modern disintegration, for it too produces "only art." And some resent the
speculation and aesthetics of which Kierkegaard was the religious spokesman. On all sides, two concepts are locked in
conflict: the pre-theoretical, Biblical concept of truth as
something to be lived, and the Greek concept of truth from
which philosophy sprang as knowledge and art for its own sake.

None other than Schiller, later editor of the periodical
"Horen," from which all politics was to be excluded, and a
principal exponent of the philosophical and aesthetic culture
of Jena and Weimar, has his Fiesko cry out to the painter
Verrina: "You overthrew tyrants on canvas but yourself
remained a miserable slave; you liberated republics with a
paint-brush, but cannot break your own chains. Go! your work
is illusory. Let appearance yield to deed. I have done what
you only painted." And in 1793 he wrote to the Duke of Augusten-
burg in connection with the French Revolution: "If the fact
were real -- if the extraordinary event had really happened

and political legislation had been put in the hands of reason,
man respected and dealt with as a purpose in himself, law
enthroned and true liberty made the foundation of the govern-
mental structure, then I would willingly say farewell to the
muses forever and devote all my activity to the most splendid
of arts, the reign of reason alone."

That the idea should become reality and philosophy, action
was, after the deaths of Goethe and Hegel, the trend of a
whole generation, including Young Germany and left-wing Hegelianism. The historical law of this dual process, they say,
must be realized anew. While at the same time Comte speaks
of turning theory into practice, but has in mind natural science and the resulting industry which lets the bourgeoisie
remain unchanged, it is here philosophy whose practical application ought to comprise the transformation of society. Intellectual freedom must be followed by social freedom, Moses
Hess demands (in his book Die eine und ganze Freiheit, 1843).
The world is the "signature of the word," as Heine expresses
it (using an older, mystical formulation) and in a poem from
Germany, a Winter Tale he personifies "the deed of your
thoughts" in an eerie man pursuing him from street to street.

Philosophy, as Marx teaches, must criticize existing conditions, point the way to their abolition and to a better
society and thus become "realized in fact." It no longer
attains its appropriate truth purely within its own medium.
The goal of philosophy is revolution. Once this goal is attained, then there is no further need for philosophy, which
was only a preliminary and intermediate phase; it has rendered
itself superfluous and obsolete. Revolutionary action, by
abolishing alienation from reality, also abolishes philosophy
as a symptom of this alienation. "It follows logically that
the philosophical transformation of the world is also the
transformation of philosophy, and that the realization of
philosophy is its abolition." Of course a terribly limited
concept of philosophy is at the basis of such reasoning. But
Marx's other works show that he also has another meaning of
philosophy not restricted only to its translation into action.
How can one "realize" categorical analysis?! Doesn't that
which is realized reveal its theoretical foundation from
beginning to end? Doesn't it need a permanent process of
realization and therefore also continual theoretical work?

"The philosophers have merely interpreted the world in
different ways, what matters is to change it" (the eleventh
Feuerbach-thesis). This is at first sight completely false,
for much about the world cannot be changed, can only be interpreted. Ontology always remains the other pole, remains the
foundation that cannot be removed. Insofar as the world can
be changed, the thesis is again false, for before I can change

it I must know in what direction to aim with the change. So
the theoretician is necessary from first to last in order to
establish the goal for the person who makes the change. The
thesis ought to read: "The philosophers must not only interpret the world, they must also establish goals and then the
man of action must change it on the basis of these goals."
But this thesis is still quite inadequate, for often one does
not know the good purely by knowledge, in such a way that
action then merely transposes the pre-existent idea into
reality, but the right decision becomes clear only in the full
individual concreteness of the action itself. Furthermore
the historical situation is constantly changed by action, and
even the good that is to be realized is therefore today no
longer the same as yesterday, and so only the person who acts
and who has no distance from the historical situation but is
completely immersed in it can know it. The person who acts
and the knower must therefore be the same. Only the man who
changes the world, one can conclude, is the true interpreter:
just as he himself becomes a revolutionary subject only through
revolutionary practice, so likewise only he is in a position
to know truth in its respective newly originating forms. He
does not first know it, then realize it, but both things happen simultaneously. If reality is assumed to be constant,
then there is also a constant truth that reflects it. Pure
contemplation would attain this truth. But, for Marx, social
reality itself is historical, it becomes increasingly self-
aware only in history. But this history does not proceed
independently of us by the action of the World Spirit, but
we ourselves must make it. This personal participation in
history is however an ethical task not only for the man of
action. Only as being is completed does the full truth about
it become evident. Therefore, to interfere in history also
becomes a task for the man of knowledge, and is in his deepest
interest. He must become practical in order to be theoretical.
He must change the world in order to wrest its highest interpretation from it. He must -- to use a Scholastic analogy --
create truth in order to find it.

As in our century Kierkegaard's existentialism becomes
formalized by abstracting from its Christian background, likewise the so-called "critical theory" of the Frankfurt School
formalizes Marx by abstracting from his revolutionary goal,
and in each case the formalization is the seat of inaccuracy
and weakness. Blindness to the truth of every form of thought
that does not fit with one's own religious or political expectations therefore is just as much a part of the greatest of prophetic figures as it is of the smallness of their followers.
Existentialism and critical theory, as violently as they
attack one another, belong together (as did the Epicureans and

the Stoics in Hellenism), insofar as both rob knowledge of its autonomy and reduce it to a function, whether it be that of the individual struggling for his "genuineness" or his "potential reality" or of society.

Two factors are behind the success of critical theory among the young students of our time (who not illogically tried to retranslate it back into a revolutionary doctrine): first, the decline of philosophy caused by the increased strength and reflectivity of the sciences, which allowed the inevitable need for "total interpretation" to be temporarily filled by sociology (though for it the whole always means the social whole, just as "reality" is only another word for "the social conditions"); secondly the entrance of science too into the age of mass culture, which substituted for its previous, as it were, "aristocratic" motivation, in which it was still understood as "self-purposeful," required a leveling, more popular motivation, more amenable to good sound common sense.

"Classical" theory is understood as impractical in this double sense: first, its stance toward reality is one of complete separateness, merely contemplating it as an object; and secondly, it persists in this contemplation and strives for no goal more real, lying beyond it: since its object -- the eternal principles, or perfect being -- is autarchic, i.e., needs no change, in fact precludes such, it too is autarchic and is its own purpose. In contrast, the "unity of theory and practice" demanded by critical theory is based on the fact that, first, theory here knows that it is incorporated in the practicality of the historical social process as a factor of it -- on the one hand, this social process is its object of knowledge; on the other, it itself constitutes an integral part of it -- and secondly, critical theory regards it as its own highest mission to intervene and help determine this process, which is never perfect but always leaves room for improvement. (Here the naive imperialism of sociology can be seen, for it extends to theory in general what may be valid only of itself because its object of study is history and society!) Because the object is still open to the future, its theory must be realized practically (a self-fulfilling prophecy!) by contributing to the attainment of that future as sociology envisages it.

As Kierkegaard responds to those whom he calls the "objective men," by reminding them of the "infinite interest" which a subject owes himself, so the analyses of critical theory too are led by what Horkheimer calls "interest in rational conditions" and "interest in the future" (here critical theory and futurology meet). Interest is not added externally to enlightening knowledge, but both are, according to Habermas, basically one. Indeed not a reason out of which interest

ensues is primary but an interest in which reason dwells.
Knowledge, as it pursues an interest, does not go beyond itself
to something else, but it fulfills itself. Theory is not
transposed into practice, but it always was practice from the
start. Reason is intrinsically also meta-logical will to
reason: will that the rational should happen. Without this
will it would not be reason. It has indeed often received its
function from an irrational will. But precisely therefore,
when it has seen into this fact, it should not retreat to
pretended purpose-free knowledge, but confess its own will.
Instead of working unconsciously for a conservative goal, it
ought to work consciously for a future goal.

Habermas differentiates between three types of science,
each with a different knowledge-controlling interest: empirical sciences, which seek to exploit the environment; historical, hermeneutic sciences, which broaden the intersubjective
scope of communication; systematic, normative behavioral
sciences, which bring about the liberation of the subject
from known and unknown coercion. These are matched by two
forms of practice: purposeful work and "interaction" or
communicative action through domination-free discussion. The
more than natural goals of emancipation, human dignity and
peace stand with equal primacy alongside the goal of self-
preservation.

It is a typical phenomenon that teachers do not hand down
to their students everything they have learned through the
tradition from which they stem. For Horkheimer and Adorno,
for Marcuse and Habermas, the unity of theory and practice is
still a dialectical unity of equal partners; it is not based
on eliminating one of the partners, on theory being explained
away as a surface phenomenon of practice. They still have
knowledge be naturally obligated to a real thing and thus to
objective truth, except that this truth, in addition to its
theoretical dimension, also has a real one: its place as a
factor in the historical process and its social significance.
In the student revolution this is changed to mean that it has
only social significance, that "all science is political,"
i.e., it has for ages been manipulated only for political purposes, and therefore can and should with all the more right
today be consciously oriented by our own purpose -- which is
so much better! The Frankfurt School wanted, in the face of
the horrors of National Socialism, to apply theory to the
struggle for a better society. This came to mean: all theory
is reduced to the level of an instrument in the political
struggle. The difficulty with this view is: theory can then
have an equally good conscience even for the worst society.
Its raison d'être no longer stems from itself, but is
prescribed for it by the party. Though "instrumental reason

is first scoffed at, because it serves interests other than
those proper to reason itself, paradoxically reason is then
intentionally subjected to other interests, which are also
alien to it. So Hitler caught up with the émigrés all the way
in the United States. Critical theory, which they created
against him, becomes the legitimation for new totalitarian
practice. "Domination-free discussion" serves as the breach
for cynical, domineering manipulation. The ethical human
factor cannot be saved without the theoretical dimension; give
up one and the other is lost.

CHAPTER 4

PHILOSOPHY AND SCIENCE

Among the Greeks, philosophy and science still stood together in common opposition to the mythical view of the world.
Both first represented the new principle of theoretical
research. Therefore, the Greeks, in archaic undifferentiation,
did not mentally separate philosophy and science as strictly
as we do, though the two were already clearly distinct in
fact. Aristotle does rank what he called "First Philosophy"
-- the later metaphysics -- ahead of all other forms of philosophy, but in his eyes these others are still philosophies.
The Greeks coined no special word for "science." Down to the
eighteenth century one still finds book titles such as
Philosophia lapidum (Philosophy of Stones): meaning minerology!
The same men studied and practiced philosophy and science
separately or intermixed (indeed to some extent this has continued down to our day). Aristotle, who was the first great
organizer of the sciences, is himself an example of this.
The Pythagoreans' conviction that everything in the
world is based on relations of numbers and size is linked
with their discovery of the musical harmonies, just as Posidonius' doctrine of the freedom and creativity of the human
mind is integral to his cultural history.
But the Greeks, precisely because of this unity, never
advanced beyond a certain stage as scientists. They asked
about the basic principles rather than the particulars, and
even as individual researchers they were always already
committed to a metaphysics which prevented entire areas of
research from coming to the fore. Basic philosophical positions will always subconsciously or -- if possible -- even
consciously point the way for science, which has to do with
the more particular and therefore subordinate reality. Hence,
the history of science can be studied meaningfully only in
conjunction with the history of philosophy. But the connection between them must never be too narrow, nor too direct.
Theophrastus' botany is better than Aristotle's zoology precisely because Theophrastus was less philosophical. Modern
science has become great always by first destroying a metaphysics: in the late Middle Ages when nominalism destroyed
Aristotelian-Scholastic metaphysics, and in the eigtheenth
century when in rapid succession first rationalism shattered
the Christian metaphysics of history and then the Age of
Goethe shattered the rationalistic metaphysics of progress.

Only when the individual object was removed from the false
framework of the conceptual system of matter and form, of
substance and accident, could it be investigated by physics;
only after the individual event no longer was harnassed to the
pre-interpretation of a priori determined historical curves,
could it be investigated by the historical sciences in its
intrinsic nature and without preconditions. The mind is
always inclined to construct premature total interpretations
from whose horizon it believes everything already understood,
and because they seem obvious and self-evident and thus do not
rise thematically to the consciousness it is very difficult
to free oneself of them and to gain a new insight into the
world as not yet comprehended. Epoch-making discoveries are
based on changes of the categorical framework.

Compared with Aristotelian physics, which (unlike that of
Archimedes) remained speculatively bound, modern physics since
Galileo sets its ambition on what was later elevated to a
motto by Newton: "Hypotheses non fingo" (I do not make hypotheses). But it has attained its successes not only through
observation of matters of fact: every natural "law" goes, as
such, beyond the describable data. The old metaphysics must
face not only empirical facts. Rather the rejection of Aristotle also allows new dimensions of inquiry to arise: instead
of asking about the essence, which is a cause of being only
in teleological thinking, the question now is about the real
causes; instead of asking about form, one now asks about
the elements (but this already is based on pre-Socratic
thought); the question of substance is replaced by that of
function; that of the general concept by the equally general
but not qualitatively seen, but mathematically quantifiable
and calculated law.

De-metaphysication serves mathematization; it helps
science to become exact. Only so did modern science free itself from the "natural" world-view, to which Aristotle was
still bound, and penetrate "behind" the "appearances." Empiricism and mathematics, two other disciplines of knowledge which
previously stood in the shadow of philosophy, join together
and rebel conjointly against it.

It was Francis Bacon's mistake to have reduced the methodology of modern science to empiricism, and yet he has the merit
of having been the first greet advocate of science's rise to
world power. Even Kant still placed a quotation from Bacon's
Instauratio magna at the front of his Critique of Pure Reason,
because Bacon had already demanded that not wings but weights
should be attached to thought: for it is too presumptuous, it
becomes fantastic instead of true, and its imagined wealth
has been the cause of its poverty.

One man who helped establish the modern self-image and

pride, after d'Alembert and Condillac, was Auguste Comte.
According to Comte, abstract metaphysics in its time replaced
fictitious religion,and so in his "three-stages law" today
both religion and metaphysics belong to the past as archaic
disciplines which man no longer needs. That an individual's
intuitive insight should unveil total reality was a childish
expectation. In the third, positive stage, the sciences have
succeeded philosophy, in which they were formerly contained.
The sciences issue successively from philosophy and they
partition reality among themselves into sectors. Philosophy
is today no better than soothsaying and astrology. Far more
than the transition from religion to metaphysics, which still
belonged together, the transition to positive science is "the
fundamental revolution which characterizes the maturity of
our mind." Metaphysics still accepts religion's question
about the true cause and the destiny of the world; like religion it still seeks the nature of things, though it tries to
give the answer in a more rational way. It is an enervated
theology. All these "absolute investigations"are doomed to
failure. The real break comes with science, which no longer
seeks to answer "why?" but still asks "how?" In contrast with
metaphysical phantasies it gives up trying to "penetrate into
the secret of the origin of phenomena" and settles for the
determination of the facts, by which every statement must be
verifiable. The mind that is modestly aware of its limits is
the one that makes progress.

For positivism -- along with the "three-stages law" itself
--as later for neo-Kantianism, what still remains for philosophy after it has become independent of the sciences is merely
their epistemological and logical foundation and methodology.
Indeed, for Comte, the sciences themselves always develop new
methods as they progress. Only by analysis of the sciences
can philosophy discover the logical structures they contain
and their interconnection. An additional task is the classification of the sciences, i.e., the arrangement of the sciences
into a system based on their intrinsic sequence (which grati-
fied mainly the librarians). Historically, philosophy preceded the sciences, now however they are first: they have
divided up all objects of the world among themselves. The
object of philosophy can therefore now be only science itself.
It is the "science of the sciences" (Helmholtz). A separate
metaphysics with a formal object of its own, however, is no
longer necessary. Metaphysical problems are only apparent
problems. While positivism has met with oppostion on the
European continent since 1900, it has held its ground in Anglo-
Saxon countries. From there it is today flooding back to the
continent, in part, in the new form of linguistic criticism.

Of present-day positivists let us mention here only Ernst

Topitsch, whose hostility to metaphysics leaves that of Carnap
and Reichenbach far behind in historical explicitness and
categorical originality. Early man, Topitsch says, in order
to rid his environment of threatening strangeness but also
because this method comes naturally to him and no one has yet
instructed him of its impermissability, interprets the world
anthropomorphically; he projects himself into it in a naive
analogical way of thinking. He sees the world, and this
applies both to mythology and to metaphysics down to Hegel,
Schopenhauer and Nietzsche, either as animate, as conceived
and born, growing and aging, or as the product of a craftsman-
God, or by analogy with his own community as a great hierarchy
(biomorphic, technomorphic or sociomorphic models). After the
macrocosm has thus been interpreted as a microcosm in terms of
it and subjected to its norms. We hypostasize perfection and
harmony, which we bitterly miss in ourselves, by compensation,
into a higher world and then elevate it as a goal for ourselves.
Earthly rule legitimates itself as an image of transcendental
rule. But since modern science has, with objective sobriety,
recognized that nature is completely different from man (Descartes already saw this) and shown the cold indifference of
the world toward man, such efforts to transform it into a
cozier home for man are of only historical interest to us.
Metaphysics did pose essential questions, but it became the
victim of metaphors.

The pragmatic world-view must stand the test of hard facts.
Limited to discoverable reality, science too is verified by
facts. Therefore both are "true" in a simpler sense than
philosophy, which -- in its basis, goal and significance --
inquires into invisible realities accessible only to thought
and conceivably different, and therefore it always contains
an element of speculation. It represents principles which cannot "be disproved by a vulgar appeal to supposedly contrary
experience"(Kant) -- any more than the idea of law is disproved
by actual injustice --, principles by which it measures
experiences rather than the other way around (Kant's beacon-
like "rational ideas"). This transcendence beyond what can be
directly documented is legitimate for philosophy because of
the type of question it must answer. Only the ignoramus will
mock it for that. But philosophy does indeed often misuse
its freedom and prove him right. Philosophy, which speaks in
the name of reason and truth and therefore seems to belong to
the "progressive" side, thereby unexpectedly falls back in its
style of thinking to an earlier, irresponsible, childish stage
and is then, on the contrary, even a retrogressive power.
Instead of limiting speculation to its necessary minimum, it
lets it run wild. Instead of being aware of its own hypothetical nature, it claims absolute certainty (by compensation).

Parmenides' being which is always at rest, Fichte's world-creating ego, Schopenhauer's inference from our heart and soul to the nature of the world (after natural science had just become great because Descartes sought a different principle in "extension" than in "cogitation"): these are the spokesmen for archaic, age-old longings of the soul which can otherwise no longer venture into daylight and which still find shelter only in philosophy.

There is such a thing as "conservative" philosophy: the human creative power already discovered by the Sophists is again restricted by Plato by pre-existent and universally binding norms. He praises immobilized Egypt, opposes individualism and democracy. While his pupil Alexander establishes a vast empire, Aristotle teaches that a state must be small enough so that a herald's voice can reach all citizens eligible to vote. While Sophism had already taught the equality of man, Aristotle's non-Greeks are slaves by nature, and he gives Alexander the inhumane counsel -- which he did not follow -- to deal with the conquered Persians not as with men, but as with plants or animals. As distinguished from philosophy it is art which legitimately has one of its functions to be the receptacle of suppressed magical, mythical and pre-scientific layers of the soul and world-views and of letting them live again as if in a dream and thus comprise a complement and counterweight to our rationalized world.

Philosophy Separate from Science

Just as Comte's evolutionistic scheme is wrong about the relationship of religion and metaphysics, so also about that between metaphysics and science. Because science came into existence after metaphysics, that does not mean it arose from it, least of all as its more mature stage. Each, rather, has separate roots and different aims. Metaphysics seeks principles; science studies the particular. They are not related to one another as stages on the same scale of progress, but as separate types. Therefore science can never make metaphysics completely superfluous, neither in the sense that metaphysics would be completely erroneous nor in the sense that science would accept its intention but carry it out better. Rather, philosophy still remains necessary even after science has originated, just as it always was more than a mere precursor of science.

Indeed, it is not even true that they appeared successively in time. Although science has grown stronger only in modern times, Heraclitus already had occasion to speak out against knowledge of all sorts of things (polydidaskala), which does not nourish the mind. The Greek metaphysicians were contempo-

raries of the Greek mathematicians, and even among the Miles-
ians, Anaximenes, the pupil of Anaximander, with his theory
that all qualities are based on density (pyknosis) and extension (manosis), is a physicist. Philosophy and science are
thus equally ancient. One can even reverse the sequence:
the Egyptians and Babylonians had science, though it was
restricted to the practical, while philosophy arose only among
the Greeks and is therefore of a later date.

Hegel, though not a typologist compared with Comte, also
assumes an upward development of intellectual forms. For him
too development takes place in three stages: art, religion,
philosophy (in Comte art is missing, in Hegel science). But
Hegel is more tolerant and fair toward the respective later
stages. For him they are not completely "overcome." Their
meaning was not totally exhausted in the fact that they were
preliminary stages for later disciplines. Rather they still
retain their own inalienable justification. Mind, when it
goes beyond them, also preserves them and continues to harbour
them in its depths. But while, according to Hegel, the process of philosophy has already been completed, Comte saw more
rightly that the process of science has just begun and is
continuing.

Dilthey came to the rescue of philosophy right in the
middle of the age of positivism. For him too, as a man of his
century, metaphysics does not contain genuine truth, which
remains reserved for science. Metaphysics is in the same
category as religion and art. The convictions contained in all
of them are only "world-view" (Weltanschauung). But, as Dilthey continues, this world-view is, in another respect, even
"deeper" than science. It contains a fullness and a vitality
which have been irretrievably lost in science.

Classifying them stylistically, as one would do with works
of art (like his teacher Trendelenburg, for whom however the
two Cartesian substances and the attempt to reconcile them
were the principle of distribution), Dilthey distinguishes
between three types of metaphysics: 1. Naturalism or materialism is based on reason. Its basic concept is natural causality. It explains even the mental world by the physical. It
leaves no room for God, or for values and purposes. 2. Objective idealism or mystical pantheism is based on feeling. For
it, things have meaning. It believes in teleology. Everything real expresses and develops from an immanent divine and
spiritual principle. (Dilthey no longer knows what Schelling
knew, that materialism generally is only the debasement of
such a pantheism). 3. Subjective idealism of freedom is based
on the will. It emphasizes the independence and sovereignty
of the human person and spirit, which itself establishes purposes, mainly physical ones. Even God is here understood as

a transcendent person, a creative principle. As contrasted
with the other two world-views, subjective idealism is dualistic. As the conviction "of every great active nature," it
stresses the ethical, while pantheism seeks to overcome
dualism in a contemplative and aesthetic harmony. Later Erich
Rothacker again found Dilthey's late views "productive" as a
heuristic principle and therefore supported all three methods
of human studies: naturalism explains, the idealism of freedom comprehends, pantheism understands.

     Thus metaphysics gives total interpretations of life and
reality which are as such unprovable, but which correspond
to a need. They are possibilities of interpretation, ultimate
perspectives. But because they cannot be derived directly
from the object, they are immediately infused with individuality: they reflect their originators, they speak not only
of the reality that offers those possibilities of interpretation but also of moods of life, characters of men and epochs,
which can be understood only by their expression. Metaphysics
gives more conclusive information about the subject who speaks
in it than about the world it speaks of.

     But Dilthey too is a positivist insofar as he believes
that the age of metaphysics has run out. He saves it only
as a historian. The only thing remaining for us late-comers
is to re-experience the metaphysical systems that have come
down from earlier ages and to carry on a "philosophy of philosophy." The phenomenological school, on the contrary, reopened
a field of study for philosophy in the present. Philosophy
indeed neither can nor should give formulations of the entire
world, for these are always constructions which abandon the
field of "description" in favor of "theories" in whose
unitary equations ("everything is mind," or the like), all
respective particularities are lost. But they are equally
lost in mechanistic science which actually, as Comte said,
though differently than he meant it, has become the "heir"
to metaphysics, indeed it is itself a constructive metaphysics.
At least it incorrectly sets up a partial truth as the complete truth. Along with and logically prior to science,
phenomenological philosophy remains the study of the immediate
"world of life" (Lebenswelt), the analysis of the acts by
which it is constructed in our consciousness, and of the
experiencing subject.

     For the scientist, the natural world-view of everyday
experience is only a subjective narrowing and falsification
of truth. Only science with its remoteness from practice and
its more refined methods improves it. Phenomenology, on the
other hand, says: science,too, in fact especially science,
is practice-connected. Its methods stand ultimately in the
service of practice and therefore cut only a narrow sector

out of the world, namely the quantitative one of what can be weighed, measured and counted, by which the world becomes accessible and processable. Its truth too is therefore of limited perspective. Far from purifying the natural world-view, the scientific one erects a filter which no longer lets pass certain data of knowledge which had already been gained in the natural world-view. It filters out form and quality, value and meaning. Homogeneous and isotropic space banishes the above and below that was still known to Aristotelian physics. All this may be relative to man, but as something relative it still has some objectivity. The subject does not only abridge being, which would exist anyway without it, but it also contributes new dimensions to reality.

It is the task of philosophy to come to grips precisely with this truth on which science turns its back. If Occam put the "knife" to the abundance of principles with his demand: "Principles are not to be multiplied more than necessary," the opposite also is true: "they are not to be reduced." On this point phenomenology (as well as the object-theory simultaneously proposed by Meinong), agrees with the Age of Goethe, to which Dilthey also traces his origin. The Age of Goethe had refused to accept the truth of physics as the only type of truth in history, in language and mythology, in religion and art.

Philosophy in Science

Phenomenology establishes itself alongside science. As it is not affected by science, it in turn does not affect science. Each goes its separate way. But as even positivism assigned to philosophy a task in the household of science, namely that of reflecting on its gnoseological foundations, so the objects of science, which are always specialized, also have more general ontic foundations and accordingly science itself has ontological ones. Every science, when it speaks of its own specialty, presupposes in effect the universal principles implicit in it. It operates with its broader concepts, which as such are always pre-existent; as, for instance, classical mechanics does with its four basic concepts of space, time, mass, and motion (to which that of causality should be added). But even beyond that, fundamental decisions on ultimate questions enter surreptitiously into the formation of its concepts. Usually science does not become aware of its dependence on them because they are decisions of a culture or an epoch as a whole. But while science on the one hand is based completely on general principles, on the other its mission is to deal not with them but with its separate field. These principles are behind and not before it; it operates with

them but does not study them. "No science tests its own
principles" (a Scholastic axiom).

Now this opens up a new task for philosophy, by which it
simultaneously gains a necessary function in the sciences
themselves, which it delivers not only from their "forgetful-
ness of being" (Heidegger) -- which actually is a legitimate
decision for the individual in process of becoming -- but also
from their "forgetting of their own most essential categoriality." It reflects on the metaphysical implications contained
in the sciences, brings their unconscious principles out into
light and clarifies those principles which had already been
given some sort of formulation by science. It performs -- to
use Kantian language -- the transcendental regression from
the fact of science to the conditions of its possibility
(which, though Kant saw it differently, are not merely subjective conditions of knowledge). Along with the conditions
which are specific to a single science or group of sciences,
there are increasingly more general ones up to the final categories of being in general, which can no longer be dealt with
by the sciences. Plato himself spoke of the chain of successively more general determinations of each point of knowledge
("hypotheses," which in Plato, contrary to the false neo-
Kantian interpretation, are determinations of being), ending
with the most general one, as most fundamental and therefore
"unconditioned, Absolute" (anhypotheton), which he called
"Archai" (ultimate underlying substance).

Positivism believes that there are only isolated individual facts. Thereby it has, though seeking to stand beyond
all philosophy, already made a philosophical assumption, in
fact a false one, an atomistic and sensualistic one. By
giving science the tast of registering individual facts, it
harnasses it to the cart of a very specific philosophy that
cannot be obtained from them. In truth all science inevitably
uses general and therefore philosophical concepts, within
whose "horizon of meaning" (Husserl) it first encounters the
individual. But because, unaware of this, it does not test
its concepts, it falls blindly into those of the handiest
and crudest philosophical prejudice. Philosophical cooperation in science, consequently, does not bring something to it
from the outside; it operates within an inevitable dimension
of science and frees it from the bad philosophy it had already
naively fallen prey to.

Only in the first third of our century did a philosophy
that again reflected on its own nature oppose science which
at that time was still positivistic. From it, Nicolai
Hartmann conceived his "categorical analysis," which starting with the highest ontological determinations of being went
on in the "philosophy of nature" without interruption to treat

of space, time, organic nexus, and thus moved into the field
of the individual sciences, physics and biology: here philosophy and science are no longer contraries, for they labor in
the same territory but under different formal aspects.

But already at the beginning of our century, many sciences,
including physics, ran into a "crisis of their foundations":
they realized that assumptions that they had made without even
being aware of it were anything but self-evident, and they
therefore began to discuss these assumptions. This, and perhaps also the influence of a revitalized philosophy, made the
sciences become self-reflective again. Today they are no
longer positivistic. The so-called methodological dispute,
which erupted in the social sciences during the sixties between
the empiricists (Popper, Albert) and the Frankfurt School,
which called attention to the fact that sociology too always
must be and is, whether it admits it or not, accompanied by
ideas of the whole and of the objective, was a dispute not
between philosophy and science but between post-positivistic
science -- which also was indebted to its pre-positivistic
origins -- and a form of science that still clung to the scientific style of the nineteenth century. Even the tirades of the
Vienna Circle against philosophy drew their virulence precisely
from the fact that they were already obsolete in their own day.

But now that philosophy has become modern again it is no
longer carried on by the "pure" philosophers who make a profession of it, but by the sciences themselves. Mathematics,
physics, biology, but also many human and social sciences
(Geisteswissenschaften) today are developing their own
private philosophies. This proves to be necessary because
philosophical problems, when they become fundamental problems
of the sciences, are infinitely differentiated. Philosophical
epistemology is much too general and unspecialized for the
physicist; likewise Dilthey's and Rothacker's methodology,
with its distinction between understanding, explanation and
comprehension, is too general and unspecialized for the style-
analytical and text-interpretative literary historian; and
the social philosophy of a Spencer or Tönnies, for the empirical social researcher. The specific categorical conceptuality
of such disciplines cannot, as it were, be seen with the naked
eye but can be understood adequately only by a person familiar
with the respective science. Only he is capable of finding
modern solutions, for he is not bogged down in philosophical
traditions. Thus, either the scientist is now the true philosopher or the philosopher must be a scientist. In addition to
philosophy he must master a science.

Certainly this does not mean that philosophy as a whole is
transformed into a study of the principles of the individual
sciences. Moreover, many philosophical problems can, even

when they are at the same time fundamental problems of the
sciences, be dealt with from other perspectives; for example,
ethics and the philosophy of history not only from the perspective of sociology; aesthetics not only from that of artistic
disciplines; concepts such as cause and freedom not only
from that of physics. Still, the appearance of science-
immanent philosophy creates a new situation for independent
philosophy. In addition there is the fact that the process
detected (though also falsely interpreted) by Comte, the
process of the exodus of the sciences out of philosophy, has
continued even more drastically in the last half century;
former philosophical disciplines such as psychology and pedagogy have established themselves as separate so-called "systematic human and social sciences" (Geisteswissenschaften).
For all these reasons, philosophy in the sense of an independent "field," has suffered a loss of substance. Compared
with the nineteenth century its conflict with science has
entered a new phase. Whereas formerly the attack on philosophy was made without sympathy for its legitimate rights, so
that it could easily defend itself, this time it cannot so
easily do so, since its rights are indeed recognized but are
with good reason claimed by others. If it was formerly supposed to disappear completely, now the much greater danger
consists in its becoming universal, in its absorption by the
sciences. "Recognize the situation!" At a new moment in
history, it has become problematic in its own eyes and must
rethink itself.

CHAPTER 5

PHILOSOPHY AND HISTORY

Essentialism Dethroned by Development and Individuality

For Platonism the essence of things is their determining
cause. The idea in which they participate makes them what they
are. Compared with the eternal being of the idea, things lie
in the dimension of temporal becoming, but this does not constitute a productive factor, for all change consists only
either of an approximation to the already pre-existent idea,
which must be adhered to, or in departure from it, which can
have only a negative result. To understand events in the real
world, one must look at the idea as their ultimate effective
cause. Carrying this to an extreme, the medieval Aristotelians explained even natural processes by the combination or
incompatibility of concepts.

Only when late-medieval nominalism refuted such hypostat-
izations of concepts, did the mind (by a renewed link with the
traditions of the pre-Socratics, Democritus, and Epicureanism)
again become free to see that the motive power of events does
not reside in a metaphysical origin but that one reality is
the cause for other reality. One must then not look upward
to the eternal in order to understand the world but back to
the temporal causes on their own plane of reality. There are
no ideal forms which attract things to themselves from ahead
in order to make them as much like themselves as possible,
but only a causality from behind which constantly produces
new and unprecedented forms. Mutability no longer has a norm
anchored in being like the polar star, but is open even to
the positive (and therefore all the more accessible to man's
normative action). Thus, essentialistic thought is replaced
by historical thought, within which causality and evolution
are only specifications. One thing is always explained as
caused by another or as arising genetically from it. What
now exists is the product not of an a priori, otherworldly
cause, but of a material earlier one. Of the four causes
which Aristotle had distinguished, the material and efficient
causes have displaced the formal and final causes.

This type of thinking is at the basis of the two great
groups of sciences which have been established successively
in the course of the modern age, the natural sciences and the
human and social sciences. Essentialism might be compared
with the dinosaurs, the sciences with the mammals, which were

already present before but developed their abundance of forms
only after they could pour into the territories left vacant by
the extinction of the dinosaurs. Nothing is more false than
to contrast the natural sciences with the human and social
sciences as if natural science dealt only with the permanent
and the human and social sciences only with changes. One of
Leibniz's writings is called Protogea: the earth too passed
through other conditions, by which the present ones can be
explained. Natural science too becomes great only when it
takes the time-factor seriously, so that time is no longer
limited to the dimension of imitation or repetition of something timeless. The liberation of the real from the apparent
power of the ideal to immanent causality is also liberation
to unabridged temporality. A thing may no longer be measured
by its eternal model but it must be followed through its various stages of transformation. it does not have a basic core
that only develops or diminishes in time; it is totally subject to time and undergoes radical transformation.

Parmenides distinguished between perception, which is
oriented toward multiplicity and therefore deceptive, and
thought, which alone can penetrate to the unity of true being.
Plato adopted both the pair of contraries and their valuation,
with the added modification that he links the individual with
perception and the general with thought. Since we have always
perceived, the individual has according to him always existed.
But we should rise above its subjective appearance to the
truth of the stronger being of the universal. In this model
the debasement of the individual to a mere semi-existence is
just as false as the assumption that we already possess it
without further ado. Bergson has shown that we generally move
neither in the general nor in the individual but in an intermediary stratum. We do not look at reality for its own particular nature, but we tend to subject the real to coarse pragmatic categories. From here there are two paths of research:
one to the more adequate and higher concept, the other to the
ever more detailed penetration of the singular. This second
way also is one of progressive mastery and by no means a mere
marking of time on the everyday level.

Rationalism and empiricism, the two methods (that is all
they are) of the seventeenth and eighteenth centuries, are not
distributed so that one seeks the universal and the other the
individual. Empiricism too (though it did not realize how
unempirical it really was) penetrates beyond mere data to laws
and formulae, with the difference that it seeks to gain them
not by deductive speculation based on innate ideas but induc-
tively and starting from observations. Natural laws are,
according to Ernst Mach, only "abbreviations" for these observations.

Following Windelband's procedure of distinguishing between "nomothetic" and "ideographic" sciences, Heinrich Rickert defined the natural sciences as generalizing sciences, the cultural sciences -- as he called them -- as individualizing, singularizing sciences. First, one comment on this. The generalization   done by natural science is completely different from that of classical metaphysics, for it does not abstract from the particular but it seeks an underlying law. Its universal is mathematically quantifiable. Even its mode of generalization thus must stand in opposition to Aristotelianism, whose still naive generalizations impede the non-representationalism of science.

But natural science also investigates the phenomenon in its particularity as well as in its temporal changeability. Formerly it had been an unquestioned axiom that the eternal and the general are the higher, now Galileo, as a scientist ("the detractors of corruptibility would deserve to be changed into statues"), and Hegel, as a philosopher of history, praises precisely that which is transitory. The highest thing seems to be that which is irreplaceably unique and does not reoccur. Galileo discovered the sun-spots with his telescope (while the Aristotelians with their hypertrophied conceptual thinking refused to use an instrument that showed such things, for it followed from the nature of the sun as the purest star that it can have no spots). On the other hand, the cultural (human and social) sciences also generalize: they cannot get along without concepts, types and genera, such as for instance "monarchy" or "sonnet," and they also have "laws," though these apply in a lesser scope and without the inviolability of natural laws. Yet Rickert is right to a degree. Natural science seeks a law even for the origin and structure of what is individual. By subsumption under the general, it covers a broader sector of objects. For the objects of the human and social sciences, on the other hand, much less is gained by subsumption. Individuality has greater priority. It is consequently more justified to spend time contemplating their respectively specific content. Therefore conflict between natural science and philosophy is primarily a conflict between two forms of generalization, while it is only in the human and social sciences that the conflict between (both philosophical and natural-scientific) generalization and individualization reaches a peak.

The Limits of Greek Historical Understanding

The greatest talent of the Greeks was insight into structure. They were under the spell of pure form which provided the standard of perfection for everything real. They saw

reality as only a repetition and variation of pure form. For
the Greeks anything real is in its basic layer only a specimen of a genus and is only secondarily unique. Therefore they
are brilliant in philosophy, while history, which through its
attention precisely to the unique is the great counterpart of
philosophy, is not as highly developed among them as it has
been among us since the eighteenth century. Nietzsche mar-
veled at the still relatively unhistorical mode of seeing of
the Greeks, though he attributed it not to philosophical
talent but to a healthy mythological instinct. Even when they
write history the Greeks remain philosophers at heart: they
still adopt the Oriental cyclic theory according to which all
states run through the same phases. Even the incomparable
Thucydides believes that since human nature remains the same
in its striving for power, everything will always be repeated
in about the same way: the same motives, the same effects.
The historical events he describes become for him surrepti-
tious examples of typical political constellations. With his
book he wants to create an "eternal property" from which those
who will come later will be able to learn for their lives.

In the field of literary history the Greeks have even less
sense of individuality, not only because they always regard
the individual work primarily as the embodiment of a generic
pattern, but also because they do not, along with the work's
relationship of imitation of the untemporal generic idea, consider the relationship of expression, by which the changing
nature of classes and ages and of individual creators finds
expression in it. Just as in their epistemology they (except
for the Sophists) overlooked the contribution of the subject,
the Greeks had but a weakly developed sense of history and
psychology and for the fact that different life-centers are
manifested in history and that this is one of its instructive
qualities. Therefore the ancient philologists, for whom
this whole dimension of classification was left undeveloped,
did not succeed very well at separating the genuine parts of
the Iliad and the Odessey from the later revisions and inser-
tions, while the modern philologist who reads the handwriting
of a unique personality in every piece of writing, immediately recognizes that there are parts in both epics which could
not stem from the same author (just as the same bush does not
yield both red and white roses, as Wilamowitz says), and
can characterize the different authors who worked at them.
No Hellenistic editor asked about the chronology of Sophocles'
tragedies; they were equally considered paragons of dramatic
perfection. Only the modern Sophocles scholar discovers in
them a development of form and technique and detects a human
and intellectual development of the author. He assigns them
to different stages and different situations of the author's

life and so penetrates, after over 2000 years, infinitely
deeper than his antique predecessor who was so much closer to
Sophocles.

History even is, as Aristotle expressed it, practically an
insult to the philosophical sense because in it -- as opposed
to nature -- no trace of rational order prevails. Aristotle,
who was enough of an empirical historian to have a collection
of Greek constitutions compiled, does not forgive history because very often in it evil is victorious and chance prevails.
Historical events can occur independently without objective
correlation except the chronological one of external connection in time; for instance, the naval battles of Salamis and
Himera because they took place in the same year (480 B.C. --
the example is extremely badly chosen since the Carthaginians
defeated near Himera in Sicily were allied with the Persians:
it was not by accident that the enemies of the Greeks chose
to attack them simultaneously). Aristotle therefore praises
literature as being more philosophical than history (his theory
of catharsis had also defended literature against Plato's
condemnation). For literature does not merely report facts,
it also reveals motives. Compared with the incoherence of
history, an artistically formed plot is systematized by its
beginning, middle and end, and all parts of it are meaningfully connected.

History as Anti-Philosophy in the Age of Goethe

For Platonism (not yet for Plato himself) the universal,
which alone gives things form, distinctness and meaning, stands
opposed to matter, which serves only as a substratum to this
universal; likewise the knowledge of thought and that of the
senses are respectively oriented to these two poles of being.
The victory of nominalism seemed to leave behind only matter
and the senses. But nominalism exists within the scope of the
Judeo-Christian religion, for which creation bears the traces
of the creator. Modern pantheism, on the other hand, regards
itself as perfused with divinity. Therefore, what modern science in its two groups, investigates, is for it not only
material, not only brute facts. The more we know things, the
more we know God (Spinoza). All being is revelation, expresses
something (Hamann), has meaning. But this meaning, especially
historical meaning, cannot be separated from the individually
unique features that it adheres to. We grasp it only in its
concreteness. Therefore it cannot be thought like a concept,
but only observed. But observation, which comes into play
here, is not the bare sensation posited by sensualism. Contrary to the traditional disjunction, the Age of Goethe and the
Historical School discovered yet another contrast to thought, a

new organ of knowledge. It is also a mental perception which
encompasses the coherent whole (synholon) or an interpenetra-
tion of being and meaning on the objective side with its own
synholon in a single organic unseparated act of perception. It
perceives significance in the individual fact precisely because
it is ineffable, a symbol. It feels its way in matters for
which rationality is too coarse-meshed.

Compared with the constructions of rationalism -- which was
hostile to history, for what could be learned from it that was
not already much better known in the idea? -- the historical
sense of Herder and the Romantics is much truer to life; compared with the one ideal of rationalism, their historical sense
is richer in pluralism; compared with the thinness of the concept, it is fuller and deeper in its interwoven reality. "Imagine aristocracy in all its characteristics, yet never could
you imagine Sparta" (Ranke). Thus, what we have here is not
merely a more intensive research in one field of objectivity,
that of history. A whole new manner of seeing has developed,
a new form of intellectual comprehension, not only along with
but beyond philosophy, and rejecting philosophy as a false road
that must be left behind. "What philosophy was, history has
become." Philosophy too can strive to appropriate the great
lesson of the Age of Goethe and change accordingly. While for
Hegel the absolute idea must of necessity appear in finite
reality, so that logical consequence and historical progress
coincide, for Schelling these two things separate, for he sees
every transition as based on a freely given surplus, an un-
derivable historical act. After a type of philosophy that
deduces from derived concepts, there must now begin, as he
says (Die Weltalter, 1811), a "narrative philosophy." The
narrating does not come from a weakness of thought, but already
stands beyond thought. In his Theses for the Reform of Philosophy (1842), Feuerbach demands that the element in man
"which does not philosophize, which rather is against philosophy
and opposed to abstract thought and which therefore in Hegel
is demoted to a footnote must be taken up into the text of
philosophy." For Nicolai Hartmann, the individual, in direct
reversal of the Platonic hierarchy, ranks higher than the
unchangeable universal -- even and precisely in its transitori-
ness, which is its criterion. The same was also true of Georg
Simmel: there is danger in the high complexity of the concrete,
but precisely the more mortal it is, the higher its value.
Phenomenology is also a form of philosophy that is preoccupied
with the individual, observable descriptive fact, and distrust-
ful of concepts. It was incorporated as the first stage in the
comprehensive structure of Hartmann's ontology. Adorno too
advocated the non-identity that was suppressed by the domination of the concept.

The Positivistic and Hegelian Misunderstandings

The manner of dealing with history that was established in the Age of Goethe is exposed to two misunderstandings. One is that of nineteenth century positivistic historicism. The turning to history as such is retained, but meaningfulness and significance are no longer found in it but only a series of random facts, or -- as opponents of this view said -- "dead matter." Positivism is "perverted Romanticism" (Karl Joël).

The other, likewise typically "philosophical" misunderstanding is that of Hegel. For Hegel things happened "rationally" in world history as a whole, and this means two things. First, he recognizes in it a coherent unity: what is later did not proceed accidentally from what was earlier, and even in apparently only external events, such as wars, more intense awareness, more freedom gradually gain ascendency under the secret guidance of the World Spirit. Secondly, it follows that not all, but only a few selected individual historical events are representative of the first appearance of these principles. Universal meaning is confirmed in the meaning of the particular.

But precisely thereby Hegel separates meaning from reality again (for all who stand under his influence, as we have seen, meaning is inseparably amalgamated with reality and concretely observable only in it) and seeks to deduce it purely in the mind, to define it and reduce it to a formula. Therefore Friedrich Meinecke in his Origin of Historicism (1936), left out Hegel when he traced the breakthrough of the sense of history in authors and historians. Benedetto Croce blamed him for this, but Meinecke replied in a separate essay in which he proved that Hegel in principle fails to recognize what is historically individual. He lets everything concrete immediately evaporate into the mental. He sees it as only a dilatory documentation of an idea which he already knew from other sources. Hegel, in an earlier essay, also wrote explicitly against "abstract" thought which subsumes a complex reality onesidedly under a single concept and eliminates all its other qualities. But his counterposition does not consist in viewing the supraconceptually real, but in encircling it by a multiplicity of overlapping and intermingled complementary concepts.

The Biblical Basis and Aesthetic Parallels

That God reveals himself in history, that he manifests his will in it, that secular events have a latent religious content -- that is the conviction of the ancient Hebrews. Therefore among them history occupies the place that philosophy has for the Greeks: the Bible is a history book. Greek dualism,

on the contrary, restricts meaning to the special sphere of the
concept, and therefore demotes the concrete to mere materiality,
the historical to   mere   contingency. In contrast the
Hebrews still lived in the primeval, unfragmented unity of the
particular with its innate forces and transcendency. Down to
our century tradition-conscious Jews cloak general statements
in the form of a story (Moschal): "The thing is so: once
there was a widow with an only son..." Christianity still lives
from this unity: the historical Jesus is also Christ the
Redeemer; the message of salvation cannot be separated from
his life and passion. Christian Gnostics sought to unite this
history-bound mode of thought with the generalizing of Greek
philosophy: they wanted to free the Gospel of its historicity
at least insofar as, contrary to Judaism and Christianity for
which the course of history is rectilinear, they thought cyclic-
ally and wanted to have a Christ appear again in each of the
many worlds (Aeons). Against this attempt, Augustine -- who in
this respect stood in a situation analogous to that of Kierkegaard against Hegel -- flung his "semel Christus mortuus est"
(Christ died only once!). In order to stress the unique and
concrete historicalness of this event, the words "crucified
under Pontius Pilate" were taken up into the creed. Decisive
for the message of salvation is precisely its inextricability
from the unique act of salvation. This is, however, true of
salvation-history in general; it is not limited to the fact
that in Christ God sent his Son. "The historical is spiritual;
the spirtual is historical." Perhaps this principle is also
the reason why Christianity won out in antiquity over Greek
philosophy. Men felt that in the "supraheavenly place" of the
colorless and formless Platonic ideas the reality of life and
the world was lost. The success of Christianity was based on
the fact that it is a mixed form: ethics based on a philosophy
of history amalgamated with a biographical novel.

    Precisely the basic axiom of Judeo-Christian religiosity --
that in the historically individual fact there resides a deeper
content of meaning that cannot be abstracted out with concepts
-- is also the axiom of historical scholarship since the late
eighteenth century, except that in the latter case it shifted
from living faith to mere theory and that it applied not only
to "salvation-history" but also to history as a whole. As
eighteenth century historians try to merely depict their
meaningful content, they set themselves a completely different
task than Greek philosophers such as Thucidides and Polybius,
who sought to highlight the typical. It is not accidental that
such history-writing of concrete meaning arose only in the
Christian West. It constitutes one more late fruit of Christianity, though it was able to ripen only after the narrow and
dogmatic framework of the Christian philosophy of history had

been broken. However, the conception of the meaningfully
individual in historicism is not exclusively "secularization."
It was rediscovered and understood as a necessary counter-
offensive against the absolute claim of abstract thought in
eighteenth century rationalism. But it has a strong ally in
Christianity, whose opposition to philosophy it continues in
its own way. Both have the same primary experience. This
experience of history was defended against philosophy, in
antiquity by a religion, and in modern times by a science.

What historians since the late eighteenth century confirm
by their activity, the aestheticians, who prepared the ground
for them, had already won in principle (A. Baeumler); both
stand shoulder to shoulder against rationalism. According to
Plotinus, whose aesthetics are still influential down to
Schopenhauer, in fact down to our own day, the artist too, just
as much as the philosopher, strives for the idea. While
nature remained far behind the idea, the artist -- who therefore has a right to stylize nature -- approaches the idea much
more closely in his work, impresses the invisible upon the
visible and makes it manifest. This is what makes art beautiful. But while Plotinus defends art against Plato in this
manner, he still remains a Platonist. For him too the philosopher stands above the artist: only he sees the idea itself
in its supersensory and transcendent purity. Hegel phrases
this in terms of the history of philosophy: since we have
philosophy, art is no longer modern in the full sense. In contrast Baumgarten had already declared: there is absolutely no
competitive relationship between philosophy and art, for each
has a different object of knowledge: art does not seek to
capture the idea, but the particular. For Baumgarten too philosophy, which aims at the universal still remains the higher
medium, while art belongs to an "inferior gnoseology": but
this is not because it accomplishes the same thing as philosophy in a less perfect manner. It accomplishes something
else. The next generation was able to start with this, and
advancing beyond Baumgarten place art on an equal footing with
philosophy because of its focus on individual reality, indeed
above derivative pale philosophy because of its original truth.
The poet now becomes not only the creator of beautiful form,
but also the possessor of deeper knowledge.

PART II

PRECONDITIONS AND OBJECTIVES OF PHILOSOPHY

CHAPTER 6

THE ROOTS OF PHILOSOPHY

Institutions that fulfill a necessary, natural and obvious
function in a vital complex do not reflect upon themselves.
They live on without interpretation; they are self-satisfied as
to their nature and performance. The same is true of the vital
complex as a whole as long as it is securely founded in itself.
There are, however, two historical moments in which this
autarchy of being is broken and which motivate awareness. One
is when a change or a completely new development is about to
take place. This must be justified toward what was before;
the new form must be presented convincingly as the better one.
The other moment (which very often coincides with the first,
but is generally experienced from the other side) is when an
existing system is threatened from within or from without. Till
then it rested matter-of-coursely upon its foundations, but now,
here too, a process of self-justification begins. In order to
protect its existence, it gives an account of itself and tries
to demonstrate its raison-d'etre. Only impugned nobility engages in self-reflection and develops an ideology of nobility.
Awareness always seems to be gained from a need to legitimize.
This need arises at two points: origin and danger. That which
is beginning projects an image of itself; that which is chal-
lenged gains distance from itself and also sums itself up in
an image. Where the new development collides with established
reality the spark of reason flashes. Reason itself becomes the
extended field of this collision.
Philosophy never goes unchallenged. Even in its origins
it is attacked by traditionalism as hybris whereby the individual claims to know better than his fathers, and as a threat to
the old inherited, sacred order. It is attacked by the world
of practical action as useless. But insofar as direct knowledge
of the basis and meaning of things fills a real need, religion
is there and believes it has always possessed such knowledge,
and it therefore resists philosophy as a competitor. Philosophy comes into a world which could well have gotten along
without it and has not been waiting for it. It has to fight
for its territory. Even after it has gained a certain consoli-
dation and acceptance through the Greeks, it is attacked again
in the modern age, this time by science: it poses false questions, it is speculative. In the one case it had been a new
upstart, but now it is considered obsolete and antiquated.
Again it must defend itself: formerly it was against those
who were there before it, now against those struggling upward.

Self-defence means, however, that it must explain and define itself, show what its nature is and demonstrate its necessity.

The philosopher is the adventurer in a world of sedate and secure men, the odd dissenter when everyone else agrees. Misunderstanding and reproach dog his heels. Though philosophy at times does become temporarily an unquestioningly recognized mental attitude, repeatedly its situation in the world becomes problematic. As self-interpretation is, according to Dilthey, a characteristic of all life, so too of philosophy. The question of its own nature has always been and remains one of the great questions of philosophy.

Philosophy from Crisis and Sickness

Because unguided by instincts, man lives by traditions which he observes and by new inventions which he creates (and on which in turn a tradition can be based): these two abilities make up his life. Both abilities, although attributed to man as such, correspond nonetheless to psychologically different types. The extrovert (the distinction comes from C.G. Jung and was not yet anthropologically motivated) follows the social and cultural patterns in which he exists and does not problematize them. His life is fulfilled, as it runs its course, in its practical purposes and vital joys. Compared with him, the introvert is not only, as the word suggests, turned inward, but above all disengaged from the direct performance of life, not caught in and captivated by it, and thus he is a contemplator and observer: both of himself and of life and things. From the point of view of daily practice he seems to be lacking something; his behavior is awkward. But this is not a weakness which he then compensates for by other strengths; rather, because he lives from these other strengths, the things immediately around him mean less to him. He sees not only what others see; he sees more, though he finds it more difficult to act; he sees structures and foundations; he asks about the past and the future, about meaning and goals. Hence he is the one who criticizes and improves the existing forms and who initiates changes of direction. That he stands outside and above things is a source of regeneration for them. Thus he too fulfills an indispensible task for the community and for the species.

Introversion, though not as such constituting philosophy, is one of its psychological foundations. Whoever finds satisfaction in his given environment and activity, does not philosophize.

Independently of a habitually introverted temperament, there are three philosophical stages in every life: 1. Once he begins to perceive objective relations, the child asks

untiringly: "Why?" It wants to learn the cause, the reason.
It also acquires the concept of the world and then it asks:
"What is the world? Where is the end of the world?" It is not
yet dulled to the boundary questions as is the adult who out
of convention or lassitude no longer poses them, or also
because he knows that no one can answer them. 2. In puberty
the childish world-view is shattered, while that of adulthood
still has not been understood and become binding. As in history the periods of transition are the most philosophical, so
at this biographical boundary-line of two world-views, doubts
and questions are stirred up. The young person discovers his
own individuality, comes in conflict with tradition and religion,
is ideologically excited and ponders on the meaning of existence.
3. The end of life frees the gaze for the entirety; questions
arise as to whether it was lived right, and whether there is
an afterlife.

But reflectiveness, otherwise unusual, is also stimulated
when the rectilinear course of life, its own free streaming
is hampered and its harmony disturbed. When a habit meets an
obstacle, according to Dewey, something analogous to what
Bergson called "the birth of intelligence" takes place (Rousseau
and Carlyle held an opposite causality, blaming awareness for
disrupting the harmony of life and they therefore called it "a
form of illness"). The crisis which tears us out of the
meaningful security of our life brings the problems to our
attention. We now seek knowledge as a compensation, comfort,
and medicine. Often an illness becomes an occasion for reflection, for it is an interruption and creates distance, and subconsciously the cause for our falling ill may be that we needed
such reflection. The schizophrenic whose ties with the familiar
world are dissolved undergoes quasi-metaphysical experiences in
the first phases of the disease. There is also an attitude of
negativeness which likewise prepares the ground for philosophy,
just as many artists gain their artistic talent through
lability, hypersensitivity, abnormality, indeed degeneracy,
which normally make a person unfit for life. But even without
any illness we fall out of the "interpreted world" (Rilke) into
what Jaspers called "boundary situations." We discover subjection to chance and inevitability of guilt and death: we lose
our hold and "fail." A solution can be sought in God, or one
can flee to a harmoniously rationalized ivory-tower world; but
philosophy brings the boundary situations undisguised to the
awareness. It smashes the secure world, puts man face to face
with his origin and his real nature and exposes him to the
movement of growth.

All such inner hardship may well sensitize one for philosophy, may activate its process in man; but it is not an
inescapable precondition for philosophy. "Existential shock"

and "engagement" give philosophy cogency and depth, yet they must be broken again by distance and scepticism, by autonomy of insight and thought, in a mixture of seriousness and play that is hard for the non-philosopher to understand. The two things can be lacking, in fact they can even decrease the freedom for the theoretical _élan_ and limit the field of vision. A person entangled in crisis and disease is obsessed with his own problems and seeks only a remedy for them. He lacks the sobriety necessary for objective, rounded, penetrating knowledge. The schizoid person will develop a philosophy of the threatened identity, and nothing more. To really open up the philosophical horizon, other factors must enter the picture.

Philosophy from Ignorance and Problems

Along with the psychological roots of philosophy there are also formal ones. Socrates uncovered a primeval self-experience of the mind when with his penetrating questions he showed that most men, including specialists in the arts and teachers of wisdom, only think that they know, but in reality as soon as one inquires, for instance, as to whether and why their a actions are good, they do not kn . Socrates said that he differed from them not through knowledge -- perhaps the gods reserved that for themselves -- but through knowing that he did not know.

A Sophistic dilemma went: there is no such thing as asking, for either one already knows, or one does not know, in which case one also doesn't know what to ask about. But this disjunction between knowing and not knowing is incomplete. As in everything else, here too there is an in-between (Plato: _metaxy_). We come upon limits of our knowledge and are thus already beyond the limits, for every limit sees in two directions: we have knowledge of the unknown, for at least we know that more could still be known. By anticipation and sketchily, in degrees of clarity, we are already in contact with what lies beyond, according to rules of the coherence of part and whole, of cause and effect, etc., that are deeply engraved in our mind; that which has already been discovered contains clues about what is still hidden. They make us feel how far off we are from genuine and complete penetration into reality. When we are knowingly ignorant in this way, then we are in a quandary, we stand before a problem. Socrates was the discoverer of the "awareness of a problem" (as N. Hartmann, whose description of it is outstanding, called it). Plato characterized it from its emotional side as a "sense of awe" and he said that philosophy sprang from this sense of awe.

For the awareness of a problem is not a stable, self-sufficient condition: its knowledge seeks to penetrate beyond

itself. We want to change our anticipatory knowledge into
founded knowledge; the unknown, of which we know only that
it exists, into knowledge of its nature; uncertainty into
certainty. Thus the problem sets a process in motion; non-
knowledge is the stimulus of an active longing for knowledge.
Socrates, as the discoverer of non-knowledge, is also the
discoverer of the philosophical question. What is knowledge?
What is justice? That is what his conversations were all about.
The pre-Socratics proclaim; Socrates asks.

Empirical and rational investigation can eliminate a problem. Knowledge attained, says Aristotle, puts us in a mood
oppostie to the one with which we set out on our quest: first
one wonders at the incommensurability between the diagonal and
the side of the rectangle; but nothing could surprise a
geometrist more than if the diagonal were suddenly commensur-
able. For Socrates, on the other hand, the question is not
merely a first step. He persists in it without firm result
except an attitude toward life. By this isolation he makes it
doubly visible as a separate motive factor. He has and teaches,
he says, no knowledge -- and this sets him apart from the
contemporary Sophists. What he does is only philo-sophia
"striving for wisdom" in the strict sense of the word (the
term acquired the meaning of stable convictions only after
Socrates). Therefore he also called his followers, not pupils,
but "fellow strivers."

Later Nicholas de Cusa (who also revived the Platonic motif
of the "hunt" for wisdom) followed Socrates with his "docta
ignorantia" (learned ignorance). But, for him the learned-
ness of ignorance resides exclusively in God. In his infinity
God can never fit within our finite understanding. Therefore
we know of him only what he is not (negative theology); we
know only that we cannot know of him. But this very thing is
already ultimate wisdom, not merely its first stage. It doesn't,
as was the case with Socrates, initiate a process whose result,
the knowledge discovered, will if possible eliminate non-knowledge. Socrates does not know because he has not yet found the
truth and still hopes to; the ignorance of Cusa is already
itself the discovery.

Normally this problem arises spontaneously: unclarity seeks
clarification; new experience seeks to be mastered by a new set
of categories; a contradiction that we have become aware of
seeks to be eliminated. But the philosopher seeks the problem:
by his higher intellectual standard he finds and poses it where
others had not seen any difficulty. He senses a riddle behind
things that otherwise seem perfectly natural. He does not
accept "familiarity" as "sufficient knowledge" (Hegel). He
goes from the solution back to questionableness; he poses new
questions that conflict with what everyone else believes:

Couldn't other _mores_ exist? Are things really what they seem?
Thus the philosopher goes against the natural tendency of our
mind, which always aims for an integral world-view, a valid
interpretation. He shatters the horizon, looks behind systems
of order, and so constitutes a countercurrent to the main-
stream. Because philosophy abandons apparent security and
goes back into open terrain, it is also a question of courage
(Nietzsche). Not only must it overcome the natural tendency
within the mind itself, but also the resistence of all those
in society who do not wish to be deprived of the shelter of a
rounded cosmos of knowledge, and who do not wish to be fright-
ened out of the peace of supposed possession of the truth. As
Hegel exemplified it precisely by Socrates, they regard the
bringer of new truth only as the destroyer of their own.

Even Kant sometimes said that philosophy cannot be learned
like geometry or history; it is by nature a quest. Lessing's
proverb that not truth but the quest of it befits man (which
Kierkegaard later appropriated and to which he gave an existential twist) stems less from the Socratic spirit than from
that of Calvinism which recognizes no "enjoyment of God" and
is the religion of the quest of God _par excellence_. Also
Fichte said: the nature of the mind is pure agility. Just as
Schleiermacher had defined religion no longer from the objective content of its creed but from its subjective religiosity,
in this century, Georg Simmel likewise defined philosophy as
formal mobility of the mind, a functional manner of dealing
with things. As in vitalism, which is the school of philosophy
to which he belongs, life must always objectify itself, and yet
the higher value lies not in the objectification but in the
stream of life itself, likewise philosophy must aim for results
but its chief significance lies in its attitude as a basic
power of the mind. Its function and its content must be kept
apart -- all the more so since many problems are not solved but
made more acute by deeper knowledge. The benefit of philosophy
does not reside exclusively in the right result, in fact not
at all in the result. "The demand of the metaphysical urge is
not fulfilled only at the end of its journey."

Philosophy from Doubt

We grow up in what the English philologist Gilbert Murray
called the "inherited conglomerate." A culture's stock of
knowledge is never a coherent system. As in geology, heterogeneous strata lie over one another. Earlier material is not
always rejected, even when it is incompatible with new convictions. This incoherence of tradition is a primary motive
that provokes criticism of it. Perhaps, as has been suspected

it was not pure chance that philosophy originated in the
Ionian Greek colonies; they simply had to be more sensitive
to the inadequacy of tradition since they had two different
traditions, that which they brought with them and the oriental
one of their new homeland, which relativized each other on
contact. This provided a basis for abandoning tradition in
general and risking one's own explanations of the world. But
this immediately provoked the same criticism again because of
the multiplicity of philosophical systems that existed from
the first, "the chaos of systems" which Kant still found fault
with.

A second motive for not blindly accepting traditional
truths lies in the rising expectations of rational knowledge
itself: it now subjects truth to an interrogation (Kant's
Critiques, i.e., court processes), in which it must satisfy
certain criteria. Descartes wanted to subject all knowledge
to the mathematical or more precisely the arithmetical ideal
(therefore he transformed geometry, which is still concrete,
analytically into arithmetic): philosophy must move in defined,
logically arranged concepts. He therefore summoned before the
tribunal of the ideal all earlier truths (vetus opinio), which
includes three things: 1) the truth one hears everyday; 2)
that of previous philosophy; and 3) the self-experienced truth
of the senses in contrast with conceptual thought (Hegel still
describes how "sensory awareness loses all sight and hearing"
when the higher forms of awareness begin). For Descartes,
philosophy must, in principle, subject all these forms of
truth to doubt and may retain only those which meet the new,
more stringent conditions of knowledge. As in Protestantism
one may not simply accept oneself in one's condition as a
creature but must "justify" oneself before God, so here opinions must justify themselves, otherwise they are condemned.

Descartes hopes to win better truth because of these conditions. And he also believes that much of the old truth will
yet be salvaged. The doubt he practices is only methodical,
not radical like that of the old Sceptics who because of illusions of the senses and false conclusions considered truth
totally inaccessible. His doubt claims to be a stimulus and
not the end of knowledge.

The difference was discussed above between whether a problem comes up by itself or whether it is intentionally problematized. There is something analogous in this context. Descartes
does not wait for doubt to arise by itself, he elevates it to
a method. But this is a revolutionary event in the history of
philosophy. Max Scheler called it "the shifting of the burden
of proof." Originally men were inclined to trust the statements of others (as late as 1900, when someone wanted to
borrow money, he did not have to undergo a "credit check").

Whoever did not trust a person's credibility had to disprove
it. But now it is met with distrust from the start, and it
must be proven. Formerly everything was considered true until
its truth is proven (just as in Locke's state everything is
allowed that is not forbidden, while in Hobbes' state everything is forbidden that is not allowed). That is why in the
Middle Ages the plaintiff did not have to prove the guilt of
the accused, but the accused had to prove his innocence, and
this was reversed only later.

What began with Bacon, whose Novum Organon in its first
destructive part starts by unmasking and casting down the idols,
the false gods of knowledge that confuse and block the mind,
and with Descartes, was continued with increased intensity in
the Enlightenment's "unmasking" of "prejudice," in the
"critique of ideology" which Marxism practices on all mental
constructs, as well as in psychoanalysis which abstracts
motives unknown to the subject himself from his ideas, actions
and modes of behavior. The modern age is the "age of suspicion."

Socrates' non-knowledge was directed at still undiscovered
being. It sought to penetrate further into it. Descartes'
doubt, on the other hand, is directed not at being but at the
structure of our knowledge. According to the "principle of
awareness," which was first formulated by Reinhold but is
already presupposed by Descartes, we possess all being only
through the medium of our awareness and of the structure of
knowledge with which we grasp it and by whose intermediary
world the apparently immediate world is transmitted. Knowledge is what must be improved: it ought to be as certain as
possible, it ought to be incontrovertible. Socrates seeks
the truth of being; Descartes seeks the certainty of truth.

Socrates too tests (basanizein) truth for its "firmness."
Descartes too is after truth of which certainty is only its
highest quality. Thus the difference seems slight. But in
fact it is tremendous. For now a type of philosopher arises
who no longer achieves primarily a direct apprehension of the
object, but only an oblique apprehension of knowledge on an
indirect, reflected level. His basic experience is not being
but error. Since it can err, knowledge is harnassed to the
discipline of strict methodology which is to lead it on the
right path to incontrovertible certitude. The result is verified or found to be false. "Ultimate proof" is required.

This pathos of caution born of disappointment, of the
trauma of being misled -- always an element of philosophy --
has entered an intensive stage since Descartes. It is, on the
one hand, a sign of maturity. It provides us protection
against the wild luxuriation of fantastic ideas. On the other
hand, it is parasitic: it already presumes interest

in the world and a turning to it. Where it becomes totally
predominant, it leads to the decline of philosophy. For it
could be that we can arrive at more certain truth about lesser
things than about more essential things. If philosophy therefore may no longer be a venture, if every statement which cannot be processed through a computer is considered ridiculous,
this would cause men to detour around the deeper problems of
being, history and existence and lead to a shallow mentality.

Philosophy from the Individual

Even in his basic structure man is more than vitality.
Since he has no instincts, he must develop his own behavior --
which for that precise reason is more than an attitude and a
reaction. In every community traditional patterns of behavior
develop. Still, in unique situations an individual faces new
decisions; he must modify the patterns inventively to fit
these new situations. As a creative being he is the individu-
ated being.

But along with the anthropology of the individual stands
the cultural history of the individual. In primitive conditions, traditions embracing all of life in a tight fabric are
dominant. They apply all the more strictly because they also
always have magical meaning: every slightest deviation could
conjure up unforeseen harm for the entire tribe. Therefore
cultures are inclined to become "fossilized" (Toynbee). Relatively without historical development, institutions, once
established, tend to be preserved for their own sake. Changes
take place only unwilled and unnoticed by the awareness. Thus,
the conservative force in such situations completely overwhelms
and stiffles the creative force. Their bearer, the individual,
cannot hold his own against communal tradition.

Only late in history, i.e., since the rise of high cultures,
but with a real breakthrough only since the Greeks, does this
basic anthropological disposition attain greater independence
and historical power. Only now does the individual become a
sufficient counterpart to compel tradition, which formerly
remained uncontested as an ancient and sacred heritage, to
justify itself. The individual now finds courage and strength
to declare his independence from tradition's authority and
expectations. Free, with his own thoughts and actions, with
new discoveries and inventions, he liberates himself in all
fields. He revolutionizes the fields themselves, creates new
ones that never before existed. The individual, who had previously not been self-aware, and had not dared to come forth,
is finally approved and called for by a complex and flexible
culture which needs the individual for its operation and
renewal.

This is the world in which, contrary to traditional self-interpretations which were handed down unquestioned from generation to generation with the total traditional heritage, philosophy comes into being as the personal discovery of one individual. It presupposes a high degree of individualization gained independently of it. But once philosophy exists, it in turn becomes a weapon in the hands of the individual, it contributes to strengthening him still more against the claims of the past and of the multitude. Thus both mutually intensify one another.

The process of individualization takes place in three dimensions:

1. In tribal feuds, if one tribe has killed a man from another tribe then a man of equal standing is killed in the first tribe as analogous compensation. But the ius talionis (law of revenge) also applies within one society: if a contractor builds a house badly so that it collapses and kills the owner's son, then as punishment the contractor's son ought to be killed! (Hammurabi). As opposed to oriental law, the Old Testament first discovers the juridical-ethical individual: "The fathers shall not die for the children nor the children for the fathers, but each shall die for his own sin? (Deuteronomy). Legal and moral responsibility is non-transferable. Each one's action is ascribable to himself alone.

2. But moral liberation from the social group does not yet mean liberation from the tradition prevalent within it. The rational individual of the Greeks first becomes independent in this respect. Reason, which is active in each individual, is the counterforce by which the individual can confidently escape from the tutelage of tradition and the pressure to conformity and no longer fear conflict with it. Reason makes the individual self-centered and autonomous.

But, in Greek philosophy, reason only discovers the reality, structure and norm that already existed before. It makes no difference whether one man's reason or another's discovers them. Truth is the same for all: otherwise it would not be truth. And likewise the power of reason that is directed toward truth is the same in all men. Socrates and Callias differ only "by flesh and bones" (Aristotle). This constitutes the limit of rational individuation. It makes for individuality but not for uniqueness. Each man becomes an ethical center -- and thus he is immunized against tradition. But he immediately exchanges his liberation for a new allegiance. He escapes the general mores only to subject himself to another universal norm, though one he personally understands and recognizes, namely that of objective truth. Uniformity prevails in the world of reason as well as in the traditional group.

3. The Renaissance and the Age of Goethe discovered the

qualitative individual in quite other sources. Here each
person was different from every other by unique, non-recurrent,
inexchangeable particularity, by a specific nature belonging
only to him. As the individuality of things is accessible to
the modern age in more definite contours, since they are no
longer seen through the veil of universals, so too the individuality of man. Since his strength and his splendor no longer
consist in participation in a higher norm, the modern age
places them in his individuality. Thus, individuality, which
always existed in fact, is approved and particularly cultivated only now. But this would be merely external. In addition,
an interiority of the soul below the level of reason is also
discovered. The Greek by knowledge found a universal norm outside himself by what his reason sees: his attitude is imita-
tive; modern man expresses his historical and individual situation: his attitude is creative.

Philosophy, though in its self-image it stems from the
rational, in reality also has roots in the qualitative individual. One empiricist can more easily be replaced by another;
but philosophy remains linked with a personality. In this it
is related with art. A school is formed around an individual
but it dissolves again when he disappears or soon afterwards.
Although philosophical ideas move history (Hegel), this non-
institutionality is the source of philosophy's weakness as a
world power.

Philosophy from Reason

1. Philosophy and Enlightenment. The individual, as was
seen above, becomes self-aware when his reason is awakened.
Reason, which previously accepted and obeyed, now discovers
itself as a revolutionary force. It calls all traditional
values before "the judgment seat of reason," it sets itself up
as the "touchstone of truth" (Kant). Reason asks in principle,
holds to facts and probability, systematizes: therefore the
individual does not merely replace the previous mythical world-
view with a new mythical world-view, but with philosophy and
science.

But reason strives not only for purer knowledge. As it
approached all convictions with the question: "Are they true?"
so it approaches existing institutions with the question: "Are
they good?" It projects from itself the picture of a more just
order. The complacent world should in time be changed in that
direction, and thus action gains direction. In addition to
being, there is now an ought-to-be: in addition to an origin
there is now a goal: the "myth of the origin" is broken (Til-
lich).

Philosophy coincides with Enlightenment to the extent that

it identifies with the special interest of reason and makes
reason a standard and lever of history. It always was so
("Be modest and learn to doubt, for that is the mark of
intellect," Xenophanes) and it always will remain so, at a
fundamental level.

But it is not only Enlightenment. For Enlightenment requires a certain situation in time, it is essentially the
struggle against prejudice and false authority. They must
be hit in their vulnerable spots, refuted by reason, and dethroned. But they also seek to build: namely a rational,
humane society; but even there they want something and they
bind themselves to practical plans. They know no purpose-free
contemplation. There are questions which they simply do not
ask. This limits them both thematically and in the depth of
their insight. Romanticism reproached the Enlightenment of
"shallowness" stemming from its neglect of the emotions.
Philosophically the reproach should be worded otherwise:
Enlightenment also represses other powers of reason which can
become free again only in the greater detachment of a less
emotional revolutionary moment. Therefore, the greatest
philosophies (Plato, Hegel) come into being after the Enlighten-
ments.

On the other hand, philosophy can, as such or in particular
systems, gain the recognition of an entire age (as in Hellenism).
It can be the official philosophy of otherwise hostile forces,
the Church (Aristotle, in the Middle Ages) or the state (Marx,
in the Communist bloc), as a form of "altar-and-throne philosophy." But by the very fact of changing from the enlightened
and progressive side to the conservative, it loses something
that it has only on that side and as long as it is "dynamite"
(Nietzsche). To be a counterblow arouses in it energies which
otherwise atrophy. A valuable part of it develops only as
long as it is contraband. The liberal philosophy of the nineteenth century which contested nothing and was contested by
no one is shallow. Only three philosophers were great, the
ones who sought to awaken the age: Kierkegaard, Marx, Nietzsche.

Another reason why it is appropriate for philosophy not to
belong to the Establishment is because it asks questions that
are necessary but not strictly apodictic in their conclusions.
As long as it struggles, this quality of uncertainty is legitimate because then its theses are a weapon with a good point and
cutting edge. The opponent can be shown to be wrong only by
proving one's own claim to be right. "The sun is larger than
the Peloponnesus" (Anaxagoras): as far as this may be from the
full truth, it dethroned the greater error of Helios driving
his chariot across the sky. The new myth of occult powers was
a scientific improvement over the old myth of final causes. As
soon however as the new thesis has won, it becomes evident how

uncertain it was, and how doubtful it too is. Because of its
dominance it must be protected: but this claim kills philosophy, which is never secure. An intrinsic feature of the
inner structure of philosophy is the urge to cross beyond the
boundaries of firm knowledge. The historical situation most
favorable to accomplishing this is one when forces are press-
ing beyond the boundaries of a generally accepted world order
-- as happens to be the case currently.

     Apparently, therefore, two opposite forces must cooperate
in philosophy, a militant attitude that provides courage for
the "adventure of reason" (Kant) and a contemplative attitude
that broadens and controls.

     2. Instrumental Reason. Reason, as was said before, as
such represents a special interest. It speaks for itself. But
on the other hand it is also merely a formal power, empty
thinking without substance of its own, "instrumental reason."
It is employed by other interests and accepts such employment.
Extra-philosophical, concrete and real needs of men often
dictate its problems, indeed at times even its results. But
since needs change with the times, philosophies also change.

     In Hellenism philosophy is ethics: it gives the individ-
ual the firm ground that he lost in religion and state. In
the Middle Ages it is the "handmaiden of theology"; it proves
the existence of God and immortality. This is also in other
cases the function assigned to it: it merely rationalizes a
pre-existent world-view. In the Enlightenment it becomes the
instrument of liberation from the feudal state and Church: it
refutes God and immortality. In the Middle Ages it systematizes existing knowledge; in the Enlightenment it prepares
for the revolution. Natural science comes into existence: now
philosophy becomes the "handmaiden of science." As epistemology and methodology it strengthens both the inventiveness and
the certainty of science.

     There are problems that always remain the same, which
philosophy must face because it exists in a world that always
remains the same: the problems of being, man, communal life,
the good, knowledge. But there is no "perennial philosophy,"
neither in the sense that it already contains a certain doctrine, proclaims an eternal truth, nor in the sense of Hegel
(and N. Hartmann) that reason by its inner logic provides
successively more mature solutions to the problems it poses.
In fact the progress of philosophy takes place not by solving
problems, but by the appearance of new principles. These
stem in part from progressive philosophical thought, but in
part also from the general historical climate that changes
independently of philosophy. The history of philosophy cannot be understood hermetically as an autonomous field, but
only in the context of general intellectual history, within

which it is one component. Every age creates its own
philosophy, depending on its particular historical purposes.
This philosophy results not from the logical development of
its same essence, but in each case by a mission assigned to
it by a new age. The continuity with earlier forms of philosophy itself is overshadowed by affinity with other cultural
domains of the same era, of which they are the common expression. The historical unity of philosophy is overshadowed
by the present unity of the spirit of the age.

Philosophy as the Mirror of Human Existence

    1. _Theoreticalness_. The behavior of animals is regulated
by the instincts. Therefore they need know about things only
enough to stimulate the respectively necessary instinctive reaction. They carry within themselves only relatively crude
apperceptive schemata of what is relevant to them. A wooden
triangle dangled at a certain height above chickens fits their
inner image of a "taloned bird" and sets off a flight reaction.
Since instinct is what guarantees behavior appropriate to the
situation, things still are not an independent counterpart
but merely signals. Drawn into the animal's stream of life,
they function as correlatives of needs.
    Man must determine for himself how he will associate with
others, feed, clothe and defend himself. He finds no pre-
designed patterns for all this within himself. In every culture certain fixed modes of behavior develop, but they must
be created and modified. Therefore man must have more comprehensive knowledge of things, must know them intrinsically in
their own constitution, in their properties and laws. Only
so can he design his behavior with the technical accuracy
needed to apply it to a multitude of different purposes. His
knowledge of things is not only greater and more accurate than
that of the animal, but there is also a qualitative difference:
for him things are first indifferent in significance, not merely correlative factors of his own practice, but distinct data
of a neutral pure world of objects. Only in man do objects
become at all independent and self-contained "things" detached
from a subject, objective counterparts to his own life center.
The subject in the full sense is constituted only as the
opposite pole to an objective world (Wundt: cf. also "constitution by the 'thou'" in Feuerbach and "dialogism" in modern
"interactionism").
    Man is not primarily a "rational animal" but a "creative
animal." Instead of "homo sapiens" he ought to be called "homo
inveniens"(man the inventor). His creative power is the reason
why he does not need the instincts. Still, he is also a
rational animal, but this ought to be given its proper place

anthropologically. The reason why he must be the creature most
capable of knowledge is precisely so that he can be creative --
that is the context and interconnection between the two factors.
All theories which describe man as merely "homo faber" (man the
maker) are right insofar as even man's knowledge is not a gift
of God for its own sake but is intended for possible future
practice. But they are wrong if they are oriented directly to
a particular practice. It is part of the specifically human
structure of practice that an excess, a surplus of knowledge
beyond applicable knowledge dominates, and that, contrary to
Heidegger's thesis, the instrument becomes such only after it
originally was an unpurposefully existent object. In principle,
the stock of knowledge is accumulated so that later practice
can seek out in it whatever knowledge is suitable in each case;
but at the moment of acquisition of any particular point of
knowledge, this practical context is not and must not be actualized. For if the link with practice ·is too direct, becomes
conscious too early and controls the learning pattern, this
hinders the build-up of surplus knowledge (which will be necessary for practice later). Even by virtue of his generic structure, man is originally a "theorist."

Yet man actually restricts himself again in every culture;
he may broaden it at any time, but the respective gap between
knowledge and practice tends to remain relatively closed. The
highly advanced astronomy of the Oriental peoples served navi-
gation, calendar calculations and soothe-saying; their
geometry was in the service of surveying and architecture
(Indian geometry is unacquainted with proofs, it simply provides formulae). It was Greek philosophy and science that
first made knowledge a purpose in itself, just as their art
too no longer stood merely in the service of magic, the conjuration of the dead, votive offerings or propaganda in the
framework of religion or the state, but became autonomous.

But pure theory does not originate, as Schopenhauer claimed,
as a slave-uprising against what he believed to be the real
function of knowledge: to act as an agent of the will. Theory
is based on the original relative independence of knowledge,
which it frees from the petty entrammelments of practice and
allows to reappear in its pristine purity. The "original"
state of unpurposeful familiarization with things does not lie
at the temporal "beginning," but is always by-passed and
betrayed by utilitarian dealings with them. The countermovement of which Schopenhauer speaks is always directed only
against this natural but distortive process of pragmatization.
Not it "sublimates" knowledge, but on the contrary practicality
causes it to deteriorate. Philosophy only regains and restores
what it always was, in its original meaning; it purifies its
natural essence of its misapplied beginning. Its implicit

wellspring is made explicit. The Greeks merely carried the
generically given and motivated independence of knowledge one
step further. They brought to maturity and energized what
had always been an ancient human heritage. The Greeks, so to
speak, rethought nature's thoughts as it created man -- including individuality and freedom. Therefore a second creation of
man takes place among them.

2. Awareness. When man appears, things not only separate
from the stream of life that also surrounds the animal, but
man in his knowledge also stands distinct from his own subjectivity. He no longer lives in total identification with it.
As he observes things, he also sees himself. There is a gap
between his existence and his awareness. Awareness, instead
of an orientation factor in the stream of life, now becomes
an independent power of reflection.

Even this anthropologically changed position and power of
the awareness was later adopted by philosophy and highly
stylized: ethically, as man gains superiority to his fate and
to his own passions and thus the nonchalance of self-existence
from his schizothyme ability to stand contemplatively outside
himself; but not only ethically. For since all being is given
to us only by means of the awareness, awareness has, since
Descartes, become the "essential reality" and therefore the
true field of study for philosophy. Its intensification to
ever brighter degrees and finally to philosophy, until the type
of philosophy in which awareness becomes aware is considered
by Leibniz, Schelling and Hegel to be the goal of the process
of nature and history.

3. The Problematic. That man's mode of behavior is not
regulated by instincts means that man is a problem to himself
(Plessner, Gehlen). This problem is one not only of practical survival but also of the interpretation of the world and
the self. He solves it in a cultural and an individual style
of life. But along with the respectively found solution, others
are possible: therefore the immeasurable, constantly increas-
ing multiplicity of such life styles. Beneath each particular-
ization the indefinition never really ceases to exist.

Philosophy isolates this element of the problematic out
of the historical answers that always conceal it, and makes it
independent and conscious. Just as the problems posed by the
very fact of being human can never be definitively made to
disappear, so too the problems of philosophy -- which is not
true of scientific problems. Hence the multiplicity of metaphysical systems, which in the medium of thought correspond to
the multiplicity of cultural forms. Thus philosophy is the
analogous repetition of an essential trait of man.

4. Conservatism and Innovation. Man lives from two
talents, one receptive and conservative, the other inventive

and creative. Instinctive guidance systems are replaced by
traditions which man generally merely accepts and learns and
passes on faithfully, and he seldom changes to anything new,
because both for the group and for the individual the power of
decision is seldom activated. But it is, nonetheless, the
underlying foundation; even the traditions stem from man's
essential free inventiveness and creativity.

This duality is also reflected in philosophy. Sometimes,
as was seen above, it merely reduces the already existing
world-view and vital structure to principles, merely systematizes and rationalizes these. At other times (when great
individuals come to the fore) it once again senses the riddle
behind the concealing fossilations, and militantly reformative
philosophy shakes the foundations of the status quo and ventures an alternate theory.

That philosophy came to be was a chance event, just as the
origin of man was a chance event in the history of living
creatures. But once it has come into existence, there is a
certain necessity attached to it. In it the principle that
makes man what he is is duplicated in the mind.

CHAPTER 7

THE NATURE AND UNITY OF PHILOSOPHY

Particular Questions

There are a number of typical lines of investigation in
philosophy. They are all interdependent and they overlap, but
the common connection can be shown only in the specifics. So
we will have to proceed by enumeration. And there is not even
a mandatory historical or systematic sequence.

1. Real and Dependent Being. Noumenon and Phenomenon.
Philosophy starts with the assumption that in particular and
in general there is an underlying reality which supports a
dependent reality; it posits a dualism between a stronger,
primary or metaphysical being and a weaker, secondary being.
Its interest centers on what really is, on "genuine being,"
Plato's ontos on ("being in a being manner"). The relation can
be so understood that everything else also is real being, but
of lesser existential gravity, since it is based upon primary
being as upon its foundation. Or the explanation may be given
that "external" reality is in truth only a deceptive "appearance" brought about by falsification through our senses.
"Behind" this surface is hidden the only true reality, which
contrasts with the subjectively conditioned appearance as
"being as such," which is independent of awareness. For
Parmenides all multiplicity and all movement exist only in our
subjective opinion (doxa).

The first task of philosophy, in order to penetrate through
to true being, must therefore be to break through the foreground
of appearance. But since this is based on our too quickly
satisfied or false knowledge, the mind must first turn back
from being to knowledge itself. Inadequate knowledge must be
destroyed, and a better form of knowledge encouraged, perfected
or created.

2. The Structural Whole and the Part. Philosophy is, in
particular fields and in general, interested in the whole. It
observes not so much particular facts (that is also a psychological propensity), but it seeks the medium and interconnection of the facts, which binds them into a unity. This unity
lies not only in the common "underlying," ontic preconditions
or genetic origins, but in structure and context, in comprehensive configurations precisely of the "whole," which "is
more than the sum of its parts" (Aristotle) and therefore is

composed of them more intrinsically than as a mere encyclo-
pedic aggregate. Although it is made up of the parts, it contains qualities which are sought in vain in the parts.

Knowledge of particulars and knowledge of the whole, both
of which are necessary, result from different distances (Simmel), which must be meaningfully interconnected. From very
near only the graininess of the stones of which a house is
built can be seen but if one moves back a greater distance
then the result is not just a worse and blurred picture but a
qualitatively different picture, for only then can the house
in its overall contours be seen. Only by means of this distance can the function of the previously isolated detail be
perceived within the whole and the context and connecting
unity be recognized. So the distant perspective adds something to the detailed view; the detail attains its objective
only within the framework of the entirety.

What metaphysics states of the whole, on the other hand,
does not need to be confirmed in all particulars: like Bossuet,
Hegel too believes in a plan followed by world history, but he
says that to trace the application of that plan in every single
fact would be "pedantic." The pious man believes in God's help,
but it would be poor taste for him to plead for it in trivial
everyday needs -- "God fills the bowl, not the spoon."

Philosophical "systems" have existed since late Hellenism.
The systematic form is late and artificial: a pre-Socratic
thinker spans the world with one single sentence. But opposition to the systems is also not lacking, not only in the name
of existence as in Kierkegaard: Nietzsche accuses the philosophical systems of a "lack of honesty," phenomenology of constructive distortion of the facts. Yet Kant rightly says that
philosophical reason is by nature "architectonic": it does
not allow the data of knowledge to stand unconnectedly apart,
it completes and connect them by ultimate "regulative ideas"
(Wundt added others to Kant's list).

3. The Universal and the Particular. Degrees of Universality.   The thinker whose gaze is directed at the universal
does not investigate the particular. As not-merely-particular,
the universal shows some relationship with the whole. Both are
inaccessible to the dogma of atomization. But the whole has
parts, the universal has specimens. The parts are different
than the whole and can also be different from one another
(Plato's example: as the parts of the face differ from the
parts of gold); together they constitute its higher structure.
The universal, on the other hand, is repeated as what is common
to all specimens, which are therefore the same as one another.
Whoever knows the part does not yet know the whole, for it
contains the part but is not "present" in it (Plato's concept
of parousia, "presence"). On the other hand, a geometric

principle can be demonstrated by a single triangle, the plant
or animal species can be understood from a single specimen by
a "view of its essence" (Husserl, Scheler).

There are universals in every field. But there are also
different degrees of universality, "a pyramid of concepts," in
which the respectively "higher" concepts become poorer in content and broader in scope. There is an Aristotelian "supreme
universal." The principle of contradiction applies to this
most universal being; the categories and modality extend to
it, prior to all particularity. Christian Wolff divides metaphysics into general and special metaphysics. His ontology
(the name has been revived in our century as a line of de-
marcation from speculative metaphysics) appeared under the
title Rational Ideas of God, the World, and Man's Soul (this
division recurs in Kant's Critique of Pure Reason for the purpose of refutation), and also of All Things that Exist.

4. Substantial Essence and Accidents. The Platonic Idea
is equated with the universal, but only secondarily. It is
the essence of things. It designates what makes a thing what
it is, i.e., what belongs essentially and necessarily to it
if it is to fit a certain concept or be subsumed under a certain class. In Aristotle it becomes the substance (hypokeimenon) as distinguished from what belongs to a thing only accidentally (per accidens, symbebekos) and what constitutes its
individuality (i.e., here lying outside its essence and
correspondingly low in rank!). Without substance there is
nothing, whereas particular accidents can be missing.

There are accidents located outside the definition of a
thing but whose co-presence in it we nonetheless expect and
accidents that can be added or not added to a thing purely externally and "by chance" (this too is connoted by the term
accident). The accident, furthermore, comprises the scope of
indifference or freedom within the necessary: thus each man
must essentially have some color or other to his hair (necessity of suchness); but which color it is, whether black, brown,
or blond, is unspecified; here individual variation is the
rule.

Descartes problematized the concept of substance by the
example of a piece of wax which he caused to lose its firmness,
shape, color and odor over a flame; and Locke went further:
there is no bearer of qualities, only a complex of relatively
stable qualities. Hume applied this also to the self: it is
not at the basis of ideas, it is itself only a "bundle of ideas."
Kant in turn contested this but said that to conclude from the
transcendental self to the empirical one is a breach of logic.

Aristotle reproached the Platonic theory of ideas with
merely duplicating the world when it added the word "itself"
to every object. This objection fails to note the difference

between the <u>essential</u> universal and the merely <u>abstractive</u>
one. Abstraction obtains the image, the outline, the <u>suchness</u>,
from the reality of a thing. Even this is not a trivial
accomplishment but a basic human faculty without which neither
language nor art could exist (Hans Jonas). Even if Plato had
discovered only this, it would have been no small achievement.
But the determining of essence involves more than abstraction:
it articulates the total complex. It distinguishes the fundamental factors from the peripheral and secondary ones, the
crux of a thing from accidental contingencies, the central
reality from incidentals. It does not merely collect all
characteristics empirically, it establishes their intrinsic
context and ranks them on a scale. The ability to abstract
is a property of man in general, while the distinction of
essence is the mark of the intellectual man.

The question of essence is related to the question of the
whole, for both are concerned with structure. The Platonic
Idea is also Aristotle's form (<u>morphe</u>). The <u>gestalt</u>-theory
and phenomenological eidetics of our century are sister disciplines that arose, not by chance, simultaneously, and both have
their roots in Platonism.

5. <u>The Normative</u>. In addition to essence, the Platonic
Idea also includes the ideal, the paradigm, the pattern. Both
are interwoven in it, and yet a distinction must be made
between the two. Essence-analysis is descriptive; the positing
of an ideal, normative (but it was Plato's belief as a metaphysical moral philosopher that the ideal is derived from the
essence, that what ought to be could be deduced from what is
-- in him metaphysics and Utopianism are still archaically
undistinguished). What belongs to the essence of the state
must reoccur in every real state as its most universal defin-
iteness of form, otherwise it is not a state; the "ideal state"
however exists only "in heaven"; all real states, even the best,
fall short of it. Compared with the ideal every historical
state is individual in the negative sense of failing to meet a
universally binding requirement.

6. <u>Category</u>. Both the essence and the ideal refer to the
whole of a thing. They establish a class of things, the
essence in the sense that particular things <u>ipso facto</u> fall
under it, the ideal in the sense that they are measured by it
as a norm or standard. But because in both essence and ideal
a single concept corresponds to each thing, they are closer ..
together than to the late Platonic (<u>The Sophists</u> and <u>Parmenides</u>)
and Aristotelian idea that one and the same thing contains a
multiplicity of formal factors which are "interconnected":
participation (<u>methaxis</u>) of a thing in its species is here
linked with the new idea of the community and the intermeshing
(<u>koinonia</u> and <u>symploke</u>) of formal factors with one another.

These formal factors, if we may here draw upon N. Hartmann's Structure of the Real World (1940), also have in
common with the essences, that they represent a universal as
opposed to a concrete thing and that they determine it into
what it is. But they are universals of a higher sort, "ideas
of ideas," and therefore no longer refer only to particular
things but to entire strata of being. Every area of being is
based on ultimate principles. The principles of Euclidian
geometry are, among others, its "axioms," space and its
dimensions, homogeneity and isotropy; arithmetical principles
are the continuity of a sequence of numbers, unity and multiplicity, finiteness and infinity. The theory of mechanism
provides the principles for optics, acoustics and thermophysics;
it supports these more specialized sciences by concepts for
what they have in common.

The scientist works with these principles, the philosopher
at them. He abstracts them "transcendentally" out of the
concrete object, describes them phenomenologically, inter-
relates them dialectically and compares and corrects the subjective categories of our knowledge by the objective categories of being.

The essence is the transposition of a being to the level
of the concept, and as such the two are simultaneous and co-
existent; the principle is a priority both ontologically as
the more underlying being and logically as the explanation or
basis in reality and in knowledge. Through the essence we
understand a thing intrinsically in and of itself; principles
have a higher explanatory value, they let the object attain
mental form from a more hidden, more general substratum. From
the point of view of the theory of principles it seems -- incorrectly -- as if the essences only explained "the same by
the same" (a doctor in Molière: the sleeping potion works because it has a soporific potency!); but the principle -- in
order to explain -- must precisely be heterogeneous (though
not too much so). Essences correspond to primitive languages
whose words are still modelled closely on visible objects, or
picture languages which have a special sign for every shape
in reality; principles, as it were, break up a composite
into "atoms" and therefore correspond to analytical languages
which synthesize the particular from more general and therefore fewer concepts. On the level of writing, they are analogous to the alphabet.

7. Arche. The concept of "principle" goes back to the
pre-Socratic idea of the origin (arche) or the origins (archai),
the first (proton), which however is first only "by nature"
as cause of being, while "for us" as the cause of knowledge,
Aristotle distinguishes, it is later. But the principles of
the older Plato and the tradition based on him are, like his

Ideas, formal and immaterial in nature. They are also aspects
of reality, but only our analytical and generalizing reason
obtains them. As opposed to this, pre-Socratic thinkers seek
the arche as a real factor in the things themselves, and they
no longer need to be explained supernaturally and mythically
but by their own nature.

The concept of arche contains many things (united or separately). First, it designates origin not in a temporal but
only in a metaphysical sense as the stronger, underlying,
meaningful reality in contrast with what has comparatively less
reality. Plato first isolated this purely metaphysical meaning,
for he was the first to consider the arche immaterial (yet he
still had it act upon the real -- in an intangible, almost
"mythical" manner -- as the basis of essence and of determination all in one. The philosophical question of the origin is
not the same as the scientific one of the beginning, but a
question of essence. Even when Hobbes has society and state
originate from a contract, he does not mean this historically,
but he is seeking to show what rational considerations these
two realities are, or should be, based on. Secondly, the arche
also precedes the rest of being in time; it does not merely
support, but also permeates derivative reality. It is at
work behind it either causally, or thirdly, genetically, as
"prime matter" out of whose transformations it arises by evolution, or fourthly, in the form of several roots of all things
(rhizomata panton, Empedocles), smallest particles, elements
(Anaxagoras, Democritus), the mixture of which makes being into
a concrete object. Here the origin, even in time, still
affects the essence, while a cause only determines a thing but
is not a characteristic of it.

The question of the origin had been posed by the ·pre-
Socratic philosophers; that of the Idea originated with Plato.
Aristotle stands in both traditions and he therefore coordinates
the two concepts, though somewhat loosely. In his Phaido,
Plato had, however, contrasted the Idea as the reason why
(therefore, also determinative of the human mind) with Anaxagoras' material source and origin. Following in his footsteps,
Aristotle too lists the form as one of the four causes (aitiai)
which he distinguishes. Actually, it is a question of two
completely heterogeneous points of departure for knowledge.
They struggle with one another for predominance in history. The
modern age replaces the Scholastic essence-oriented mode of
thought with the principle of causality; phenomenology in
turn reproaches modern science with explaining things by prior
stages and elements instead of describing and understanding
their real content.

8. The End or Purpose. The opposite question to that
of source or origin is the question of the end, purpose and

motivation. Does the individual thing have a purpose? Do the
world and history have a goal? The end or purpose can be so
understood that man alone invents it and perhaps attempts to
shape things toward it, without a guarantee of ever reaching
it, or religiously (God guides him to the goal), or metaphysically and teleologically, as in Aristotle (the telos works
as entelechy in all things; as "final cause" it draws them
toward itself). It was modern natural science that replaced
this type of teleological thinking, which is a projection of
human purposefulness into nature, with causal thinking.

The concept of purpose seems to contain the idea that it
is a "good purpose for the one who seeks it (though it can
objectively consist of destruction or worsening). The question
of purpose is not a purely ontological one, it is also ethically colored. With the reversal of direction, it brings a
change of dimension, subjecting an event to the criterion of
goodness. To this extent, it is only a partial aspect of the
contemplation of things -- both events and conditions --
under the aspect of the good, of the question of the "highest
goods." For Lotze and the so-called Southwest-German Neo-
Kantianism, science deals with being, philosophy with meaning.
Philosophy must be a "philosophy of value."

The "essence" of things is what always stays the same in
them. Things change -- for Plato this is even their definition, as opposed to aei on, the Eternal Being -- but no change
takes place in their metaphysical core. One thing perishes,
but another again realizes the same immortal Idea. Whoever
seeks the essence understands things in terms of what they have
always been: essence (Wesen) means "to have been" (Gewesenheit:
Ernst Bloch). Therefore, nominalism, as the destroyer of
essences in the metaphysical sense, radically subjects reality,
down to its core, to the fate of time and change. Then, with
Darwin, species can even lose their permanency and evolve one
from the other -- an idea impossible for classical antiquity.
But only the person who sets a goal is changed from a passive
observer of events to an affirmer of progress or an active
participant in the effort to accomplish such goal. This
involves a forward projection of the idea: it is no longer
only prior and older, but still unborn and new. The social
and cultural world -- and, in Ernst Bloch's bold new metaphysics,
even matter -- no longer appears against the background of the
eternal which it merely repeats as a "mobile replica" (Plato)
but on the horizon of the future, open to Utopia and directed
toward the ultimate.

9. Awareness. All the above questions, however they differ,
resemble one another in pointing to dimensions within the world,
within being itself. They all stem from the philosophy of
Greco-Roman antiquity. In contrast, the specifically modern

point of departure (though anticipated in the Sophists and
the Sceptics) is a viewpoint that has become clear since
Descartes: everything in the world is given to us only through
the medium of awareness.

This insight is gained from a negative starting-point. For
if our knowledge is true, then it itself disappears and the
truth resides in what is known. Only in the case of error, in
which there is a wide difference of content between what we
think about the thing and the thing itself, does the specific
performance of awareness become distinct and pronounced.

For us, then, and for our knowledge, awareness precedes
the world. It is the first thing; it comes before everything
else. Philosophy, as the science of the first things, must,
then, begin as a philosophy of awareness. More radically
formulated it can be nothing else but that.

10. Knowledge and Truth. Another point is closely related
with this. That we possess things only through the medium of
the awareness means: we possess them only because of our
knowledge, which from them constructs for us the knowledge-
structure of truth. This knowledge and truth now become the
great new themes of philosophy. How do we know the world? Are
we at all capable of knowledge? What is truth?

Epistemology (the theory of knowledge) is joined by
methodology, which has a dual task. First, it seeks to guide
the mind so that it avoids error. It seeks to make truth certain. Secondly, it should help us to discover new truth.
From a primeval confidence in the correspondence between the
world and man, Aristotle still believed that all attainable
knowledge had already been discovered. The Middle Ages sought
only to describe and classify the stock of knowledge. Now,
however, interest centers on what we do not yet have in the
scope and quality of knowledge. Cast out of our cozy and con-
natural cosmos, we no longer trust the data of our senses and
the given facts. However, distrust of prior achievements of
reason can arouse the hope of improving the mind's performance
by an "emendation of the intellect" (Spinoza). The basic
feeling now is: we stand at the beginning, the ocean of know-
able reality still lies before us (Newton). Progress is being
organized.

The Philosophical Movement of the Mind

From the superficial to the real, from the part to the
whole, from the chance particular to the universal, the essence,
pattern and principle, from the subsequent to the origin, from
what is accepted as such to the question of meaning and purpose,
from the objects to the awareness that presents and forms them,
from the problems of being to the problems of truth -- the

trends are always different and yet related. Together they
comprise but one single movement of the mind in various modi-
fications, made necessary by the structure of the world, which
is composed of these dualities, and by man's place in it as he
strives to understand it more deeply. All declarations that
philosophy is unnecessary, no matter from what camp they may
come, are refuted by this necessity. So this movement is not
restricted to philosophy: it is expressed ethically in the
ability to keep the momentary, near, small and accidental at
arm's length, and to withdraw from its urgency in view of the
greater universal good. It is also expressed in the sciences:
it is always easy to tell whether a grammar was written by a
pedantic or a philosophical person. The historian too must
separate the non-essential from the essential in his field,
leaving out many details for the benefit of the context. But
philosophy presses even beyond philosophically-oriented history
to the philosophy of history, i.e., to fundamental questions
such as whether repeated cycles, progress or decline prevail
in history, whether there are historical laws, what their
motive forces are. Philosophy also finally advances beyond
such "regional ontologies" (Husserl) to "fundamental ontology."

Philosophy moves, as was said above, from the superficial
to the essence. But it could not make this move, if it did
not already have an anticipation of essence. Man always has
prior knowledge of a greater depth. But in the intent pursuit
of practical goals and particular tasks, this primeval knowledge is eroded by everyday concerns. Man loses it intentionally by "distraction" (Pascal) because he wishes to avoid the
claim made on him out of the depths: if he faced it, then
he would have to recognize too much of his previous activity
as worthless -- "Man, become essential!" (Angelus Silesius).
So he habitually lives in guilty omission and non-genuineness
(Heidegger). Philosophy does two things: it tells us, in
Plato's metaphors, to wake up, it turns our face around in the
other direction; it has us look toward the light instead of
into the darkness. It corrects misconceptions, while at the
same time causing us to reflect upon the self which we have
always carried hidden within us. It is anamnesis, remembrance
of what was buried and forgotten, which it merely educes by
its art of midwifery. We return to the homeland where we
have never been (Bloch). Philosophy's movement of knowledge
is existentially the direct countermovement to our own tendency to decline. However, this existential movement cannot
be philosophically isolated; it succeeds only in conjunction
with the movement of knowledge.

CHAPTER 8

IMPLICIT AND EXPLICIT PHILOSOPHY

The Subconscious Preconception and its Elucidation

Philosophical questions necessarily result from the nature of the world and of man. But mankind has lived for hundreds of thousands of years; philosophy is very young compared with man, and even since its origin only few men have been affected by it. How can this contradiction be explained?

Reflectiveness, as Dilthey showed, is a natural and spontaneous property of all life. And this not only externally: life begins and develops only with an interpretation of itself and the world. Even this innate interpretiveness is more than merely "practical"; it goes beyond the particular and obvious, coordinating all events into a system of categories, processing and deciding basic questions. It knows something about being in general, about the essence and context of things, about the origin and purpose of the world, about man's place in it, his destiny, the purpose of his existence. Early interpretation knows all this not in the form of a structure of thought, not expressly but by anticipation. This supra-objective knowledge lies at the basis of all expressions of a culture, its social structure, technology and economy, its religious worship and its art, and even all the objective contents of its sciences, controling them and depicting itself in them. As in early conditions the individual unreflectingly accepts and passes on the entire traditional good of his society, so also the stock of categories is inextricably interwoven into the pre-philosophical interpretation.

No act of life is without "a design of the world." We always stand within a "metaphysical horizon." Long before the founding of autonomous "advanced philosophy" as a separate intellectual field of objectivity, there exists a germinal implicit philosophy that has not yet awakened, a philosophy prior to the word "philosophy" itself. It is not true, as Aristotle claimed, that a first phase of exclusively practical knowledge was followed by a second one in which the question of the universal and the causes was first raised; rather, both are equally primeval. All thinking is based on ultimate metaphysical convictions. They are inevitable to thought; there is no way it can avoid them.

Of course, the mind is generally not conscious of these convictions as such. On the one hand, they are the precondi-

tions not only of thought but of all life and behavior, which
are impregnated through and through with them and obtain their
"style" from them. But, on the other hand, it is precisely
within their nature as preconditions to be located not within
view of the mind but behind it. Within their framework, the
mind is constantly focused on particulars, while the categories themselves, in their universality, are taken for granted,
left unexpressed and not framed in concepts and sentences.
"The greatest thoughts are mute." The mind is as little aware
of its philosophy as Molière's Monsieur de Pourceaugnac knows
that he is speaking in prose. Primitive man does not say
expressly: I distinguish between two forms of cause, the physical one and that of mystical participation (Levy-Bruhl); but
these two forms of causality are implicit in all his thoughts
and actions.

Yet pre-conscious knowledge can rise by degrees to greater
explicitness. Preconditions become convictions. New experience which does not readily fit into the previous form of
thought and therefore compels it to become more precise and
improved can be the occasion for this. In the social field it
can happen when an institution or a pattern of behavior are
contested from the outside or by a younger generation; defend-
ers of the institution or mode of behavior, protecting themselves, must speak their mind, state arguments, reflect on
their principles, and therefore they become self-aware. Along
with the latent principles that existed only as "effective
structures," there now arise "world-view" convictions that
have been distilled out of implicitness to a certain degree
of clarity or that have been re-established on an earlier
level of reflectivity.

The term "world-view" (Weltanschauung) was coined -- not
accidentally, in the Age of Goethe -- by Schleiermacher and
Humboldt as a designation for pre-conecptual knowledge that
clings to immediate experience and yet aims at knowledge of the
whole. World-views are more emotional, more closely connected
with an ethos, and make less rationalistic claims than philosophy, yet in their universality they are related with it as
preliminary and parallel stages. All philosophy grows in the
soil of a world-view and retains elements of world-view, though
it is false to equate philosophy with world-view, as Dilthey
did.

Even the natural languages contain numerous so-called
"protometaphysical concepts," which even as concepts already
contain a fundamental thesis: space, time, world, nature, power,
cause, mind. While the user believes he is merely naming something that exists, such concepts are really interpretive constructions on the part of cultures. Their suggestive appearance of objectivity is based only on their fixation in language.

They often stem from religion or are religiously toned. For
instance, "necessity": Horace still speaks of "dire necessity"
(kratere ananke); also "soul": it is originally contrasted
with "the divine outside us" as the "subjectively numinous,"
indeed there is a whole series of religious concepts in psychology. Philosophy later adopts these concepts, adapts and
clarifies them, while still remaining dependent on them: thus
the religious concept of soul still is operative not only in
Plato, but even down to Wolff's rational psychology. On the
other hand, philosophical terms also wander, usually without
anyone noticing it, into the colloquial language: infinity
(Anaximander), cosmos (Pythagorean), substance, subject
(Aristotle), allotria (the Stoics), from the first (a priori),
everything possible (Leibniz' omnia possibilia).

All concepts of a language, however, and the manner in
which it forms and combines them, already contain a world
penetration and articulation. The languages of advanced cultures have already performed a tremendous task of generalization compared with primitive languages; the words are less
burdened with sensory detail, more analytical and therefore
more broadly applicable. Logical relationships are isolated
and clarified by specific conjunctions such as "because,"
"although," and "so that"; these are marking-stones of intellectual development. Thus, prior to every statement of content, the language as such already provides a system of
articulation, a categorical apparatus.

Positivism started from the assumption that isolated naked
facts exist in the world. This is ontologically false, for
every particular thing is based on more general foundations,
stands in contexts, receives causal impulses, serves purposes.
Our knowledge, positivism continues, is primarily sensory experience of the facts. These experiences are its basic components; only from them does the mind progress to more comprehensive interpretations. This is a false description of
knowledge: we never grasp "naked matter" which has not already
been formed symbolically (Cassirer). All experiences stand
for us, from first to last, in the context of a "world" (Kant,
Husserl), of a "horizon," a "design." As awareness of a problem already takes us beyond the given facts, so also the
framework in which we place them. We always perceive the
particular under the "interpretative anticipation" of a total
conception. The particular is interpreted only within the
broader field of an "anticipatory decision" (Heidegger). We
do not first have fragmentary impressions, which we then
transcend by classifying and completing them according to
mental guidelines. Every judge who has testimony to check,
every historian who has sources to examine, knows this. Even
the impression itself, in its supposed immediacy, is saturated

with a more comprehensive "fore-knowledge." The given facts
become given only through permeation by an ungiven "transcendental" schema contributed by the subject (Kant). "The word
transcendental does not mean something that goes beyond all
experience, but something a priori that precedes it but is
destined to no other purpose than simply to make experiential
knowledge possible" (Kant, Prolegomena). But in addition to
the subjective contribution, one can distinguish an "anticipatory" fore-knowledge derived from the thing itself (Schleiermacher's "divinatory" apprehension of the whole).

     Even positivism realizes that the path of investigation
does not lead directly from the factual experience to the
theory based upon it; first, the preconception -- theoretical,
as well as ideological and interest-conditioned -- must be
detected and gradually reduced and beneath this overgrowth the
"pure facts" must then be discovered and isolated (Bayle). The
independent fact is as much a late cultural product as the
independent individual. Only starting from it can the mind
then go a step further to an improved theory. Here a basic
movement of philosophy is repeated: the Socratic method itself
began with a destruction, with the refutation (elenktic) of
"vain apparent knowledge. Knowledge must free itself from
confusion by the senses and passions (Plato, Phaido; analogously
nominalistic reduction; Bacon's "casting down of the idols";
the Cartesian doubt). After having accepted supposed certainties and assumptions, philosophy always must start over again
from the beginning. But positivism, like the Enlightenment,
from which it stems, does not admit the existence of a kind of
preconception that opens the way to knowledge, but only the kind
that blocks the way, the "prejudice" that must be removed.
Because of this purely negative and militant perspective it
fails to see the fundamentally transcendental structure of our
mind. As soon as the prejudice is removed, positivism reverts
to the naivete of natural man, who believes that his knowledge
is pure "experience." It stops much too soon with its critique
and at this point already accepts as "fact" what in truth is
still the product of human cognition. It does not yet turn
from the outside to the inside, from preoccupation with the
object to creative awareness. Only through this shift of
perspective do we learn how much of ourselves we inevitably
contribute to knowledge.

     Yet, as the example of Kant shows, even awareness of the
a priori structures does not as such necessarily undermine
confidence in their validity. In contrast with Aristotle, Kant
considers the forms of perception and the categories to be merely
subjective; but like Aristotle he also considers them to be
primeval, unchangeable, and therefore again intersubjectively
binding, though within the limited framework of our earthly

reason. Opposed to this is the insight that the categories --
ultimate formal conditions, for Kant -- are in fact historically
conditioned; but if they are historical then we can remodel
them too and give them greater adequacy to being, by the continuation of the historical process. To arrive at such an insight there is need of dynamic experiences, intellectual work
on the a priori itself or comparison with the aprioristic
systems of other peoples and times, which make evident the
historicity of one's own.

The ethnologist Bastian spoke of the common "elementary
thoughts" of all peoples. Yet the world-views of even the
simplest tribes differ greatly from one another; only modern
science imposes itself cogently on everyone. The so-called
"natural world-view" is itself a historical outgrowth.

Even we modern men still fall into the illusion of mistaking the forms of our insight into the world as simply a
matter of fact. For example, we cannot imagine it otherwise
than that the soul is attached to an earthly body; we distinguish between dream and reality; we regard the substance as
remaining the same despite a change of conditions; we accept
only one causality, one space and a unilinear time. For other
cultures, however, soul is diffused and distributed in the
world; for animism fire and water also have souls. If a
primitive chieftain the next morning tells his dream in which
he made a far journey, the tribe congratulates him on his safe
return. If a thing changes one quality, then it is, for the
primitive, who experiences totalities, a new thing and receives
a new name. More important to him than the natural cause,
which he considers secondary, is the influence of things on
one another through similarity and spacial proximity, and he
interferes in this magical happening. Humboldt, like Sapir
and Whorf (the "linguistic principle of relativity") already
noted such differences on the basis of language structure.
Levy-Bruhl also built his system (which he later rejected) on
them. In our global age, the "intersocietal theory of knowledge" has acquired even a practical significance.

Spengler has shown that a physiognomic unity of form exists
between the ancient value-preference for the limited, the near
and the stable and Aristotelian physics, on the one hand, and
the Western preference for the infinite and the changing and
Galileo's and Newton's physics, on the other. Cultures differ
even in something apparently so natural and self-evident as
the idea of space. Therefore Antiquity had Euclidian geometry,
and the modern age has infinitesimal calculus. Thus even science, though it is more than an expression of the time, seems
to remain dependent upon fundamental determinations of the
respective culture as a whole, which are prior to and more
basic than science and, though subconscious, determine all its

manifestations. According to this view, it is not thought
that brings about decisive changes in the world; only new
peoples, a new faith, a new historical constellation can
change the more fundamental factors, which in turn change the
thinking that follows from them.

Consequences and Forms of Explication

Philosophy performs a change of perspective: both within
the world in another direction or to other dimensions and also
from the direct intention, which looks outward, to an oblique
one involving observation of the vantage-point from which we
look. It elevates categoriality, which otherwise lies in the
background of the awareness, into a counterpart. It makes
what is otherwise a tool of knowledge into the goal of knowledge. It separates out the form of interpretation, which is
normally intermixed with particular data of knowledge.

This changes what was formerly a fixed form into a question. The form previously was the answer to a problem no one
had yet asked. Now the problem behind this answer is made
visible. The scientist, for instance, was already establishing
laws; the philosopher asks: "What is a law? What forms of laws
(moral or natural) exist? Are there laws 'as such' or do they
exist only in the mind?"

This also implies a further point. This retroversion does
not serve only for clarification, it does not merely explicate
what is already contained in the implicit modes of apperception.
It is not only a question of fact, but a question of what ought
to be: "Does this way of seeing things exist rightly?" The
explication imposes the need for legitimation. Philosophy is
radical thinking: it mentally dismantles established institutions and lets them stand only if they can be justified.

Thus the attention, which had just turned from the external
particular object of knowledge to its inner schema, returns to
the outside, but now not back to the particular, but from the
subjective categories to the objective principles which they
contain, from the a priori of the mind to the ideal aspect of
being. It checks, corrects and broadens the a priori against
this ideal aspect. And finally it no longer asks at all about
the previous forms of apperception of our awareness, but leaves
them behind as something empirical and historical and works
strictly systematically only on the material of the "ontic form."

Aristotle's philosophy is limited by the fact that he still
trusted excessively in the analogical adequation of our mind
and the world. He mistook the Greek mind for the human mind as
such, and took into account neither the variability nor the
perfectibility of the mind. Consequently he merely formalized
how things are generally thought of by us and obtained his

categories in this way (Wolfgang Wieland). Only the modern
age has attained the critical distance from our understanding
which allows the mind to regard itself in its momentary state
as accidental and has changed its traditional forms into mere
material of creative formation, into a "conjecture" (Cusa)
which must be progressively renewed and corrected by science.
What for Spengler history achieves through the changing of
cultures without philosophical participation, philosophy here
itself undertakes. It discovers not only objects of thought,
but also modes of thought.

    Yet reflection on the forms of direct awareness, as exempli-
fied in classical times by Socrates in thought and deed when he
questioned the generals on courage and the politicians on
justice, will always remain a first stage. Hegel still assigned
to philosophy the task of merely translating into logic "what
is otherwise considered known," of framing in concepts what
an epoch already carried in itself in a still unthought manner
-- which however does not succeed if it is something that by
nature remains inaccessible to the concept: for the pre-concep-
tual can be what is more true, and Hegel himself, as seen above,
distorted the great idea of his age by conceptualization. Husserl's phenomenology is transcendental self-analysis (egology):
in an infinitely more minutious way than ever before he brings
to light the constitution of the world of objects through the
frequently intervening acts of the awareness. This point of
departure with the constitutive achievements of one's own
awareness proves to be necessary because, as long as we do not
reflect on them, we remain caught within their historicalness.

    Dilthey and phenomenology give a different twist to inves-
tigation into the categories: the categories of science do not
have exclusive power to discover the world; in fact, their
abstract, quantifying and analytical stringency loses information that was framed much more realistically in the natural
world-view, in language, religion and art; Descartes' doubt
provides certainty by depriving us of fullness and depth. Therefore research into the pre-rational and extra-rational world-
views now begins (as also in Ernst Cassirer). Philosophical
treatises now begin by studying the basis of the concept in the
original context of life, and by seeking to explore the contents
of words and idioms with which language already pre-structures
the object. Some scholars stress the gap betwen philosophy
and all other intellectual endeavors: others seek continuity.

CHAPTER 9

PHILOSOPHY UNDER THE SPELL OF SCIENCE

Inductive and Hypothetical Metaphysics

In addition to epistemology and methodology, the second
half of the nineteenth century gave philosophy another task:
to be an "inductive, hypothetical metaphysics" based on the
sciences, after the older metaphysics had made its deductions
from highest concepts (the "world as will"!). Science, as a
progressive discipline, still has gaps; and as a strict discipline, it dares make no decision about ultimate questions.
Moreover, the continuum of the sciences is not solid everywhere; gaps still exist between the individual sciences. Philosophy, it was now said, should close these gaps in an anticipatory manner. If physiology deals with the body, psychology
with the soul, then philosophy with the problem of body and
soul. It should unite the sciences, which are divided into
numerous, sectorally distinct and unconnected disciplines. In
doing this it is more than an encyclopedia: the question which
only it asks, the question of the contributions of the sciences
to the total picture of the world, produces their "creative
resultant" (Wundt). This synthesis goes beyond what was already
contained in the sciences.

Just as Taine's historical works contain more than his
methodology would lead one to expect, because he is by nature
a great narrator, and just as Rohde's _Psyche_ though positivistic in outlook, is based, in its content, on a constructive
philosophical theory of religion, namely animism, so here analogously those who claim to be philosophizing only as a completion
of the existing sciences actually go beyond their own program.
Spencer, whose sociology is positivistic, comes close to Schelling in his evolutionism. Likewise in E. von Hartmann and W.
Wundt the elements, an old metaphysical heritage, are still
alive and these even lead the two thinkers to remodel the sciences: Hartmann's biology is a non-Darwinistic, vitalized one;
and by his principle of creativity, Wundt even overcomes
association-psychology and becomes the founder of the _gestalt_-
concept.

The "unity of the scientific world-view" was discredited
because it misused science as a pretended support for a world-
view established from other sources. Pan-psychism, pan-vitalism
and many other _isms_ were involved. Even the philosophy of

synthesis degenerated into a "conceptual poetry," "a philosophy of emotional needs" (F.A. Lange). Today the sciences have become so complex that the derivation of a total conception seems possible only on the level of a world-view and is therefore avoided by scientifically responsible men. When they lose confidence in the possibility of an integral interpretation of the whole, they also lose their longing for it. The unity of the sciences today is not based on their contents, but on their methodology: disciplines which only a short time ago were alien to each other (e.g., technology and psychology) are beginning to communicate with one another in the language of structuralism, mathematical models and cybernetics.

But unity, as an allergy and asceticism, poses a grave danger in the current historical situation. The need for transparent coherence, for a world formula, refuses to die even in the age of specialization. Since it finds no fulfillment suitable to the modern level of intellectual responsibility, it resorts to an "uncontemporary" "salvational knowledge." It exposes youth to sociologism and, as the next step, to historical materialism, leading them from dictatorship in the universities to political dictatorship and so casting the world into the ideological intolerance of a second Middle Ages, from which no liberation will ever be possible, because it will no longer be a naive Middle Ages, as was the first, but a reflected one. Because science gave us no totality, we obtain one through totalitarianism. While the first Middle Ages was caused by the cultural disintegration accompanying the migration of nations, we fall into the second one from the height of civilization through the eschatological madness of pseudo-leftist academic Torquemadas. The whole planet is becoming Communist as an _ersatz_ for a missing metaphysics.

Philosophy as Science

German Idealism still professed the "speculative" nature of philosophy. In the course of developments which led to the "collapse of idealism" around 1850, precisely this factor became the main reproof against it, just as "metaphysics" at that time was debased into a pejorative term. "A thesis is speculative" now came to mean: it exists only in the mind and is a purposeful product of the imagination stemming from certain ideological intentions. However, in the age of science even philosophy should become "scientific." This is demanded not only by the sciences, nor only by the opponents of philosophy. Kant himself writes _Prolegomena to any Future Metaphysics that Can Present itself as a Science_; and "Philosophy as a Science" is the title of a famous essay by Husserl. Philosophy must at last become sober and honest, must hold to a

solid method, learn the modesty of a division of labor and
check its statements against the facts. Then it too will become certain, cogent, and universally valid.

Philosophy deals with the most universal principles. Its
theses are neither subject to pragmatic validation, nor can
they be empirically verified. Therefore philosophy always is
a romping ground for dilettantes and enthusiasts, where their
confused and loose thinking sees its chance. Philosophy must
protect itself from these bad pretendents and so it too demands
greater stringency. Under the influence of science, philosophy
becomes more disciplined, and indeed itself becomes a science.
The process by which former disciplines of philosophy have
declared their independence could progress still further: the
philosophy of history will produce meta-history; ethics will
split up into behavioral study, law, psychology, etc.

But the precisioning of philosophy, as many advantages as
it brings, is not only a plus for knowledge. For, when precision is elevated to the highest ineluctible criterion, the
tendency is to deal only with those areas where such exactness
is attainable. All other fields, in which statements cannot be
checked directly for congruence with the object, are then left
aside from the start as not scientifically admissible. Because
it is impossible to proceed scientifically in them, one capitu-
lates with regard to entire dimensions of reality: one must
remain silent about what one cannot speak of (Wittgenstein).
The other side of precision is thus a loss of thematic scope,
in fact of essential themes: in questions of totality, goal
and meaning, there seems to be no ultimate precision, no incontrovertible proof. A "school concept," to use Kant's distinction replaces the "world concept" of philosophy, which goes
on struggling "for the great objects of mankind." Thus philosophy, when it tries to emulate the example of science, declares
bankruptcy: it reduces itself to a minimum and   thus   no
longer speaks where its opinion is expected. Kant still reflected on eternal peace, Jaspers on the question of guilt;
natural scientists today reflect on the political and moral
consequences of their discoveries. Where however the philosopher is a semanticist, his book on ethics is concerned only
with how we symbolize ethical material in language. He makes
no statements himself, but only explains statements (Wittgenstein).

Above and Below Science

Philosophy must, despite its fear of not being scientific
enough, avoid so diminishing its scope that it finally bypasses
all deeper problems: in the Germany of the extraordinary
1920's, this idea led to a revival of metaphysics though it had

already been declared dead. As Kant had formulated it, our
mind reaches further problematically than assertively; it
faces insoluble yet inescapable questions. Philosophy is the
attempt to deal with these questions. Consequently, it never
attains the cogent reliability, the striking provenness of
verifiable science. It always retains an element of adventure;
it does not, as it were, carry on merely coastal shipping, but
it dares a Viking journey out to the open sea. Because its
results do not   scientific standards does not mean it must
be abolished as an enterprise. On the contrary, it remains
forever necessary. "Beautiful is the danger" (Plato). Beyond
the petty certainties, it keeps us alert for the great questions.
At the price that its results remain controvertible, it at
least brings us into contact with those questions, opening up
areas of whose existence we would otherwise have no knowledge
though they are more essential than many fields where incontrovertible proofs are accessible. It causes us to reflect on
things required by both the structure of the world and our own
needs. It places us in ultimate horizons of meaning. But it
thereby also transforms us, opening otherwise dormant depths
in us, placing us in a region of both greater seriousness and
greater breadth and brightness. Like love, religion and art,
it serves to fulfill our true mission.

Of course, philosophy does this not only by exposing the
questions as such, nor only by drawing a line on a graph showing where the possible answers lie, but always with a definite
answer. What is only a possible solution, precisely because
it cannot be confirmed, leads philosophy to appeal, in compensation, to higher sources of truth, and so philosophy pronounces
its respective answers apodictically as permanent and certain.
This puts it in the wrong -- though it is also merely the other
side of its rightness. It provokes the opponent, who gives
another solution, and it provokes the sceptic, who contests the
ability of philosophy to reach any truth. Both are dialectically necessary counterfigures.

Truth and error are also intermixed in the sceptic. For
he who answers falsely may at least have seen the problem
rightly (though his answer as such immediately conceals the
truth again). The mere discovery and framing of the problem
can be an accomplishment. Nicolai Hartmann's method was to
disengage the perennial problems from the systems which speculatively anticipate solutions, for he regarded these systems as
the unphilosophical aspect of philosophy; though progress in
knowledge is only partially possible in the perennial problems,
they also in part point toward the "trans-intelligible." As
in Hartmann's view the best thing about philosophy had always
been its "bewilderment" (Aporetik), so today philosophy should
have the courage to face unresolved antinomies and satisfy

itself with a "metaphysical minimum." Admitted ignorance is
better than supposed truth. As religion too was formerly a
universal interpretation of the world but drew back into its
innermost germinal cell after philosophy and science took over
this task, so now philosophy ought to reflect on what little it
has left.

Philosophy, because it makes statements which are in part
not derived from the object, always has a stronger infusion of
subjectivity than science does. In this, philosophy is related
to art: the subjectivity of the author's individuality, of his
type, but also of the language, the nation, the culture, and
the times, all play a part in it. Philosophy is never only
expression, as its contemners such as Carnap maintained; only
because he was a sceptic could Montaigne say that the subject
of his book was himself. Yet philosophy is also expression --
which is not, as relativism would claim, an exclusively negative factor that holds it back from the truth. For, first of
all, the subject too is a being whose truth must be obtained by
a confession, and secondly, subjective preconditions are also
observation-posts for objectivity. Therefore, the expressive-
ness of philosophy does not only impede, it can also stimulate
and broaden its objectivity.

Hence also the social form of philosophy (Scheler). Science
is based on verifiability and not on authority. It imposes
itself cogently on each interested and informed person. It is
universal. Philosophy however lacks cogency, at least a cogency
of the same kind. An esoteric circle of always just a few
students, or often disciples, gathers around a philosopher, who
himself has "a sense of mission": some schools of philosophy
in fact have a touch of sectarianism about them, with personal
reverance for the head of the school (autos epha, "he himself
said it!" was the Pythagoreans' manner of speaking; opposed
to such tendencies is the Aristotelian dictum: "A friend of
Plato, but a greater friend of truth"). An "elitist mentality"
prevails within each school. Since it is unprovable, philosophy is also undisprovable. Scientific theories are refuted
by arguments; philosophies decline because their supporters
die out.

For positivism, metaphysics was nothing but an error to be
abolished. Karl Jaspers' answer to this was: it was indeed
wrong, for it still hoped to grasp supra-objective reality
scientifically and objectively -- and all our knowledge is objective. Because we know today that this is impossible, we can
no longer ourselves become metaphysicians -- in this positivism
is right. As apprehension of the "comprehensive," metaphysics
is refutable. Nonetheless we ought to vicariously "appropriate"
the earlier metaphysics, which were prophetic and self-styled
as scientific. Their false pre-conditions allowed something

which we, because of our better pre-conditions, can no longer
attain and yet which remains indispensable for us, if only we
interpret it rightly. We can no longer consider metaphysical
statements directly binding, as their originators did, but
as symbolical, transparent signs. They have become for us
"signs of transcendence." In this perspective, even their
untruth proves to have depth. Their "failure" causes a
brilliant light. As soon as they are freed of their self-
misunderstanding, they reveal a valid core. In an indirect
mirror they catch something of what it is impossible for us
to know directly. But to do this they also appeal to the
"supra-objective in us," which otherwise is lost amid the
things of the world and interprets itself falsely by them (cf.
Bergson): namely "existence."

CHAPTER 10

PHILOSOPHY AND THE HISTORY OF PHILOSOPHY

Philosophy's Necessary Connection with History

In science there is only one truth about a thing, while many philosophies are possible simultaneously and successively because their claims always go, if not beyond reality, at least beyond the tangible and visible world. Philosophy lives essentially in a plurality of conflicting movements and schools. (Though at times they seem compatible, that is only because they not only give different answers, but also ask different questions.) Measuring their approach to truth by that of science, people have always reproached philosophers for this. Again philosophy shows an affinity with art, which has a multiplicity of styles.

Science progresses toward its one definitive truth: correctively, by rectifying former error, and cumulatively, by accepting former truth and complementing it with new truth. In philosophy it is different. Philosophy too aims for progress in objectivity and logic: Anaxagoras walked "like a sober man among drunkards" (Aristotle). It participates, moreover, in the progress of the sciences: pre-Socratic natural philosophy or Augustinian philosophy of history today would be a monstrosity. But no line of progress runs between the philosophers. They stand unconnected and separate. The individual system neither refutes the earlier ones, nor does it complete them, as the sciences do, but it constitutes a new beginning; it heads in another direction. Scientific results are cooperative; philosophy is solitary. Scientific results can be understood as a contribution to the whole of science; philosophy however makes pretensions of being itself already the whole, final and perfect.

But because philosophy is not related progressively with other philosophies does not mean it cannot be without any relationship to them. On the contrary, precisely because it knows no progress, philosophy always essentially involves the processing of its own history. It does not progress, but it has a history. It is not only conditioned and formed by its history, but it stands in full view of it.

This is another trait that distinguishes philosophy from science. In science, there is a state of the question. As soon as the scientist has studied this, he turns his attention to the object of study. Formerly gained results are either true and still belong to the present state of the question, or they are false and there is no sensible reason to bother with them anymore. Thus science, as such, takes no interest in its own past. (Generally belief in progress and preoccupation with history are antithetical: for example, the rationalist designs the idea of the best state to strive for, but he does not observe the multiplicity of empirically real states, which for him are all just faint reflections of it.) Contemporary philosophy, however, is neither the whole nor the best, but only one possible type of philosophy among others that appeared earlier. So the present by itself is scanty. Only by incorporating the older philosophies into co-presence with it, does it obtain the accumulated wealth and level of differentiation of philosophy. Our power to invent a new philosophy is proportional to our memory of the past.

The philosopher cannot, like the scientist, conduct strictly objective research. The object of philosophical study is indemonstrable; it is mediated by philosophy itself in formulations, questions and theses. When the philosopher discovers other theses than his own, which make the same claim to validity as his, he must take them seriously and analyze them as competing possibilities of thought. A new philosophical system crosses the threshold of relevancy only on the horizon of its own history and visualizing the entire gamut of other forms of thought, delimiting itself from them and clarifying itself by them. Research into the current state of the question is thus replaced by dialogue with fellow philosophers. As nature produces richer forms than the boldest imagination, so the exclusively internal dialectics of the mind is excelled by the historical dialectics of the philosophers, and therefore every philosophizer must participate in this dialectics. All unhistorical, merely direct philosophizing remains dilettantic.

That philosophers must deal with their predecessors and contemporaries is true not only, or even primarily, in late, Alexandrinic ages. Plato and Aristotle already did so because of an immanent necessity of philosophy. Theophrastus' history of Greek philosophy has its roots in them. Even such unhistorically inclined thinkers as Kant and Husserl are forced into the historical arena by the law of philosophy. The division of philosophy since Descartes into rationalism and empiricism that is still current was first made by Kant.

When someone else's opinion is accepted uncritically, it is, since believed true, independent of history. It may have been discovered at a particular time, but its validity prevails timelessly, in an "eternal present." The philosopher feels dissatisfaction with earlier opinions. Often it is this dissatisfaction which causes his own position to originate,

out of opposition. But that not only separates him from the
other opinion: to oppose it, he must know it and think it
through more soundly than its own adherents. Furthermore, because he does not consider it true, it becomes for him something "only historical" that has to be explained by individual
conditions. Philosophical opposition is one of the great mid-
wives of the recent ability to see things historically.

The philosopher does well to familiarize himself both with
the earlier opinions he opposes and, apart from that, with the
history of thought in general. For only then does he realize
how many of his own opinions, which he uncritically considered
natural and apodictic, have actually been transmitted down
through history. Only when the lived tradition is transformed
into objectified history does it become clear that it arose in
unique situations and often from motivations that have long
since become obsolete. "When words open their wings, millennia
fall out of them" (Benn). Thus the philosopher gains a new
freedom: either he retains the old, though now no longer as
something accepted blindly, but out of his own insight and
reasoning: or he rejects it because it no longer bears its
former meaning for him.

The historical view helps us shake off a heritage maintained only out of habit and frees us for new knowledge. It
thus shows itself to run parallel with the Cartesian doubt:
for Descartes the heritage is abandoned because of its irra-
tionality, here because of its historicalness. The same experience is gained in different ways. Descartes says that we
should doubt all our opinions; but if historical reflection
and comparison did not teach us of them, we would not even be
aware of many of our opinions, for they are too deeply
engrained in us (the most fundamental is known last). Despite
some differences, historical awareness -- as opposed to conservative enthusiasm for history it springs from a seed of
enlightenment -- and logical analysis are related and compatible.

Knowledge does not generally proceed, as in mathematical
deductions, from one secure point to the next, but in hermeneutic simultaneity with the first experiences of detail the
mind designs a still uncertain model of the whole. If this
holistic model, on further progression, proves inadequate, the
mind takes it in hand again and reconstructs it. So it does
not begin by penetrating further into the object but it returns, in a "loop" movement, to its former starting point,
works at it, and then ventures, better equipped, back to the
object (C.F. Bollnow compared this with the fact that in
psychology and ethics we progress only by correcting mistakes
we have made, by regretful "conversion"). This general law
of knowledge is repeated in the disputes of the philosophers

with the systems invented by earlier philssophers.

To know and understand older philosophy is thus a part of
the structural pattern of philosophy itself. The history of
philosophy is based on this, but philosophy is also something
else existing for its own sake (Kant himself complains about
those who reduce philosophy to the history of philosophy).
In the second case, history is no longer criticized in order
to oppose it with one's own truth, but contemplated for its
own sake. Certainly, in the history of philosophy, some
evaluative accents are made, depending on the historian's
standpoint, but the objective is understanding, prior to any
evaluation.

And yet the history of philosophy, even when pursued in
this way, is still a part of philosophy and not only of
historical studies. The systematician still wants to refute
his opponent; only in the historian do the pluralism and non-
progressiveness of philosophy come to full development. For
the historian all philosophies are in principle equally valid
as basic possibilities of apprehending reality. He sees in
all of them something that makes it worthwhile to rethink them
once again. We said previously: one can no longer philosophize like the pre-Socratics. That does not mean they are
"obsolete," any more than pre-perspective painting ceases to
be beautiful because of the technical discovery of perspective.
When the first philosopher Thales of Milet, at the turn from
the seventh to the sixth century B.C., says that everything
came from water, that has an extremely archaic form, but insofar as it implies that the multiplicity of the world is
united by evolution from a transformed basic substance, it
remains -- whether one approves it or not -- an indispensable
idea.

Therefore historical writing is itself already a part of
philosophy, while the history of physics is not a part of physics. Still, the sciences are more interested in their own
history now than formerly when their history was mostly a
collection of anecdotes. For many of them have undergone great
changes during and after the turn of the century. These changes
were based on a shift in the view of principles. And just as
today they have, in contrast with their positivistic phase,
started investigating their own principles, they also investigate the history of their principles. Both things prove that
the sciences have become more philosophical.

Hegel's Identification of History and System of Philosophy

Everything that has developed in history is meaningful in
its way; it is, in its very variety, wiser than our own ideal
constructions: on this individual-pantheistic belief Herder

had, as a counterblow to rationalism's "critical-analytical"
history, established the new historical science with its
affirmative attitude toward the genetic products of the world;
through this belief Herder first liberated and intensified the
sense of history. For the historian, the past can never be
only past; otherwise why would he try so hard to understand
it.

The very fact that many equally valid languages, artistic
styles, and forms of government coexist is no reason to take
offense, or would be so only for a complete rationalist. How
can this principle be applied to the field of philosophy? How
can many truths be equally justified, since truths are mutually exclusive?

In Leibniz' great conciliatory system, every monad in its
individuality reflects the entire universe in a different way,
each with respective fidelity; likewise in what it denies.
"All of them are right." Hegel then blended his own system
and the whole history of philosophy into a questionable myth
of the philosophy of history. Hegel starts with the assumption that truth has many facets; it cannot be exhausted in a
single attempt. Every metaphysics that has appeared in history is just one component, one building-block of truth, and
vice versa every attempt at truth produced its own metaphysics,
so that we possess its historical counterpart. Every metaphysics at first claims to be the complete truth, but it is wrong.
An antithesis arises to correct and complete it, and from both
of them a systhesis results that reconciles the contradictions,
which then in turn evokes an antithesis, etc. But subsequent
metaphysics does not eliminate previous metaphysics completely.
Some factor remains. The German word "aufgehoben" applies to
it not only in the sense of "abolished, invalidated" but also
in the sense of "kept, preserved" (and "elevated"). Only in
a multiplicity of historical stages is the whole truth gradually established. It is not enough, as in science, to hold to
the last stage: the earlier ones were also necessary and remain irreplaceable. In a simultaneity that is only an apparent paradox the previous stages are eternal stages. "The truth
is the entirety," not only the last step.

We do not therefore, according to Hegel, find the historical counterparts of our own truth at chance passages in history, one here and the other there. The historical anticipation of the truth applies to both the content of its particular
theses and to their inner sequence. "The succession of systems
in history is the same as their succession in the logical
derivation of the conceptual determinations of the idea." Not
only were the metaphysics true, but the temporal sequence in
which they succeeded one another was also meaningful. Their
real origination one after another reflects the necessary

development of the ideas one out of the other. The position
of their origin designates their place in the total structure
of thought. Accordingly, the history of philosophy coincides
with the objective structure of the system of philosophy. We
can figure out the structure of a particular system from its
position in history, just as we could deduce its history, if
we didn't know it already, from the system. The historian is
already, provided he understands correctly, a systematician;
and the systematician must refer to history. Just as for
Hegel (and Schelling) history as a whole opens up the book of
the mind, which is identical in history and in our thinking,
this applies especially to the history of philosophy.

Though this clever mental construction identifying history
and logic did not gain general acceptance, Hegel did thereby
deepen the writing of the history of philosophy and give it
its real start. All the significant historians of the nineteenth century are right-wing Hegelians: Rudolf Haym, Eduard
Zeller (Greek philosophy), Kuno Fischer (who had modern philosophy begin first with Descartes, later with Bacon, while only
the otherwise unoriginal Falckenberg has the merit of having
it begin with Cusa), Johann Eduard Erdmann (who is more exact
than Fischer), Albert Schwegler (who, as a Hegelian, reads too
much order into history).

In the later nineteenth century, then, Hegel's idea was
turned directly around. As positivism in general, though it
adopted the Age of Goethe's turn to history, saw in it no longer
meaning but merely content, so now the history of philosophy,
which for Hegel had been a history of truths, became a history
of errors. Hegel's pan-logism was replaced by historical relativism.

Three objections can be raised against Hegel's description:
1. Although for Hegel, every "stage" is given its due,
the next one just happens to be "higher." The earlier one was
necessary at its point in history, but what is of duration in
it is all that is adopted by the continuing development. Here
Hegel betrays the historical principle of the Age of Goethe in
which he has his roots, and reverts once again to the theory
of progress. According to that principle, the historical
phenomena have full value precisely in their individual particularity, and they are all of equal validity. Hegel constructs
a defective synthesis between the modes of viewing history of
the Age of the Enlightenment and the Age of Goethe (and thus,
by his own real example, disavows his philosophy of synthesis).
2. Hegel, by arranging the philosophies in an ascending
line, makes them into a unity. Together they constitute the
whole truth, indeed from the first they move in continuous
necessity -- for in them the World Spirit thinks and develops
toward truth as its goal. Thereby, Hegel fails to see the

insularity of the philosophers. He reads too much and too
systematized a meaning into their sequence. That one system
comes from the other and integrates it is only a surface fact.
Such lines of development can be drawn within a single epoch,
although here too book titles and lecture announcements such
as"From Kant to Hegel" are false; in principle and from the
point of view of universal history the systems are unconnected.
Each opens up new dimensions. Like species of animals or cultures, they arise in genuine historical heterogeneity and
contingency, and are not interrelated like links in a chain
of logic. Hegel projects logic into the history of philosophy,
just as he does into history in general, and he thereby robs
it of its historical firmness and actuality.

3. Because a system was meaningful in its historical
setting does not mean that it is viable and true today -- after
antitheses and syntheses have knocked off all its jagged edges.
Nor need it be viable and true for study of it to be meaningful
for us. Hegel accords too little truth to the earlier systems
by having them all contribute to the final shape of philosophy.
On the contrary, it was the method of the Historical School
not to measure other cultural goods by one's own or by a
rational standard, but to take them seriously in their very
differences and to reconstruct them mentally from their own
center. Only this assumption of other standards made possible
more subtle understanding. In the same way the historian of
philosophy must give second place to the question of the truth
or falsehood of a system; paradoxically, he is more likely to
answer it correctly in that way.

Precisely because we do not transform the other philosophy
into our own ideas, but record it in the mind as a permanent
counterpart, it carries out, as Humboldt showed, its function
for us: because it represents another type of humanity, it
leads us to a higher totality; our own individuality is shaped
by its counterindividuality and becomes self-aware. So too
here. We grow philosophically even, and perhaps especially,
in conversation with false philosophies. All the more so,
since truth is not at all the ultimate criterion of philosophy,
whose task, rather, is to discover possibilities of thought.
Hegel brings the history of philosophy as close to us as a
theologian does the Biblical text, which he applies to our own
moment in time; but there is also an elixir of distance.

As in other areas, knowledge of other men's possibilities
does not lame us, as Nietzsche feared; on the contrary, by
teaching us that thinking had to, and therefore could be historically different, by freeing us from one single valid norm,
it gives us the courage to develop our own new possibility.
The sense of history itself "heals the wounds it inflicts"
(Dilthey). The awareness of historicalness goes hand in hand

with creativity.

Types and Styles

In our century typology was a counterdevelopment to Hegel's
conception. According to typology, the philosophies do not
collaborate and reach the same goal, but basically irreduce-
able and irreconcilable positions stand in non-contiguous
opposition. The great number of systems existing in history
are classified within a smaller number of typologies. The
later system does not presuppose the earlier one; they can
coexist at any time. A dispute between them is senseless --
like the Spenglerian cultures they can neither affect nor even
understand one another -- for each one uses different concepts,
or gives a different meaning to the same concepts.

Dilthey's world-view typology has already been mentioned
above. Hans Leisegang distinguished between "forms of thought":
some thinkers build concept pyramids, others arrange everything, including history, in circles (the discovery of this
form of thought in St. Paul was Leisegang's point of departure).
A third group derives a whole system from a few principles, as
mathematics does. Error always begins when thought that is
trained for a certain field of objects is transferred to
objects of a different structure (cf. N. Hartmann's "error of
stratification"). For Georg Simmel, though he did not propose
a particular typology, all philosophies remain one-sided because of the disproportion between the ambiguity of the world
and our limited possibilities of interpretation. Objectively
incompatible, they still somehow are united by the subsequent
observer. At the end of his book <u>Schopenhauer and Nietzsche</u>
he says that the convictions of the two thinkers could be
reconciled in a higher unity but "the value of what can be
called their synthesis consists precisely in the fact that
mankind has created this span of tension of its vital feelings.
Therefore a unity between them can lie only in a completely
different dimension than that of their objective content, i.e.,
in the subject who looks at them together. When we feel the
vibrations of intellectual existence through the entire span of
these oppositions, the soul expands -- even if and precisely if
it is dogmatically obligated to neither of the parties -- until
it can encompass and enjoy despair of life and jubilation in
it as the poles of its own extension, its own strength, its
own fullness of form." Similarly at the end of <u>Kant and Goethe</u>:
"Perhaps the question of a stable balance of the two world-
views is falsely put: perhaps the true rhythm and formula of
modern life is that the boundary line between the mechanistic
and the idealistic conception of the world should remain in
continual flux, so that the movement between them, the change

in their demands on the individual, the development of their
interactions to infinity, gives life the charm which we sought
in vain from the definitive decision between them. That is
admittedly an epigonal existence; but it is also the extreme
development and exploitation of the favor that the nature of
things grants to epigones, that in failing to reach the greatness of onesidedness, they also escape the onesidedness of
greatness."

Among the themes of the art historian are, in addition to
the artists and their works and the values revealed in isolated
contemplation of the individual masterpiece, the "styles" within
which the individual works often have a valency that does not
fully coincide with such individual value (Wölfflin's "art
history without names"). Likewise the historian of philosophy
will classify the systems in major lines of development. He
will show how a common problem is approached by different
thinkers, how a basic common idea is modified like a motif. To
this extent, there are again, as for Hegel, connecting lines;
there is however not only one, but there are many and they not
only ascend, but they branch off, and they also decline.

Indirectly, following lines also contributes to an understanding of the individual system of philosophy. One limitation of the "interpretive method" is that it isolates authors
excessively from the contexts in which they stand. The author
often does not express his own preconditions because they are
too obvious or even not fully conscious. He works with them
"implicitly," rather than intentionally. Therefore, one must
understand an author "better than he understood himself" (a
treatise on this by Bollnow). One must know the ideas that
moved the times, recognize which was the traditional, which the
opposition party, etc. If we return to the author equipped
with this knowledge, then he has much more to say than when
we believed we could read everything from his isolated text.
For a time, the textual idolatry which radiated from the
Staiger school of German philology also gained some ground in
philosophy; but it was only a reaction to the excesses of
Dilthey's idea-historical overall view, and like Wölfflin's
stylistic history caused the contingent particular to evaporate
into the necessary and universal by fitting it into the continuity of a development as a mere example.

Finally, Greek art is treated by the art historian as a
specific actualization of the universal possibility art alongside its actualization by other nations, and also by the arche-
ologist as an expression of the Greek character along with its
expression also in the state, religion, etc. Likewise, besides
its interconnection with other philosophies, before, beside and
after it, philosophy is also interlinked with non-philosophical
factors, with the "spirit of the times."   Thus the loneliness

of the Calvinistic soul is transposed into Leibniz' monads.
Just as decisive for Kant as his reading of Leibniz is his
family background in a pietistic household and his historical
situation as a contemporary of the French revolution. Therefore the historian of philosophy cannot study philosophy as an
isolated strand of reality. As a system forms a context with
other systems in succession, it also forms a simultaneous context with the underlying contemporary social and religious
strata, with which it interacts and which also express the
situation of the times. A stylistic relationship exists
between the Gothic cathedrals and the High Scholastic summae
(Worringer), between Racine's tragedies and the contemporary
mathematics and physics (Duhem, Cassirer). Hegel himself knew
this and if he gives the impression that the systems only spun
forth on the thread of the concept, that is only because in
his view the total progress of world history crystalizes in
the concept.

On the other hand, the history of philosophy should not
be allowed to dissolve into universal cultural history. A
supra-epochal continuity of philosophy continues to exist, and
even when philosophy takes up current problems they are transformed when translated into the consubstantial medium of the
concept and drawn into relationships and developments that
result exclusively from the laws of conceptuality. Someone who
is exclusively a philosopher, such as Natorp, interprets Plato
falsely, because he fails to see what is historically conditioned in him; someone who is exclusively a philologist, such
as Wilamowitz, also interprets him falsely, because he does
not see his philosophical side: the history of philosophy
here becomes the literary history of philosophy. The systematician must, as seen above, also have rapport with history,
otherwise he remains empty; similarly the historian of philosophy must have systematic ideas, otherwise he remains blind.
The different dispositions become distinct only over a common
substratum.

But as a historian's system is his strength, it is also
his limitation: he finds only his own problems in his field
of study. Epistemologists of the nineteenth century saw the
history of metaphysics as dead; they understood even the pre-
Socratics (partially as primitive physicists, partially) as
epistemologists; and the same with Plato. Leibniz himself
was, for Russell, Couturat and Cassirer, only a logician. Only
eventually, after metaphysics had undergone a renewal, did
the historians -- such as Heimsoeth in his Six Themes and
Schmalenbach in his Leibniz -- rediscover it in the past.

PART III

PHILOSOPHICAL DISCIPLINES

CHAPTER 11

SOME PERSPECTIVES ON PHILOSOPHICAL DISCIPLINES

Karl Jaspers, who thus represents a unified concept of philosophy, considers its division into separate disciplines as something extrinsic. A philosopher's basic insight is revealed in all areas he treats of and he often does not draw a strict distinction between them. Philosophical ideas are always interdependent; one presupposes the other and leads to a third. So an individual's original intuition and the comprehensive internal unity of his system militate against the multiplicity of statements into which it fans out only secondarily. For Jaspers, the history of philosophy was made up of "Great Thinkers." One motive for this viewpoint, in Jaspers' mind, was that he traced the objective content of philosophical theses back to the reality of experience: what counts about these philosophical theses is only the upsurge of existence to transcendence, which they impart and for which it is indifferent what factual material occasions its achievement.

If philosophy is described discipline by discipline in the following chapters, this presupposes not only a firmer confidence in its power to attain truth, but also a concept of it analogous to that of science, which does not let itself be captivated only by its great conceptions. Existential objectification, if it seeks to be philosophy, must be filtered through work on objective problems. Even within the philosophical systems, the individual disciplines have something like autonomy. They contain perennial interconnections of problems and traditions which resist change by the formal laws of the system into which they happen to be incorporated. One example: Plotinus' aesthetics, in which art represents the "idea," still lives in Schelling and Schopenhauer, although the idea otherwise has no place in their systems. Thus the homogeneity of the systems is not total. Moreover, outstanding systemizers are not the only ones engaged in philosophy. Individual research can promote individual questions.

Aristotle combined physics (i.e., knowledge of nature, the highest part of which is metaphysics) and logic into theoretical philosophy, and contrasted it with practical philosophy, which he divided into economics and politics, which deal with communal goals, and ethics, which deals with the goals of the individual. In addition, Aristotle lists poetic or technical philosophy, which deals with man's artefacts. The distinction between theoretical and practical philosophy can still be found

in Kant. Physics and ethics, which deal with reality and
action, were ranked by the Stoics below logic and dialectics,
which deal with thought.

But this ranking is itself only logical. Historically,
metaphysics and ethics are the two roots of philosophy. In
these two disciplines, philosophy deals with questions which
mankind had already answered differently. Logic and epistemology however are more recent; they treat of questions which
were first raised by philosophy itself.

This is far from a complete listing of philosophical
disciplines. Since Plato it was customary to coordinate the
beautiful with the true and the good (Scholasticism then pro-
pounded the false thesis that these three so-called trans-
scendentals are interchangeable with one another, as well as
with being and the one). Thus aesthetics is a further discipline. Generally it is traced back to Plotinus because
theories of beauty and art intertwine in his work; but both
are much earlier (cf. the Pythagorean doctrine of harmony). The
Sophists already knew anthropology and cultural philosophy.
But Platonic ethics and metaphysics relegated these disciplines
to the background. In addition, classical antiquity already
had philosophy of history (of both the progressive and the
cyclical theoretical types); however this discipline was improved and changed by the more intensive Judeo-Christian idea
of history. Finally almost every science can be accompanied
by a philosophy of its own: philosophy of mathematics and of
nature, philosophy of law, of government, religion, language.
And furthermore internal distinctions can even be made within
the special philosophies: the metaphysics of history, for
example, claims to know about the laws and meaning of history,
the logic of history asks about the possibilities and forms of
historical knowledge. But all these interdisciplinary philosophies are on the decline today. Originally they still formed
a unity with their respective sciences, then the sciences
became independent, but were at first positivistic and still
allowed room for a parallel philosophy; but today the sciences
themselves pose their fundamental problems and so absorb the
respectively applicable philosophy.

What field of problems is most urgent to a philosopher
decides what type of philosopher he is. Nietzsche, for
instance, is decidedly a moral philosopher: if we are clear
about this, we have already made a first step toward understanding him. We will then be able to classify all his statements about non-ethical matters from the right perspective if
we try to correlate them with his central point of interest
and interpret them in that light.

It is not at all as if the disciplines of philosophy lay
peacefully isolated from one another or as if they divided up

the realm of principles among themselves as the sciences do
the realm of objects. That for one philosopher a particular
discipline and for another a different one is predominant is
not merely a question of division of labor, and of course
one cannot piece together the entirety of philosophy from the
various sector-disciplines. Antinomies exist: a metaphysician
of unity like Heraclitus cannot be a moral philosopher, for he
considers being as a whole to be good and thus relativizes the
contrast of good and evil; epistemology in turn tends to pre-
clude metaphysics, for it is concerned more with certainty
than with truth-content and it regards the doctrines of
metaphysics as insufficiently proven. Historically therefore
the disciplines do, in part, run parallel; but as the various
arts exist simultaneously and yet, as Pinder showed, there is
an Age of Architecture (1200), of Painting (1500), and of
Music (1800), so particular philosophical disciplines often
stand in the foreground and claim to be all of philosophy or
at least the one real philosophy. This struggle of the disciplines for predominance is also a part of the history of
philosophy.

Since ancient times, metaphysics has claimed the highest
dignity because it deals with the first principles (prota) and
the most universal reality. When metaphysics is obscured by
ethics, as in Hellenism, it is not so much from enmity toward
it (though ethics can be linked with metaphysical scepticism),
but only because men have greater need of it. Philosophy now
becomes the "teacher of life" (Cicero), the art of right
living (Seneca). Ionian metaphysics shattered myth, Stoic
ethics draws close to religion again, and much of it was later
incorporated into Christianity. On the other hand, when in
modern times the analysis of consciousness and epistemology
become dominant, this is based on an explicit opposition to
metaphysics, in the conviction that philosophy ought to take
a completely different point of departure. For awareness,
with its immanent structures, stands between us and the world.
If philosophy always directs its efforts at fundamental problems, then its concern must be not the world but consciousness,
and the certainty and progress of knowledge. Aristotle had
put logic, as an agent and implement of thought, ahead of the
other disciplines only methodologically, but now epistemology
claims objective precedence over them, in fact it seeks to
replace them: "The proud name of an ontology which presump-
tuously lays claim to synthetic a priori knowledge of things
must be replaced by a more modest analytics of pure reason"
(Kant), i.e., transcendentalism. One discipline which almost
always held a subordinate position is aesthetics. But twice
it also had its great hour. First, in the Renaissance, when
it opposed the aesthetics of classical imitation and ascribed

to the artist the godlike power of creating a "second world,"
and secondly in the seventeenth and eighteenth centuries, when
it proved that there is a third possibility between the
dilemma of judging by general rules and sheer subjectivity:
namely an accurate subjective judgment. Subjectivity, since
Descartes the starting point of philosophy, though still
rationalistically misinterpreted by him, first gained its
modern leverage, in principle, through his discovery. Natural
forms of awareness are not the only ones that exist, if they
exist at all, but awareness moves in categories that were prepared for it by the various languages, which are historical
in origin and undergo historical change. When Humboldt under-
took to deepen Kant's transcendentalism, this took him into
the field of cultural history. Linguistic analysis is a modern
form of transcendentalism that developed among Humboldt's
followers. For all forms of thought which comprise the data
of our world are also forms of language. Language pre-filters
the material of the world. But while Humboldt still believed
in a revealing power of language, linguistic analysis shows
rather the opposite, namely how subjective and misleading language is. Another modern variant of transcendentalism is
philosophical anthropology. It becomes philosophical not
because it studies man as a particularly interesting being
among other beings. Rather, the priority of our world, which
for us is always one reflected by man, just as man likewise
remains the utlimate point of reference for every artefact he
makes, is broadened again in a new manner. Max Scheler, therefore, said that the modern fundamental discipline is meta-
anthropology. In another way, finally, the philosophy of history also claims a key position. For all being is in the process of change. Therefore, in its view, ontology and anthropology, which still believe in fixed structures, are, even as
disciplines, based on a prejudice. Everything must be seen
temporally, dialectically, and teleologically. Anthropology
is a form of naturalism; it arises only when the philosophy
of history, which associates man with a rational future, declines (Odo Marquard).
        The same is true of the claim to priority by the various
disciplines as of the claim to truth by the various philosophical systems: opposition and conflict can be an enrichment
in the multi-dimensional structure of reason as it emancipates
itself from the compulsions of its own rectilinearity.
        There are numerous other philosophical subdisciplines;
but only the above-named claim to be fundamental disciplines.
only these will be discussed in the following chapters.

CHAPTER 12

METAPHYSICS

The Three Mataphysical Dimensions

The neo-Platonic philosopher Simplicius understood in the
title of the Aristotelian books Ta meta ta physika the "meta"
in the sense of "trans-" (beyond): these books dealt with
what lies beyond the physical world, with the transcendental,
which the neo-Platonists too were interested in, the supernatural, compared with which earthly things have only a weaker
reality. Metaphysics is "the science of supersensory things."
Even today many repeat this and are usually surprised to discover that the denial of every "world beyond" (Nietzsche) and
the belief that only this world exists, as the unique and true
one, is also a metaphysics -- though perhaps a poor one.
Actually this "meta" does not mean "trans-" but "post-":
it indicates those books which the first publisher of Aristotle, Eudemos, placed "after," or "behind" the books on Physics
and which, since Aristotle himself had given them no title, in
this way came to be called Metaphysics.
The second misunderstanding associated with this book-title
since the Renaissance is that this mistranslation was only an
editorial accident. What Aristotle deals with in that book is
"hae peri ton archon theoria," the theory of principles
(Grundlagentheorie). He himself calls metaphysics "prota
philosophia," first philosophy, and as such the "most advanced
of the sciences." But exactly because it deals with the
"prota," the first principles, it cannot stand at the beginning, it must be at the end, according to Aristotle's general
conviction that the more universal is harder to know and must
therefore, for pedagogical reasons, be presented later for the
benefit of the student and the reader. The position of this
book after the more specialized Physics in the editorial canon
is in onformity with this idea.
Three dimensions of the discipline of metaphysics can be
schematically separated, although in fact they overlap:
1. The horizontal dimension. Metaphysics deals with the
most general determinations of being, which precede every
special area and recur in it. Here belong for Aristotle dynamis
and energia (potency and act, possibility and reality, of
which a further modality is necessity). hypokeimenon and symbebekos (substance and accident, the thing in its essence and
in its qualities), hyle and morphe (matter and form, the real

and the ideal), but also the categories and the types of
causes. Metaphysics could be subdivided as follows: being
and nothingness, being and becoming, being and appearance,
being and knowledge, being and what ought to be, being and ·
meaning.

2. <u>The vertical dimension downward</u>. <u>To on hae on kai ta
touto hyparchonta kath hauto</u>, being as being and what is at
the basis of it: so Aristotle defines the two themes of metaphysics. Analysis of the constitution of being is added to its
general characterization. Both can be the same in content, in
which case only the point of view is different. But the intra-
material components which pre-Socratic philosophers had been
seeking are also constitutive of being. Insofar as "what
lies below" is also "what lies behind," Simplicius indirectly
turns out to have been right after all.

However, the distinction between fundamentals and what they
support, determinants and what depends on them, principles and
what they control, is not restricted only to metaphysics.
Science too penetrates beyond the natural picture of the world
to a more fundamental reality. One can evolve from the other:
for Democritus, atomic theory was metaphysics, but later it
became chemistry and physics. Science fathoms a depth of
reality beyond that of everyday knowledge, but the substrata
it discovers belong to particular regions of being. Metaphysics inquires one step further, into the underlying principles beyond these substrata, into the ultimate foundation of
all reality.

This ultimate foundation has for metaphysics, stronger,
"truer" reality than the structures that evolved out of and
beyond it. This can be understood in two ways: a) Either the
difference runs within being itself. Then the more essential
does not have more being but only a priority of ontological
significance. One can distinguish between the "surface," the
foreground where the ordinary view normally stops, and the
depth which only the expert unveils; but the foreground too
exists. Normally the question then arises about how the connection between the two is to be pictured. Do the prior factors determine the secondary ones as simultaneous entities, as
in Plato ideas determine reality by their presence (<u>synousia</u>)
or in Democritus atoms determine everything by their combination? Or are the prior factors earlier in time, and everything
else comes into being only by their evolution or emanation --
whoever accepts only one prior factor or "world foundation"
will tend to hold this latter opinion. b) Or is the more real
to be understood as if it alone really is. The less real
comprises only an apparent world, which ultimately does not
exist at all. It is only an appearance for the subject. This
way of thinking is both metaphysical and scientific: the

mechanical equivalent of wave-lengths in modern physics becomes qualities of the senses only through its transposition
as a reflex in us. Physics also moves within the world of
experience; but new experience, which reaches further, reveals
that the first experience is merely phenomenal. Often the two
models described above are confused with one another: higher
"metaphysical dignity" with exclusive "being as such," secondari-
ness of being in the metaphysical sense with mere phenomenality.

3. <u>The vertical dimension upward</u>. Besides the Aristotelian definition, a third objective of metaphysics, together
with the universal and the fundamental, is the unconditional
to which Aristotle devotes only the last-written Book XII of
his <u>Metaphysics</u>. In contrast with this third type of metaphysics which classically deals with God and the immortal soul
(since the causalistic modern age also: the "free" soul), the
two first dimensions of metaphysics are very similar.

The first two dimensions can be grouped together as ontology, and the name metaphysics be reserved only for the third;
or one can distinguish between ontological and religious metaphysics. Kant opposes both types of metaphysics, which were
still very close together in Wolff, but the metaphysics of the
unconditional is what stimulated Kant's opposition: only because of it can there be no metaphysics of the "thing in itself" either. The autonomy of religious feeling militates
against metaphysics of the unconditional and the sharpened
responsibility of reason against that of the "thing in itself."

Metaphysics' Claim and the Sceptical Response

Long before the advent of philosophy in human history a
decline of naive credulity took place. Even monotheism is the
product of such a lessened credulity. Metaphysics itself
participates in it by reducing immediate experience to super-
ficiality or mere phenomenality. But its scepticism is always
only partial. Its denunciation of <u>doxa</u> (opinion, appearance)
flows from the certainty of its <u>episteme</u> (true knowledge). It
is always supported by the confidence that mind and world are
ultimately attuned to one another. Whether by identity as in
the pre-Socratic philosophers: "the same is known by the same,"
just as in Goethe the sun and a sunlight-receptive eye are
attuned to one another, or in Schelling's "philosophy of
identity" the unconscious mind that is present in nature corresponds to the human mind. Or in the sense of a partial correspondence of our categories of knowledge with the principles
of being (N. Hartmann). "The order and connection of things
is the same as the order and connection of ideas" (Spinoza).
At a time when this confidence had already been shaken by Des-

cartes and more recently by Kant, Hegel renewed it again in an exaggerated form. Both in content and in sequence he posits a correspondence between the dialectical development of our concepts in the mind and the dialectical development of being in reality. "Man cannot think highly enough of the power of the mind. The hidden nature of the universe contains no force that could resist the courage of knowing. It must open up before the mind and lay its wealth and depths before its eyes for its pleasure." Hegel felt, he said, "mistrust of mistrust": pretended fear of error is really fear of truth.

The believer, though he neither can nor should grasp Luther's God by means of reason, still can melt overtenderly in a _fruitio dei_ (enjoyment of God). He receives an experience by God's grace. German metaphysics later sprang from this traditional feeling. Calvin's God, on the other hand, is a voluntaristic God. His action consists of individual spontaneous acts of the will; the choice of his grace is not guided by rational considerations, it remains incomprehensible. The experience of grace could be a deception of the devil. God, in his infinite majesty, casts the soul that thirsts after him back into its loneliness. Therefore, in countries like Holland and England, where Calvinism won, the absolute in philosophy too is unapproachably transcendent. The results are empiricism and positivism which surrender substantial unity, causality and inner necessity, and stress the individual and actual (Troeltsch).

Calvinism reflects the loss of analogy between the world and modern man, who, no longer united with it by any common standard, feels lost and strange in its infinity. Descartes gave philosophical expression to this loss of analogy, first by his doctrine of two substances: _cogitatio_ (mind) is so heterogeneous in nature and follows laws so different from _extensio_ (matter) that, according to him, no contact between the two is possible; secondly, by doubt in principle: could the world be only the dream of a single solitary self? The feverish man too thinks that his delusions are real. An evil _genie_ could make fools of us with deceits and at the same time give us the feeling of reliable evidence (just as the earth, though it seems immobile to us, was proven by Copernicus to rotate -- Descartes, in view of Galileo's fate, does not dare to state this). What guarantees to us the existence independently of awareness of what is first immanent only in awareness?

Descartes answers: methematical knowledge is true. In the field of pure reason, God cannot be a deceiver. But that is only a theological proof of truth, and even a defective one: Occamism had, because this further increases God's transcendence, so seriously weighed the idea of _deus deceptor_ (God

as deceiver) that it speculatively anticipated Copernicanism.
For Kant, geometry too is unmetaphysical because it is subject
to the phenomenal category of space, and arithmetic because it
is subject to that of time. Descartes furthermore trusts the
immediate self-evidence at least of awareness, of _cogitatio_
itself, as opposed to the phenomenal _cogitata_ (objects of
thought); this was later taken up by metaphysics of the self,
in Fichte and Schelling's "intellectual intuition" of inner
creativity and then in Bergson. In Locke and the later psychol-
ogists, on the contrary, the "evidential advantage of inner
perception" (Brentano) was no longer metaphysically toned. But
it too has been contested by many: first by the critical Kant,
whose "transcendental subject," extra-temporal because of its
"momentariness," can become objective only in the fact but not
in the modality of its existence, and only projects for us a
poor substitute of itself (cf. also the "supra-objectivity" of
Scheler's "person" and of Jaspers' "existence"). For others,
however, the lack of self-knowledge is our own fault and they
therefore demand a "new truthfulness" contrary to any masque-
rade and self-deceit in which we live (Schopenhauer; cf. also
Nietzsche's "Each one is furthest from himself"). Man ought
to see himself as he really is. Psychoanalysis (also French
moralism prior to it) holds that we hide our true motivations
from ourselves, because they contradict our moral self-image.
This counter-interest in self-knowledge must however be
broken (at least for the neurotic, who regains his health thereby). Conversely, according to existentialism it is not our
immorality but precisely our highest moral claim that we flee
from interiorly and fall prey to façades and conventions, out
of which however we ought to rise to "genuineness" (cf. the
contemporaneous Espressionisn).

When Parmenides said that the world of our senses was a
deception, laughter echoed throughout Hellas. "Scepticism
accompanies metaphysics like its shadow" (Dilthey). But in
a different manner. Positivism opposes metaphysics with the
experienced factual world of science. Metaphysical problems
are for positivism not only unsolvable, but falsely posed even
as problems, partly through seductions of language, which must
therefore be critically examined. But in some respects Kant's
distrust of knowledge goes even deeper. For him even scientific truth is valid only intersubjectively but does not reach
the thing in itself. Yet for Kant, the metaphysical drive
(cf. Schopenhauer's "_animal metaphysicum_" and "metaphysical
need") remains an "ineradicable root" in us. "That man's mind
should ever give up metaphysical investigations completely is
as little to be expected as that in order to avoid inhaling
unclean air we should stop breathing altogether." "Metaphysics is, perhaps more than any other science, placed in us, in

its general traits, by nature itself and can by no means be
regarded as the product of an arbitrary choice or as a chance
expansion in the progress of experience." Speculative ideas
of the mind are for Kant only noumena (mental entities), but
as unexperienceable regulatives they show experience its
directions; in "practical confidence in reason" they recur as
postulates.

Unity and Multiplicity

There are metaphysical dualisms, which trace back all of
being to the work of contraries (the Pythagorean table of
contraries, Aristotle's matter and form, which are always together, Descartes' two substances, which never touch), and
pluralisms, which trace it back to an irreducible multiplicity
of heterogeneous principles (for instance, "the four elements").
On closer examination, however, atomism and molecularism very
often seem secondary compared with faith in a homogeneous oneness which is articulated only modally in multiplicity. From
Averroes to Malebranche even the individual soul is thought
of as individuation of the "one universal soul" (the synecho-
logical concept of the soul; antithesis: Leibniz). It is
always a tendency of metaphysics to relate all multiplicity to
a point of unity. That springs not only from a subjective need
for as simple an explanation as possible ("simplicity is the
mark of truth"), for a "world formula," but even objectively
philosophy as inquiry into the ultimate seems to reach the end
of its quest only -- and this could be disputed -- when it has
found one single ultimate reality. (In religion, parallel
basic impulses lead to monotheism. But while for metaphysics
the desire for unity is the occasion to pass from faith in the
gods to conceptual thought, monotheism is neither one nor the
other: it is theistic without the advantages of polytheism
and monistic without the advantages of conceptuality).

If unity is at the basis of multiplicity, then the truth
is completely different from what is revealed in everyday life.
What we see, what we deal with, the reality we take for granted
-- all this is not the true world. Truth lies at a hidden
depth and is directly opposite to what is otherwise considered
true. This "complete otherness" is not merely a logical consequence of metaphysics, but may also itself be a motive leading to it: reality cannot be as disharmonious, as full of
suffering as it seems! From this ethical and eudaimonistic
postulate a metaphysical conviction follows. Since the negativeness of reality is caused by its multiplicity, which first
makes any conflict possible, that is another reason why the
underlying unity must exist: it must not only explain reality,
but redeem it. Metaphysics here has a common root with Messian-

ism, except that it seeks to possess as an eternally existing and ever discoverable truth what Messianism hopes will be "given at a future time" or, in its secularized forms, assigns as a task to be realized.

If a unity lies behind everything, then it is natural to seek unity in everything: metaphysical unity is interpreted as factual homogeneity. There is a common standard even between the most different things. Quality is only a changing quantity of what is recurrently the same. Thus metaphysics of oneness develops into mechanism, indeed not only in the Renaissance, but already in Anaximenes of Milet: inner necessity leads to this typical sequence. Bergson, Scheler and Marxian ideologization even of science trace modern science back, as was seen above, to the fact that whoever wishes to master the world by his work must divide it into measurable particles of mass. This derivation, in its directness, is false. It makes a secondary thing primary. First mechanism had to become a possibility of thought by a complete internal transformation of metaphysics on a theoretical level. And only when this possibility of thought was available could the will to rule now use it for itself. Each of the four "strata" of the real world, which Hartmann, following Aristotle and Thomas Aquinas, distinguished, has at one time or another been made into an absolute, a world-spanning unifying principle.

1. Materialism starts with the inorganic. It was originally not yet "crude materialism," which it became because of Platonist, Christian and Cartesian dualism which by contrasting matter with everything "higher' left matter behind, barren and empty. Pre-Socratic material was, as Cudworth called it, hylozoism; he could also have called it hylozoopsychism. Only when, after Descartes, some retained only spirit, others only matter, while denying the opposite principle, did both sides become radicalized. The League of Monists, usurping the broader concept of monism for itself, held that thoughts are movement processes of the atoms of gray matter, as Haeckel worded it. It is to Ernst Bloch's merit to have rethought the philosophical concept of matter, purifying it from time-conditioned attitudes, and so once again developed a new kind of materialism, quite different from "crude materialism."

2. Vitalism seeks to understand life as such, as an independent layer of reality, and not mechanically (Driesch). It goes back to before Descartes who subjected even living things to the laws of inorganic matter. Another form of the metaphysics of unity is panvitalism. It regards life as the primeval principle, and thus it to some extent reverts to animism, which projected life into inanimate things. Similar views, following Gnostic, neo-Platonic and medieval patterns (Gabirol's "fountain of life"), were held by Schopenhauer with

his metaphysics of the will and also by Bergson, who saw matter as a weakening of the "elan vital."

3. Related with this and likewise a reversion to animistic, anthropomorphic thinking is panpsychism. "Things have souls" (Thomas Aquinas). Untouched by mechanism, Leibniz, who engaged in it but understood it only as a system of beautiful methods and not as a materialistic metaphysics, has the world consist only of "monads" which he expressly conceives of by analogy with "what we call 'I' in ourselves." The monads contain "ideas" with different degrees of clarity. Where they still lack awareness as in "small perceptions" they are unconscious soul elements -- which makes Leibniz the discoverer of the unconscious. But for him the unconscious still has a negative valency: it ought to become aware. The whole inner process of the monads, which form a hierarchy according to how far they have progressed, aims at ever higher awareness. Herder and the young Goethe first established a positive concept of the unconscious: the unconsciious wisdom of nature or of genius stands above rational knowledge (the same contrast of two conflicting concepts of the unconscious still exists in Freud and Jung respectively). For Leibniz conscious "apperceptions" stem from unconscious "perceptions" by repetition and intensification; the individual blows of the waves reach our ear, but we hear only the roaring of the sea (while for Kant apperception is an act of awareness).

For Fechner not only the plant has soul-life, but even the star-souls of Plato's Timaeus and Kepler reappear in him: everything has a psychic inside and outside, a day- and a night-side reminiscent of Romantic natural philosophy (Ritter). Aristotle and the Scholastics had already ascribed a "vegetative" soul to the plants and a "sensitive" soul to the animals, and let these two first levels also exist in the human soul, below the spirit. Descartes first denied categorically the "life-giving" soul: of other beings and also in man. He established the concept of the "conscious soul," according to which the soul -- still a property only of man -- no longer merely has awareness as it formerly did but is identical with awareness. Thus Fechner bypasses Descartes and goes back to an older tradition. The concept of the conscious soul, however, has dominated academic psychology down to Freud.

Schopenahuer ought also to be mentioned here; while the soul is rational and meaningful in Leibniz and in Romanticism, Schopenhauer depicts his "will" as decidedly irrational. He takes his emphasis on the non-intellectual parts of the mind from the Age of Goethe but his evaluation or rather depreciation from the Enlightenment. The will, which resembles a prehistoric monster in its insatiability and blindness is the essence of the world; only the "idea" deserves approval, and

that only when it frees itself (and thereby us too) from the
will.

4. Fichte and, in a different way, Schelling and Hegel are
spiritualists (though wrongly called idealists). In Kant the
subject merely gave form to a "thing as such" independent of
itself. In Fichte, therefore, spiritualism is also subject-
monism. Not so with Schelling and Hegel: the spirit exists
behind nature; the world process and that of history are its
development to awareness and to ever higher stages of awareness. Nature is the "Odessey of the spirit" (Schelling).
"Everything real is rational" (Hegel).

5. Strata of real being can be considered the only thing,
or also ideal being; e.g., the tendency in Plato to regard
the medium in which being appears to us as a form of "non-
being" (Avicebron: "the form gives being to the thing").
Aristotle first elevated <u>hyle</u> (matter), the construction material, into an independent counterforce which, though indeterminate, is passively <u>to hou ouden aneu</u>, "that without which
nothing can be." Therefore empiricism gains a higher rank in
Aristotle. For the late Plato reality comes into being through
combination of the highest types of idea that are mixed in it.
Plotinus is again an immaterialist. Hegel's panlogism, which
replaces the idea by spirit, therefore goes back to Plotinus;
German Idealism is neo-Plotinism (Ziegler).

6. Those types of monism which make higher stages of
reality or ideality into absolutes are also related with pantheism. But pantheism always retains a stronger dualistic
element than purely philosophical theories: the cosmos is
divine; God acts in it, but it is not God. With its concept
of "<u>natura naturans</u>" (active nature) based on neo-Platonism,
pantheism (though the name dates back only to Toland) has been
competing with the transcendent God of theism since antiquity.

7. But it is not necessarily something already known from
the world that is selected and laid at the basis of all other
things. By analysis of reality the mind can also gain a concept of some fundamental prime material (<u>Urstoff</u>) which is
nowhere to be seen as so constituted but must first be
obtained from the data by analysis.

8. Finally it can also abstain from any contentual identification of the cause of unity. Plato and Plotinus did this
by calling it simply <u>hen</u>, the one. Spinoza calls it nature
or substance, of which Descartes' two contentual substances
are only attributes among an infinity of others. Heidegger
speaks of "being," Jaspers of "transcendence." But while
Plato's and Plotinus' "one" is the final product of abstraction, these latter terms remind one of the contemporary "New
Objectivity," which limits itself to the simplest essentials,
from fear of any decisive style.

Primary and Secondary Being

What is the relationship of the postulated unity to visible multiplicity? In what way does the one contain the many?
For if it did not contain it, then the multiplicity would fall
outside it and the unity would not exist at all.

1. The theory of development. A frequent answer is:
Multiplicity comes into being by the transformation of the
one -- whether really in time or only by structural priority
is another question. The one is changed into the many, it
develops into it or, if the one is not placed "below" but
"above": it emanates it, releases it from itself in the
Plotinistic procession (prohodos) -- and takes it back again
in the return (anhodos). Thus the idea of development can be
a consequence of the point of departure with a metaphysics of
unity.

Looking back from what it becomes, the one at the base of
everything itself acquires new qualities. Compared with multiplicity it is: (1) not only the basis of everything, not only
the stronger determinant; but rather a temporal priority also
follows from the ontic priority: it is also older in time, the
first thing, not in the sense that a second thing is added
independently of it, but that it is the origin of everything
that is and without it nothing would be. But then in relation to what develops from it, it is (2) also eternal, unchangeable being. (This contrast can also be posited when
the many does not develop from one "basic substance: but is
conceived in general as the "realm of becoming." In contrast
with it, the longing for "the eternal" can even be primary and
so attain the quality of fundamental being.)

But development within the framework of a metaphysics of
unity is predetermined. Nothing can proceed from it that was
not already contained in the original unity. For otherwise
something would exist outside the unity and it would no longer
be a unity. Thus, development is here not a true development.
It "develops" or, as the etymology of the word suggests, it
"unfolds" seeds that were present from the first. Only then
can the one be preserved in the many. But then one could ask
whether the unity is not merely formal and one only in name.
The many, though it was only manifested by development, was
already implicit in it. Development merely brings it out.
The merely external temporal development proves to be essentially only ontic explication. The concept of development in
a metaphysics of unity accords with the Aristotelian metaphysics in having the result of development be pre-formed as
telos (end, goal) in the mind. But because this telos is merely translated into the other language of reality, it also can
claim no independent originality. As in one case the develop-

ment is explicative, in the other it is only a realization.

Not until the eighteenth century does development begin
to be understood as completely causal and productive of something new that is not pre-formed. Time now becomes an increase and intensification. What becomes, transcends its
origin qualitatively and produces something categorically new.
This marks the end of a metaphysics of unity. Though it spoke
of development, its development was static: everything was
already there. Now history, which sees nature and the world
of men as in process of change, replaces the metaphysics of
unity. Earlier the differences of being were not given their
full weight compared with the substantial bond; now the
combining factor recedes as a mere substratum compared with
the more real differentiations. Its multiplicity is not less
valuable being of a secondary degree; it itself contains
"ultimate truth."

In addition to the absolute origin, there exist fundamental determinants in every area of being, and it was a false
rigorism of metaphysics to limit itself to the former. Although
life stemmed from the inorganic, completely different laws
are intrinsically at work within it. Similarly with the soul:
it is not merely an inner space in which ideas and laws of
association are linked just as mechanically (Herbert) as in
external space atoms attract and repel one another, or in which
because of the "narrowness of consciousness" they are "repressed" below the "threshold" but it is a context and structure of meaning that must be understood on its own terms
(Dilthey): the relationship of object to perception is not
one of natural cause and effect, but one specific to the soul;
it is an act of apprehension not reducible to "stimulus" and
"perception" (Brentano). Thus in every particular stratum of
being the principles that apply to that stratum must be studied
in their specific particularity. Differential ontology wins
out over metaphysics of unity. In our century phenomenological
anti-reductionism wins out over the reductionistic naturalism
of the nineteenth century (which did not realize that it was
a metaphysics). This is not to deny that the higher can come
from the lower, or meaningful events from natural processes.
But because one sees it proceed one should not level it down
to what it came from. Development is "emergent evolution"
(Morgan).

2. Phenomenal theory. The other solution to the unity/
multiplicity problem conjured up by metaphysics, in addition
to development, is phenomenalistic. Multiplicity, this theory
says, doesn't really exist; rather, we are merely surrounded
with appearance. The relationship between metaphysical being
and what depends on it is not that between first and second
being, stronger and weaker being, but between being at all

and merely supposed being. As the basic reality becomes manifest by contrast with what ensues from it as its eternal
origin, so here again a new quality is added by contrasting
being as such with appearance.

The phenomenon can be understood as "objective appearance."
In a religious version a deceitful demon dangles illusions
before us. Or, in Plato, the idea is reflected back to us
by the medium of reality, which then must be allowed something
like a "second being."

The more frequent line of reasoning, however, is to explain
that only we, with our imperfect equipment of knowledge, evoke
the phenomena. Without us knowers only the bare object would
exist; the phenomenon is subjectively conditioned. It is
falsified when received by our senses which are inadequate to
it. They translate it into something relative only to us (as
did the Sophists). Kant says that our senses, like our understanding, contain aprioristic forms for grasping reality, but
these do not completely match true being -- at least as far
as we know. They construct the phenomenon by impressing these
forms on reality. Kant is here still thinking religiously:
human weakness lags behind being, much as we would like to
reach it. In this context, later thinkers see interests at
work here: they intentionally remodel reality to fit the
pattern of vital pruposes.

On the other hand, the metaphysician, since he believes
he has knowledge of the thing as such, generally arrives at a
theory of the dual division of our powers of knowledge into
one vulnerable to or even actually causing error, and one
receptive to truth. Generally then the senses are considered
erroneous, and thought is seen as the "metaphysical organ"
that leads us to the noetic sphere, the intelligible world;
but sensualism and positivism were also able to reverse this:
sensation sticks to the facts, only conceptual thought goes
beyond them. Kant, on the other hand, saw subjectivization
in both forces.

But the subject is only one factor of the phenomenon, which
results as the product of two factors. The other factor is the
thing as such, itself, the "objects which affect our senses"
(Kant). In part, we fail to grasp them and therefore only
phenomena result; but in part they contribute to the phenomenon, which is therefore always a "well-founded phenomenon"
(Leibniz) with a basis in reality. The phenomenon is not
merely phantasmagorical illusion. It receives error from us,
but truth from the thing. Therefore Plato calls the world of
doxa (appearance, opinion) "a middle thing between being and
non-being." No thinker, says Aristotle, can ever reach truth
completely, but none can ever miss it completely.

The same degrees of nearness and distance can prevail in

the relationship between phenomenon and thing-as-such as with
the analogous relationship within reality of "surface" and
"depth." The phenomenal world can be explained as completely
dissimilar,as Parmenides does: here unity and rest, there
multiplicity and movement. In that case there is no transcendence from one to the other, except by a turning back.
Compared with this concealment, Plato's phenomenon is indicative: it approximates the idea at least to a ceraain degree;
it does lag behind and obscure it, but despite this imperfec-
tion reality participates in the ideal representationally.
Our normal image of the world does not lead us astray; despite
the gap between the two we can rise to the idea. In Hegel
(and differently, in Goethe also) the phenomenon manifests and
reveals; it is epiphany, logophany: "phenomenology of the
spirit!" The phenomenon does not have to be declared a separate field in Hegel. (There is the same ambivalence in the
concept "symbol" as in that of "phenomenon": a "mere" symbol
or a meaningful symbol.)

The determination imparted on the phenomenon by the knowing subject stands in reverse proportionality to the determination by the thing itself. If the shaping of the phenomenon
by the object is slight, then almost the entire content of the
phenomenon stems from the transformation of the noumenon into
knowledge. But if there is a close relationship between the
thing and the phenomenon, then the subject must contribute
correspondingly less to the phenomenon.

If one attributes ultimate, true reality only to atomic
matter, as modern mechanism does, then all structure and
coherence in the world, everything that was formerly seen in
it, is transferred to the subject which itself projects this
into the world. Then we stand, as does Kant, inside a shell
of pure phenomena in which our reason prescribes laws to
nature. In Platonism the form had been self-existent, and
even reality became fully existent only by participation in
it and was known in its metaphysical center only from the
priority of form -- that is the meaning of "a priori knowledge"
in the Middle Ages -- now the form is just a function in us.
Our knowledge is restricted to it and incapable of attaining
reality, which is completely different. Since, on the other
hand, the world created by the subject is the only one we have,
the role of the basic metaphysical reality, which was formerly
sought in the depth of the world, now is ascribed to the
"subject" (which is so called with the old metaphysical term).
This idea remains just below the surface in Kant himself, since
for him the subject is still a competitor with the "thing as
such," which is only modified by it. Maimon and Fichte however already denied the "thing as such." What was still a
modulation in Kant, therefore is lifted to total creation in

them. Subjectivistic epistemology again becomes metaphysics:
the metaphysics of the creative subject. Fichte thereby
influences the Romantics and, more recently, the Symbolists.

The psychologism of the nineteenth century was still based
on the fact that mechanism demoted everything that it could
not explain to a mere appearance, which then is blamed on the
subject. Psychologism is a corollary of mechanism, and fills
the gaps it left behind. Everything general (including, for
example, a law) is now only psychological; for in the physical
world only individual things exist; even society exists only
in the awareness of the individuals that are its bearers. The
meanings and institutions of "objective spirit" and values are
psychological; beauty consists only of our experiences of
beauty.   Therefore in the nineteenth century so many sciences
psychologized, just as today they sociologize, etc. (cf. W.
Wundt's Völkerpsychologie, which aims to present total history.

Only the critique of the metaphysical scope of mechanism
by phenomenology made possible a critique both of Kantian
transcendentalism and of psychologism, which both had been
reactions to mechanistic rigorism. In addition to extension
and mind, the physical and the psychological, a third area,
that of meaning, becomes visible. Therefore the human and
social sciences, which had previously been entangled in the
investigation of causalistic influences and biographism, now
are undergoing an upsurge.

CHAPTER 13

EPISTEMOLOGY

Its Origin

Logically epistemology comes before metaphysics: only after it affirms the fact of knowledge and teaches how knowledge is possible is the way clear for metaphysics. The neo-Kantians were therefore convinced that philosophy had begun historically, too, as epistemology. In actual fact, however, metaphysics stands at the beginning.

Normally we put our trust in knowledge's natural sense of direction: we let it be our guide to the world, live in and with things and find no occasion to reflect back on knowledge itself. This occasion arises only in case of differences of opinion, disruptions of knowledge, recognized error. Even in everyday life mistakes of experience are discovered and corrected: the approaching ship does not get bigger, we know that only distance made it look small. But metaphysics, from its new interpretation of the world, declares illusion, which otherwise had been only a particular single experience, to be the usual thing in principle: most things which we generally consider to be true are superficial or apparent; the truth is completely different.

Two things follow: First, the metaphysician must not only proclaim, but -- as Parmenides was the first to do -- proves his doctrine of true being, in order to consolidate and distinguish it from the apparent plausibility of the general error. Secondly, he must explain untruth as well as prove the truth: why, so he asks, does the world as a rule not show itself to us as it is deep down and as such? What leads us to our error? How does the phenomenal world originate, since it must ultimately be supported by the world as such? The answer usually given (the arguments are presented in Plato's Theaetetus and are later summarized by Sextus Empiricus) goes: Our perception is deceptive, it is only subjective. Thus the metaphysician becomes, by intrinsic necessity, an epistemologist -- he also necessarily becomes a "historian," as seen above. As the theologican has the world as subject-matter as well as God, so the metaphysician must deal with the phenomenon.

The impulse to epistemology, which in antiquity came from metaphysics, stems in the modern age from physics. Therefore it investigates preferably knowledge of the physical object rather than of other human beings (Feuerbach, Buber, dialogistics) or of the cultural structure (Dilthey), although the latter is prior in our knowledge. Even mechanistic physics originally makes metaphysical claims, which were given up only by Kirchhoff and Hertz (though Newton already dared to say: "Perhaps what we call movement is, in God, power). Again, then, metaphysics comes first, and again it is the evidence of the senses that is contested. Galileo in Saggiatore (1623) sets the program: what we perceive as qualities must be traceable to different quantities of homogeneous matter, to their graduated greater or lesser amounts or their faster or slower motion (in later language: the mechnanical equivalent of violet is vibrations of 400 millionths millimeter). Like Democritus before and Locke after him, Galileo distinguishes between natural primary qualities (size, shape, situation, motion) and merely subjective, secondary, non-tactile qualities -- "subjective" meaning not "exclusively psychological" but "psychically co-conditioned."

Later also physicists have at the same time been epistemologists: Helmholtz, Mach, Heisenberg. That is not mere ambidexterity of talent; they are led to this by their own science, which includes a general thesis about being. Helmholtz even posed the (false) thesis that Kant too had arrived at epistemology by way of physics (after all, he wrote a "theory of the heavens"). In the middle of the nineteenth century such scientific positivism still goes hand in hand in hand with neo-Kantianism, even in Liebmann and F.A. Lange, in whom Cohen and Nietzsche as a pragmatist have common roots (science must be materialistic but that does not necessarily make materialism true, it may be only a practical assumption). Ernst Laas in his book Idealism and Positivism -- which made the word "positivism" current in Germany -- first introduced the bifurcation that distinguishes between a Plato-Kant tradition and a Protagoras-Hume one.

Empiricism and Transcendentalism

Our senses falsify objective reality, as Kant develops the old teaching, because they act only through inner forms. Science's hope of finally catching up with nature through more refined observation must therefore fail. But reason too is caught in a system of inner forms. Therefore philosophers too must bury their old dream of flying in pure thought to the truth hidden by the senses.

Kant concurs partially with Hume. Hume said: what we learn is always "after the fact," never "because of it"; we add the "because" ourselves. But, as Kant interprets this, science cannot and must not for that reason give up causality and the other categories. It uses them legitimately, but whatever it

accomplishes thereby has only inter-subjective validity and
is not ultimate truth. Later Dilthey argued, against both
Kant and Hume, that causality could indeed be an object of
experience, namely when the cause or the thing exposed to an
effect was our own subject.

Kant further distinguishes himself from Hume (whose line
of thinking continues in the physio-psychological epistemology
of Helmholtz, among others) by not introspectively analyzing
the subject's real experiences of knowledge, but starting with
the "fact of science" and its results, which are recognized
as valid, and from there inquiring into the general and necessary "conditions of their possibility." Kant's method is trans-
scendental retrogression" from the known object to our a
priori concepts and rules, by which "awareness in general" as
the subject of science has always formed the object in the
"synthesis of apperception." These concepts must therefore be
regained from the object like out of a mirror. The specific
nature of this method became clear only gradually to Kant himself, therefore in the second edition of the Critique of Pure
Reason he inserts the idea that space makes geometry possible
and time the theory of motion and he asks in the three parts
of the Prolegomena how mathematics, natural science and metaphysics are "possible." Therefore the neo-Kantians (Cohen,
Natorp) based themselves on the Prolegomena for their question
about the logical "validity" (Lotze) of the sciences. For
them the retrogression became an infinite one in which the
given data -- in reality something imposed on us -- were traced
back more and more to determinations of thought and finally were
transformed completely into such (as already in Maimon and
Fichte). Philosophy, according to them, no longer merely
elaborates on what the spirit has always solidly possessed: a
priori does not mean "innate."

Transcendental method, moreover, and not merely epistemological meaning, is at work when Feuerbach seeks to return
man's qualities to him, since God is only an unconscious projection of oneself; and also when Dilthey makes the entire cultural world of expression, which reveals nothing more than
self-observation, into the "organon of anthropology" -- man's
history tells him what he is --; when Spengler discovers
behind every culture a "soul of the culture," from which he
then interprets the culture; and when Gundolf, starting with
the work, finds the principles by which an author creates, i.e.,
not his empirical individuality, whose biography is indifferent,
but his "transcendental subject."

According to Democritus, the atoms, which are the alphabet
of the world, write on the wax tablets of our soul (therefore
he calls them stoicheia, "letters" --"elements" also originally
had this meaning). Locke adapts this image (tabula rasa) from

Plato's <u>Theaetetus</u>. The sensory im-pression (the <u>typosis</u> of
the Stoics) still corresponds directly and without falsification to the external world; perception (<u>Empfindung</u>) corresponds to the "stimulus"(<u>Reiz</u>) -- to state it with a pair of
concepts later used by Albrecht von Haller, which Herder and
Kant adopted. According to Locke, not only does all knowledge begin with the senses (Thomas Aquinas), but it also
stems from them. "Nothing is in the intellect that was not
first in the senses." The generalized triangle of geometry
is only a pale relic from memories of individual triangles
which we have seen. There are no "innate ideas" (also not
that of God): Locke is the father of both empiricism and the
religious Enlightenment). Contrary to such empiricism, rationalism (Descartes, Leibniz) reduces perception, indeed also
feeling and will, to merely confused, obscure thinking (therefore the term "cogitation" designates for Descartes not only
thought, but the entire awareness). For empiricism, thought
is defective perception, for rationalism perception is deficient thought.

But Locke's segregation of a pure sensoriness corresponding to physical reality and mirroring it faithfully is naturalism. Kant (like Leibniz, who added "except the intellect
itself" only extrinsically to Locke's statement and made too
little use of it) compromises too much with this naturalism,
for while he admits of no perception (<u>Anschauung</u>) without a
concept, it is only because a second, accompanying act of
thought ("I think") is added. He thereby criticizes sensualism, but begins too late with his critique, allowing it to
stand as fundamental within a limited field (as Plato had done
with the analogous sensualism of the Sophists). Only the act
of thought ("I think"), according to him, introduces form as
as a triple achievement into the "confusion of sensations,"
and makes them conscious and objective (which in Leibniz happened mechanically by repetition and not through one's own
action). In reality, all sensation is as such already flooded
with categoriality, inevitably and without borrowing from
"thought." Kant himself was aware of this distinction; in his
"transcendental aesthetics" he expressly distinguishes --
though in a constructively narrow sense -- between the doctrine
of the "forms of perception" and the "concepts of the mind"
(the neo-Kantians later did not follow him in this). "Spontaneity," which he contrasts with the "passive receptivity" of
the senses, is just one other such association.

The analysis of perception in our century has made one
thing prefectly clear. To mean "something" is always to mean
it "as something": that is the more complete meaning of
Brentano's "intentionality," as interpreted by Husserl. The
gestalt-theory, too, showed that the senses never deal with
disorderly matter; every perception already stands in context,

is sustained by an interpretation. As we classify a thing by
an anticipatory inner image of it, so we see the individual
detail as an element of a composite, and therefore as something different depending on the nature of the composite. And
vice versa, within an analogous composite, we see different
things as the same if they fulfill the same function. A
melody that has been transposed to another key still seems to
be the same melody, though all individual notes have been
changed. Animals too experience relationships; for instance,
they assign a certain reaction not to a certain color but,
when the sequence is changed, always to the brighter color.

Matter completely isolated this side of mind and exclusively sensory is only a construct and an empty postulate of
the naturalists.

Theories of Truth

Epistemology (which like "theory" is descriptive) does more
than study the process of knowing (this is done by non-philosophical psychology of knowledge). It subjects its result,
knowledge, to the criterion of truth: knowledge must be knowledge in more than a neutral sense, and not error. As a methodology it specifies how truth can be assured and discovered. As
the science of truth (alethics) it determines the nature of
truth.

Truth does not reside in the thing itself. The object may
be "unhidden" but it becomes so only because we have a truth
about it. Heidegger's concept of "ontological" truth is,
firstly, not a concept of truth, and secondly, even logically
derivative. Truth is a quality of our opinion of a thing, of
the "image" or "structure" of knowledge, of which we are generally not aware because its task is precisely to open up a
thing for us: truth coincides with the object and so disappears in it. As little as we generally think of the fact that
we possess the world only through the mediacy of awareness, so
little do we think of the medial function of truth. By truth
we live in things; only in the case of failure, in error, does
the structure of knowledge attract knowledge to itself. We
first detect the function of truth via the detour of error.
But truth no more inheres in the knowing subject than it does
in the object. A judgment written down in language is true,
even if no one is thinking it at the moment (Bolzano's "sentence as such," which Husserl drew upon for his anti-psychol-
ogism in logic).

A concept becomes true when it coincides with something
independent of itself (transcendent) and preexistent:
"adequation of the thing and the intellect." How this adequation is to be understood raises a problem, but being

has priority; knowledge seeks to approach it, while being itself remains unmoved; knowledge fits the object (more or less accurately) and so gains a truth about the object which it may then transmit by language (or even in another form: every structure contains truth). The Pythagorean doctrine had to be discovered at some time or other, but the conditions of being which it expresses always existed. However, knowledge can also change things, not only in microphysics, but in all living organisms. Things are not as "indifferent" to being known as Hartmann claimed.

Immanentistic concepts of truth try to define truth independently of its relation to the object. For pragmatism truth is what stands the test of life (but often truth is destructive and illusion stands the test: Machiavelli, Leopardi, Nietzsche, Sorel, cf. Ibsen's "lie of life"). Even in Marburg neo-Kantianism, which is related with pragmatism on this point, truth is what stands the test, namely in the system of science where it must fit without contradiction (since science progresses, the particular truth is increasingly verified by it, and thus science gains a futuristic dimension). This recalls Hume, who gave as a criterion -- not a definition -- of truth that it must be compatible with the context of experience. For Southwest German neo-Kantianism, truth is a "value": that which is scientifically "valid." But all these concepts of truth cling to something secondary. They presuppose mental adequation to the thing, even when they deny it. An exception is mathematical conventionalism ("it is neither true nor false, but convenient," Poincaré; cf. Hilbert).

Originally adequation is thought of as a relationship of depiction. But the perfection of the portrayal ought not to be judged by its containing as many elements as possible of the object depicted. Depiction that coincides with the complete content is impossible: it was Hegel who said, "If I wanted to describe the wood of my table down to the smallest splinter, that would be a task lasting all my life." Nor is it desirable; on the contrary, knowledge can fulfill its objective only by simplification or reduction. It does not duplicate being; it selects contour, structure, elements. Only so does it give a comprehensible, overall picture. (The artist faces the same problem in portraying his object: cf. Balzac's Chef d'oeuvre inconnu.) The depiction theory was dealt its hardest blow by the proof of the subjectivity of the image of knowledge since the Sophists. The qualities which we believe to derive impartially from things are "posited" by the equipment of knowledge we happen to have, which varies from animal to animal and even within the world of man; these qualities exist only "for us."

Therefore the depiction theory was improved into the correspondence theory. What represents for us the thing we

relate to is no longer -- or perhaps only partially -- understood as a similar image, but as an indicative sign. Objective matter in vibration is perceived as a red carnation. In
context, red is completely heterogeneous to the vibrations, but
still an unmistakable context of references exists. Despite
its dissimilarity it is caused by something objective, and we
react to a different wave-length with a different nuance of the
sensation red. Therefore red is not <u>the</u> truth, but <u>a</u> truth
about the vibrations. It is relative, but to man as such and
not to the individual subject and it cannot be arbitrarily
changed. We possess being, but unless metaphysics or science
open it up to us in another manner, we know it, so to speak,
only by translation into our own language, which though it
sounds completely different still retains the meaning (just as
script does not copy language but likewise renders it by un-
ambiguous coordination -- in this case established by convention).

The image imitates the object, the sign points to it or
signifies it. Knowledge hosever means it. What is partially
right in both theories must be integrated into the theory of
intentionality. All knowledge is, as Plato correctly says,
identification of a given fact with the universal inner image
which we already have of it within us, with the category in
the broadest sense. Everyone can observe this in himself in
cases in which the category does not coincide simultaneously
with the data: for instance, in the case of something approaching from a distance, at first indistinctly. We must first seek
the right category, we vacillate about which of the possible
empty forms we should classify the approaching object under.
But both Plato and Kant were wrong to regard the schemata of
knowledge as innate and eternal. That may be true of the broadest of them, but generally they have been formed only by
experience (of the individual and of the generations which pass
them on). Therefore they can be expanded or modified by new
experience.

It was therefore false when philosophy so often sought an
"Archimedean point" (Bollnow), an unshakably secure foundation
from which it hoped to progress inerrantly. Evidence does not
constitute such a foundation, for it is only the experience of
evidence; in the non-Euclidean geometries axioms are assumptions about whose applicability a decision is made only on the
basis of the consequences derived. Nor is perception such an
absolutely reliable point of departure, for it is already pre-
interpreted by its function in the total perceived <u>gestalt</u>.
But the discovery of an unassailable basis of truth as a
starting point is not only impossible but unnecessary. It would
contradict the process of knowledge, which proceeds quite
differently. It is a paradox that in order to understand we

must already have understood (Humboldt). Knowledge is interpretation of an interpretation. The "hermeneutic circle"
(made famous by Dilthey) characterizes not only interpretative
understanding, but all knowledge. The first step is always a
tentative preliminary understanding, the establishment of a
horizon. The second step checks the data to see whether the
preliminary understanding is adequate. If it is not, then
the third step goes back to the preliminary understanding
and corrects it. The movement is thus not simply progressive,
whether inductive or deductive, but zigzag or, rather, circular. That the first tentative design was only hypothetical
does not militate against it, for we are not totally dependent on it. By its assumptions it sets in motion the process
that will abolish it, if necessary. Theologically: sin is not
error, but persistence in error.

If reflection thus builds upon its own categoriality, if
to work at the system of categories is a property of all knowledge, then the next task of philosophy is to make us aware of
the most elementary stratum of our understanding, which had
been taken for granted and left unquestioned. Yet if philosophy contents itself, as Aristotle does, with explicating this
basic stratum, then it takes for eternal and final what has
in fact undergone development and change. Instead of questioning the origins of our understanding by reflection, as it
should, and thus rejuvenating them, it reifies them. Along
with its merit of finding philosophical language for the general implications of the "natural world-view," it was the
"original sin" (Plessner) of phenomenology to confuse meaning-
analysis of the natural world-view with the justification
thereof. While positivistic non-philosophy bypasses the transcendental, the immanent retrogressive danger of philosophy
itself is to know it but to fossilize it.

But philosophy has the power to oppose this danger. After
Aristotle had rationalized the world-view of everyday experience, which traces heterogeneous things to identical elements,
it was the venture of modern times -- after some precursors
in antiquity -- to understand a still greater number of phenomena from a unitary point of view by forming not abstractive
but constructive concepts. Euclid starts with the existing
circle and defines it by the equal distance of its points
from the center; the modern age has the circle come into being by moving a point at the same distance around the center.
Nothing in nature need necessarily correspond to concepts born
of reason (imaginary numbers, non-Euclidean geometries). But
by their greater universality such concepts then constitute
new ways of thinking reality: e.g., Galileo's universal theory
of movement, which is not movement of a certain type of bodies;
relational logic, instead of the object-connected Aristotelian

categorical logic. In mathematics there are three levels:
arithmetic, algebra, quantitative analysis.

Yet, prior to content, the modern age seeks to advance
knowledge through methodology. Pre-philosophical man may well
have believed that the world provided him with such methods
ready-made and without him having to work for them. But if,
as Greek metaphysics already showed, truth lies below the usual
aspect of things, then it can be reached only by certain ways
of access and mental equipment. Knowledge becomes work and a
process. This awareness of the necessity of methodology is
further intensified by the modern "alienation of man from being (which is understood too narrowly and secondarily only as
social alienation). Method, as Bacon states, makes excep-
tional talent no longer necessary for science; it becomes a
wide road for everyone. Method makes the results follow almost by themselves,"as if mechanically." Yet one must be
patient with it: "Truth is the daughter of time." Method has
a qualitative significance: it guarantees us real truth
instead of error; and a quantitative one: it broadens the
scope of truth.

The Subject of Knowledge and the Subject of Life

All being is, according to the theory of awareness that
goes back to Descartes, given to us only by means of the awareness; though ontologically being may be prior, in reference
to us awareness comes first. All philosophy, it is concluded
from this, must begin with the "contents of awareness"; and
its first question would have to be: where do we obtain certainty that what these contents of awareness refer to also
exists independently, outside the awareness? How do we go
outside, how do we break the circle of awareness? Since Descartes, Dilthey scoffed, man has been busy trying to build
bridges.

According to Schopenhauer and Helmholtz, our faith in the
reality of the outside world independently of awareness can
be traced to an unconscious causal conclusion from our perceptions, which we interpret as effects of a stimulating cause:
namely, the thing as such. Jacobi already objected against
Kant, whom he reproached with drawing the same conclusion, by
referring to Kant's argument that causality itself was only a
subjective category. According to Hume, along with the above-
mentioned classifiability into the context of experience, the
intensity with which we perceive something vouches for its
reality. According to Maine de Biron and Dilthey this is done
by its resistance in tactile experience.

Finally, phenomenology, weary of this incessant tuning of
the instruments, so that the concert never began (Lotze), gave

up the entire problem of epistemology. Starting with Franz
Brentano's theory of the intentionality of awareness, which
thus does not primarily have "contents," it performed a
"turning to the object," whose reality it assumed. The next
step after this was a "turning to ontology," in N. Hartmann
still with numerous epistemological arguments. Prominent among
them was his allusion to what he called "phenomenal transcendency," which counterbalanced the point of departure with
awareness, i.e., the indication within the phenomenon itself
that it is not merely a phenomenon. On the other hand,
according to Heidegger, the question about the reality of the
outside world is falsely posed, even as a question. It starts,
on the pattern of general modern atomization, with a world-
less, isolated subject which appropriates the world only subsequently. In contrast, according to Heidegger, being-in-the-
world, which Husserl had already described as part of the
natural attitude (but from which he nonetheless turned back
to Cartesian isolationism), being-with, and being-in, habi-
tation, is from the first an existential fact of life, without
which it would not exist. Human existence, as it acquires
things, can never be doubtful of reality. Only the pure subject of knowledge is susceptible to this, but it is a secondary and ungenuine subject.

Ideas from vitalism and pragmatism are absorbed in this
view. Both schools have no need to prove that knowledge
reaches through to the world, because they understand it as
being by nature an innerworldly process. That it needed such
a proof was both a sharp-witted and a shallow idea. Knowledge can be rightly understood only as a part of two totalities. First, all its powers are organs of a living whole
which sustains them; secondly, their relation to the world
is built into broader relationships which connect the whole of
life with the world in a greater totality. Knowledge is not
autonomous. It is not put into practice only accidentally and
subsequently. It does not originally seek truth for its
truth-value. Interests of a living creature impart its mission
upon it. It has a function to fulfill toward the will and
action. The truth it discovers must provide them with an
orientation. Therefore, life knows only what is relevant to
it (Rothacker's "principle of significance"); therefore each
creature, depending on its respective "radius of action" (Wirk-
welt) lives in a different "perceptible world" (Merkwelt,
Uexküll), which except in man who is "open to the world" is
restricted to a directly vital scope (Scheler). And the rule
applies even to man, though not primarily, as pragmatism held,
but secondarily, that things are not pure objects of contemplation but a "basis for action": "What a thing means is simply
what habits it involves" (Pierce).

The incorporation of knowledge into the vital processes also makes it evident that knowledge is not always, not even in its highest concept, a sober, disinterested constatation by "cold reason." Interests direct the radiation of knowledge into the world and give it intensity and revelatory power; the object of knowledge is also grasped by the emotions. This can be linked with Franz Brentano's insight that even feelings, which the older tradition had declared to be merely "conditions" of the subject, or "colorations" of the "ideas," which ideas were given first rank by intellectualism (Herbart), can have an intentional function (not that they always do, as he claimed: there are also "conditions" of feeling). "Moods," according to Dilthey, Heidegger and Bollnow, open up our access to the world; it remains enveloped in them. Values are given to us emotionally (Meinong) or by loving intuition (Scheler). Old knowledge from as far back as Augustine and Pascal is here revived. Knowledge, on the one hand, presupposes a drawing back from entanglement in reality to a contemplative counterposition and distance, on which ethical freedom and the overall-view are based, yet on the other hand it matures by "engagement" in life together with things and men.

Starting from scientific knowledge taken as the real knowledge, truth was formerly regarded as a quality of the logical judgment. But we have truth already in perception and reaction. The person who says, "It is cold," but also the person who wraps himself more firmly in his blanket knows that it is cold (Rothacker's example). Many truths cannot even be stated: what a hammer is, is known not by the person who stares at it and describes it, but by the one who hammers (Heidegger). Non-linguistic art also says something in its fashion, and even a style of activity or workmanship contains an interpretation of the world. There is no such a thing as unstated, non-apophantic, pre-predicative truth (Heidegger).

Though the involvement of knowledge in life has been increasingly discovered, still the classical prejudice against practice and the "passions" which only confuse it has continued to hold its ground. Under its sway, knowledge automatically seemed to turn only to one segment of the world, coarsely and selfishly. But necessity is the mother not only of invention but also of discovery. And how could we live meaningfully and successfully in the world, if the image of it conveyed to us by feeling, will and action were completely distorted? Bacon, who established the definition: Scientia est potentia ("Knowledge is power," Hobbes), also knew that "Nature cannot be overcome except by producing new reality." Precisely the man of action must submit to truth, just as vice versa applicability to action is an indication of truth. It provides a control which the mere knower lacks -- therefore he can so easily become lost in speculation.

The Concept of Ideology

According to Marx, who gave a sociological turn to the
idea, the ruling class is motivated not by just any interest,
in the sense of everyday practice, but by one specific interest, namely the preservation of its power. Religion, law,
morality are, for Marx, only "sublimations" of this interest,
in part its "apologetic" expression, but in part also its
intentional concealment. Under the appearance of objectivity
they really serve to maintain the existing conditions of
domination. The Enlightenment already saw that every class
has its "prejudice." For this, Marx, who reaches back to pre-
Hegelian thought in the Enlightenment and links with Hegel
only externally, uses the concept of "ideology," which comes
from Destutt de Tracy, thought it had a different meaning for
him and was first given its negative connotation only by
Napoleon. But the Enlightenment still believed that we are
rational beings: a prejudice understood is already half
abolished. For Marx, on the contrary, the bourgeoisie,
because it inescapably oppresses and exploits, has a "false
awareness." Because of its conditions of existence and the
state of its interests, it can have no other: in a reversal
of Hegel, being determines awareness. But if thoughts are
derived only from real circumstances, then philosophy must
result in power: it cannot remain in the realm of thought,
it must change the real circumstances in a revolutionary
manner. After this has happened, pure knowledge of the truth
will begin. The mind had only been distracted from its true
destiny by class interests and now it returns to the truth.
Marx has only a specialized concept of ideology: the
proletariat, since it has the "right" interests by which it
finds itself in agreement with the direction of history, is
already in possession of the truth. And so will all men be,
after the classless society has been established. Marx's
concept of ideology is polemic: it seeks to unmask and destroy. In contrast, Karl Mannheim, in his Sociology of Knowledge, combining Marx with the line of historism, developed a
comprehensive concept of ideology. All thinking is, for him,
inevitably anchored in history and society; it is "being-
connected." Kant's logical extra-temporal transcendentals are
here joined by real and historically variable transcendentals.
Though Marx and Schopenhauer still believed that knowledge
could ultimately free itself from interest, according to Mannheim it is as incapable of this as in Kant's view it is incapable of freeing itself from the categories. And for Mannheim the bondage to a viewpoint does not, as it does for

Scheler, who also developed a sociology of knowledge, have only a selective relevance for an independently pre-existent truth that simply does not show itself from all viewpoints (Scheler and also N. Hartmann). For Mannheim the viewpoint has constitutive relevance for the content of knowledge. It is here fully absorbed into history. There is not truth and falsehood, opinions are not object-adequate but only situation-adequate. This is, according to Mannheim, not relativism, which still measures by the idea of an absolute truth, but relationism, since such an idea is abandoned entirely. What remains for us is only to work out the connection between the situation of life and our view of it in terms of the sociology of knowledge.

A concept in circulation in the Frankfurt School is a theory that sees the whole, even though it is itself a part of this whole: its "object" is not pure "counterpart"; it must reflect itself along with it, or it is to a certain extent itself reflected in the theory. Thus it differs from the Greek theoria, which is posited as outside its own content. Since all reality is subject to historical change, it sees itself as historical, i.e., not merely historically conditioned (that could still be interpresed in Scheler's sense), but as "totally historical" and transformable by history. This need not impede its militancy for the truth it stands for -- since except possibly in mathematics and natural science there is no other truth.

Once again we come upon immanentistic concepts of truth. This time they do not reduce truth to validity or applicability in system or practice, but they are historical and sociological concepts of truth established by sociologists. Philosophy, for its part, can accept the proof of the intermixture of truth with subjective reality; but it will not surrender its link with objective reality.

CHAPTER 14

ETHICS

Metaphysical Ethics

The oldest, constantly repeated attempt of philosophical
ethics, a dream of humanity, is metaphysical ethics. With the
world foundation, so it claims, we possess at the same time
the principle of right behavior. What ought to be, must be
deduced from what is, meaning from being. In fact "real being"
is itself the ultimate authority; there is no higher court
of appeal by which it could be negatively valuated. Up to
this point the equation "being, or the good" still applies.
When Schopenhauer declared the will to be "metaphysical being"
but at the same time negated it and recommended aesthetic
escape from it or its ascetic taming, he did this not out of
metaphysical consistency -- this congruent conclusion was first
drawn by Nietzsche after his affirmation of the will even in its
terribleness -- but only because the will causes suffering.
There is an inconsistency in Schopenhauer's system; his pessimism is, as E. von Hartmann saw, only eudaimonic, not metaphysical pessimism, which doesn't exist.
       Yet, in the metaphysics of unity true being is not only the
foundation of the world, it also encompasses the whole;
nothing falls out of it. But then the following statements are
true: "Everything is good." "For God everything is beautiful
and good and just; only men call some things good, some things
bad" (Heraclitus). One could resort to the subterfuge of evolutionism: the good wins out only gradually, indeed it demands
not specific content but only development (Spencer); but then
even what has not yet been attained, or the hindrance itself,
would have to be considered good (Nietzsche's affirmation of
the eternal return). In the Middle Ages there were sects that
paid special honor to the serpent in Paradise and the traitor
Judas, because by their ethically evil actions they became
metaphysical instruments of salvation; in fact others wanted
to bring about the Last Judgment by sinning.
       Metaphysical ethics thus denies something that no ethics
can do without: the opposition of good and evil, the "value-law
of bipolarity." For it, everything is already completed. However, a viable philosophical ethics needs a new point of departure to make it self-reliant. Even historically it is not by
chance that ethics originated in the "post-metaphysical"
Sophistry of the second half of the fifth century B.C. But

philosophical ethics cannot be satisfied with describing ethical phenomena, it must also justify the ethical. Since this
problem of justification is never completely solved, metaphysical ethics makes a resurgence again and again in altered
form down the ages.

Mores and Morality

Originally man's behavior is guided by living customs. He
repeats things that he has seen done around him. Pre-established patterns of behavior make communal life run more smooth-
ly. They relieve the mind of finding and deciding on new forms.
In early times man submits so unquestioningly to customs and
society watches over their observance so strictly, punishing
every deviation with sanctions, because they have proven valuable as conjurations and because of the primeval dread always
latent in a world of magic effects. The entire life of primitive man is a permanent unreeling of traditions that exist in
his tribe for even the apparently most insignificant things.
The later so-called sphere of adiaphoria (indifference "between virtue and vice" -- the Cynics), in which it does not
matter whether one acts in one way or another, does not yet
exist.

Since originally all behavior is ritual, there is still no
distinction between the fields of the practical, the cultic,
the legal, the conventional and the "moral." which were later
differentiated. A sign that morality became a separate field
relatively late in history is the fact that all its terminol-
ogy was developed from a pre-ethical stratum of language (for
example, the German Tugend, "virtue," from the more general
taugen, "to be worth, useful"). Even the word "morality" comes
from the Roman mos, moris "custom, habit," which rendered only
a part of the meaning of the Greek word "aethos," which also
meant "inner nature, character," i.e., not what is visibly
done, but the entire attitude, mentality and basic habit
(Aristotle's hexis) of a man, from which individual actions
follow (e.g., medical ethics). Decisive for morality is, contrary to what the word might suggest, not conformity to the
mores but this emanation of an action from an internal attitude.

The living custom is not transformed into an expressly
formulated moral code of commands and prohibitions except for
pedagogical reasons, or in cases of violations or of the clash-
ing of different customs, or when reflectivity increases from
independent causes. Though attributed to the seven wise men,
moral pronouncements can also be proverbs; for in tance:
"nothing too much" (Solon).

Philosophical ethics, as distinguished from moral training,

does not provide particular casuistic instructions for the
concrete case. Its mission is to base morality on more general principles. By deriving it from them, it legitimates the
binding force of morality. Morality, once understood as right,
is justified. But the principles can also show that the existing morality is unjustified, that it should be replaced by
another, a new morality. Philosophical ethics thus can be conservative; Kant, for example, wanted to trace Christian,
bourgeois morality, whose validity he was certain of, and on
a theoreticaal level the Newtonian world-view also, back to
a priori principles. Or it can, like the Enlightenment's
critique of religion, criticize the prevalent morality, though
not necessarily religion in general. It can also seek to
revolutionize, as do the Sophistic doctrine of natural law and
Nietzsche, in which case it gains affinity with the type of
(non-philosophical) prophetic ethics.

Morality does not merely cut a narrower segment out of the
totality of custom (and add new contents which appear only on
its own level). It also produces an internalization of general
custom, adding subjective factors to the "objective good." As
long as the good is followed only externally and its form
observed, all that we have, in Kant's language, is "legality."
Involvement of the person is a necessary ingredient of "morality"; Kant calls it the perception of the imperative of "duty"
so that "when one is speaking of moral value, it is not the
actions which are seen that count, but the inner principles
behind them, which are unseen." Legality does the good either
from habit, to gain recognition, or to avoid suffering contempt. Morality, however, acts from an ethical motive, or in
Kantian language from a rational a priori, independent of experience, and it would if the prevalent custom is bad (as in
the Third Reich) also violate it.

Philosophy, as was seen, presupposes the independent, autonomous individual who no longer merely obeys traditions but is
a law unto himself. This same individual, who is the source
of philosophy on the theoretical level, is the source of morality on the ethical one. Though he may act in conformity with
custom, he raises it to a higher level by making it his own:
his activity, though adopted from other sources, now truly
springs from himself. But in addition to autonomy of approbation there is also a creative ethical autonomy which discovers
a new good. Existing custom does not ask about the autonomy
of the individual: it approves it as long as it is used only
in conformity with tradition. But as soon as autonomy denies
or transgresses against tradition, custom turns against it. Of
course, the individual cannot be autonomous in all areas; in
many he will merely imitate heteronomous patterns as before.
The morality of the ethically "heroic individual" rises like

an isolated mountain peak over continuing bondage within custom.

The Subjective Factors of the Ethical

Morality begins where the good is done not only by habit because custom does not know any differently, or out of obedience to the authority of God who commands it, but out of an internal affirmation, on one's own responsibility. Such an affirmation is also possible within tradition and religion. But complete ethical approval can stem only from an insight into meaning and into the reasons for the good that is to be done (a similar insight is necessary for assent to philosophical truth). Here the connection between morality and philosophical ethics is striking. Morality claims to do the good only because reason recognizes it. Therefore no further divine commands are needed, in fact they would be detrimental to morality. (Wolff had to leave Prussian territory within 48 hours because in a speech he had referred to Confucius' high ethical doctrines that are not founded on religion!) Yet if morality is based on knowledge, it faces the following danger: as a craft is mastered by only a few and the unskilled majority must rely on them, so according to Socrates technicians and specialists in the field of ethics (including politics, which was not yet a separate discipline) would be necessary and the majority would have to submit voluntarily to their greater insight. Morality would thereby be reserved for only a few, and the majority would be subjected to heteronomy by the very principle of ethical freedom.

Under the exclusive rule of custom it is not asked whether it is accepted of one's own will. Hence the so often bemoaned formalism and externality even in religion, when rules are observed without any feeling of religiosity. A main point of Jesus' teaching was that purity of heart counts more than cultic purity; the widow's penny thrown into the alms box out of devotion counted more in God's eyes than the greater donations of the rich man only in order to observe the law. For Kant, if behavior stems from "good will," it is good even if it fails to accomplish its corresponding "good action." "In great things, it is enough to have wished them" (Propertius). "Though the strength is lacking, the will is praiseworthy." Hegel, in contrast, again stressed the moral quality of the real act: people are what their deeds are.

Medieval law was concerned only with the deed, punishing the violation as such and not investigating the motives. Also among the Greeks, Oedipus was guilty (aitia still means both "cause" and "guilt") of murdering his father, even though his act was unintentional. In far earlier times, even Draco had

distinguished between intentional murder and unintentional
manslaughter. If there was no evil intent, this lessened the
punishment; if the killer had acted in self-defense, he was
set free. The symmetrical consequence would be that the criminal intent of itself, even if it did not go as far as the deed,
should be subject to punishment. Law does not draw this conclusion with the same scrupulosity: it restricts itself to
the visible event. Religion, however, knows "sins of thought"
and ethics knows guilt in the form of evil will, shame, qualms
of conscience, remorse.

From the French moralists down to Nietzsche and Freud, it
has often been shown psychologically that the true motives of
behavior, even when it follows the external ethical guidelines,
are not ethical ones, but selfishness, ambition, greed for
power. Whoever does the good only to stand forth as a phil-
anthropist in the eyes of others is a Pharisee. But even the
man who does good in order to do good fails in goodness. The
desire to do good should not be contained in the intention. It
is a question of doing the right thing in a given situation for
its own sake. The moral act must not be self-reflective; it
carries the "good on its back" (Scheler).

Another necessary ingredient of morality is freedom. The
good must be done not only by compulsion or out of fear of
punishment. It would have to be done, in Plato's example, even
if one possessed the ring of Gyges which would make it possible
to commit any crime without being discovered. For this reason,
according to Schiller, there are no laws commanding the higher
virtues such as fidelity, magnanimity, gratitude, otherwise we
would practice them only out of legality instead of "from un-
defiled moral grace." Conversely, morality does the good, not
from fear of punishment, but also not in expectation of rewards
(although both Plato and Kant reintroduced such rewards
secondarily), but for its own sake. The good is the reward of
the good (Spinoza). Instinct would have led to happiness more
easily than freedom does (Kant).

The idea of ethical freedom can also be given a different
turn: we must chose between good and evil, we must decide for
the good against the attractive and tangible possibility of
evil. Only when we could also have decided differently, when
the doing of the good is based on an overcoming of oneself,
does it acquire moral merit, only then do we deserve credit
for it. If a man does the good from a natural disposition,
without having to overcome himself, if he knows of no contrary
impulses, is courageous because he feels no fear, doesn't steal
because he is not in need, his behavior cannot be accounted
meritorious in the same sense.

Emotions, interests and drives, which themselves seek to
determine behavior, stand in opposition to the good. Since

the Stoics there has existed an entire system of ethics for
which the basic ethical situation is a conflict between higher
"reason" and lower "desires," and "virtue" consists in opposing and hampering the desires: Thou shalt <u>not</u>. In part its
focus is thus narrowed down with a pedagogical intent. Virtue
results only by a victory over these "lower desires": docility
is good because we are inclined to anger, justice because we
are inclined to partiality. In Kant this pair of opposites
(reason/desire) recurs as "duty/inclination" -- though he
doesn't mean this in the sense that inclination would always
pull in a different direction: it could in principle advise
the same action as duty does, but we act ethically only when
reason, rather than inclination, is the "decisive cause of the
will": we need not, as Kant has been misinterpreted, act
against inclination, but we should not act because of it.

Two Ethical Paradoxes

    Two paradoxes follow from the subjective conditions of
morality. Morality places the man who decides freely above
the one who simply accepts a custom without reflection. But
now suppose a man decides freely for evil. Does he who "knowingly does wrong" (Socrates, though he denied that such a
person exists), stand above the man who unwittingly does right,
because of his greater ethical autonomy? Augustine said: God
had to permit evil so that we would be free to do the good.
That is the basis of Augustine's theodicy. Temptation and
danger have a function of intensifying the ethical dimension.
The evil man who falls prey to sin has at least the advantage
of freedom over the unfree good man. Diabolical perversion
even has greater ethical potential; therefore the fascination
it radiates. Yet obviously the ethical cannot be defined just
subjectively in terms of freedom; the "subjective good" must
be joined by the "objective good." The two factors are equally
valid, analogously to form and content in art. Both the free
evil man and the unfree good man are ethically deficient.
    Furthermore, a man may at first find it hard to master him-
self and to do his duty; but gradually the duty becomes a habit,
he likes to do it, and he would even find it hard not to do so.
Likewise in cultural history: what was once a step ahead and
had to be fought for against barbaric custom, now is instituted
as a refined but all-pervasive custom. Which condition should
be considered the best, that in which the good is still done
by effort and self-mastery or that in which it has already become habitual? The former is subjectively more ethical, the
latter objectively so. The subjectively ethical achievement
is only transitional; it creates a new situation where it is
no longer needed, just as cultural creativity is always engulfed

by the created geniality of culture. Against Kant's exclusively personal morality, Hegel defended the more objectivized
morality of institutions such as marriage, the state, and law,
whose ethic is retroactively reimparted upon the individuals
they support.

Generally we do not judge the qualities of men only by
the subjectively ethical criterion of their responsibility
for them. This is true at least of non-ethical qualities: we
admire strength, beauty, abundance of ideas, genius, charisma,
which their bearers receive freely without any merit on their
part. It is true also of ethical qualities: are courage, per-
severance, strength of will really morally indifferent even
when possessed only as natural dispositions, as Kant claimed?
This boundary between psychology and ethics is artificial.
The valuation can even be reversed: Schiller, in disagreement
with Kant, held that the "beautiful soul" for whom, as for the
"naturally Christian soul," the good flows spontaneously from
its nature is preferable to the moral person who must strive
for it in inner struggles. Nietzsche's thinking was similar:
we can claim credit only for the least, not for the best in
us: "Everything good is inherited." The ethic of morality,
on the contrary, is the ethic of the free individual: it
overestimates the capacities of the individual. It stresses
what he can do by his own effort, it calls him to greater and
greater achievement of the good, and it leaves in obscurity
what he owes primarily to his origin and his basic nature.

Such considerations could lead to scepticism in principle
toward ethics. Ethics isolates the individual excessively;
it thrives on the fiction that his decision between good and
evil is completely free. For only then can merit and guilt
be ascribed to him. In reality, his decision is dependent on
how he has previously been formed by his tradition and his
social and economic situation. They also give him the tendency
to evil that he lacks the strength to overcome by himself.
Instead of prosecuting crimes with draconic justice, Thomas
More advocated that society eliminate the causes of crime.
Likewise Helvetius and Rousseau: society, rather than the
individual, belongs on the prosecution bench; it blames the
defendent for something that is primarily its own fault. It
provokes to evil deeds by letting men grown up in oppression
and poverty.

Later, Marx also professed a form of anti-ethicism: the
moral awareness of man is not, as the philosopher believes,
stimulated by moral demands, which are impotent, but only by
changed empirical conditions. How can one speak to exploited
people of the categorical imperative! The circumstances must
first be changed. And thought alone cannot do it. The revolution is the fundamental moral deed. For only it reverses

all circumstances that keep man oppressed and enslaved. The
revolution far excels goodness from man to man, which leaves
the wickedness of the general institutional framework unchanged. In a better economic and social system, men will
themselves be better (though, as the late Marx corrects himself, not overnight). Egoism, which in former times was
necessary for the survival of the individual, will recede.
Helpfulness and self-sacrifice will become natural inclinations and will need no such moral exertion as they do now,
for they will coincide with the individual's own strivings.
They will also be less necessary in a society happier as a
whole. Spokesmen from the modern Communist camp are less opti-
mistic. Roger Garaudy says that the constitutive morality of
the individual will recurrently conflict with the general
norms of constituted morality. No society can remove man's
own responsibility. Society, furthermore, needs the responsibility of the individual, who thereby shows himself to be a
part of it, for if it should err morally only the individual
can control it and lead it back to true morality (Adam Schaff).

The Three Types of Ethics

We have duties toward our fellowman, toward ourselves,
and toward objective value-systems. Accordingly there are
three necessary and complementary forms of ethics: communal
ethics, individual ethics, and value-ethics.

1. Communal ethics. Communal ethics applies equally to all
men. It demands those reciprocal modes of behavior without
which it would be impossible to live together. "What you do
not wish someone else to do to you..." The individual, so
Durkheim states, because he knows no other ethic than this,
has of himself alone no morality: morality arises in and for
society. Hobbes, on whom this analysis is based in its general lines, developed this point of departure in a crudely schema-
tic way. For Hobbes, ethics and society cast light on each
other. In a conceptualizing hypothesis he assumes that
originally only individuals existed and were dominated by
their egoisms. A merciless struggle of all against all pre-
vailed (for man does not, like the animal have an instinctive
"inhibition against killing" within the species -- Konrad
Lorenz). So that each man will not have to suffer constantly
under the egoism of the other, they now make a contract to
restrict egoism and no longer to live against, but with each
other. They transfer their rights to society, which returns
only a few of them, and they act in such a way that society
can survive, i.e., morally. Morality is the precondition for
the possibility of society. But they do this not for society's
sake, nor for the good of others. Selfishness dictates the

limitation of selfishness. They remain internally the old
egoists. Only externally do they behave morally, because this
is in their own rightly understood interest. What is good for
society is indirectly also good for oneself. Society and
morality are purposeful products of egoism that has become
intelligent.

Now the individual, who would very much like to murder,
steal and commit adultery, and society, which forbids it, are
opposed. As hard as he finds this prohibition, the individual
submits to it for the advantage which he enjoys from society
in return. The individual is therefore internally divided: one
part of his nature denies society, which so curtails him,
another part approves this curtailment as ultimately advantageous to himself also. A struggle ensues between himself as
an individual and himself as a conscious and willing member
of society. Thus his tension with the social order is transformed into an intrapsychic tension. "Desire" now arises to
represent his individuality and "reason" to represent his
sociability. For Kant "inclination" (Rousseau's penchant)
is selfish, while duty is recognizable by its suitableness to
be made a "principle of universal legislation."

Now the process of interiorization begins, as Mill, Darwin,
and Spencer have described it. After theft has been severely
punished long enough, "conscience" afflicts the thief at his
deed or even at the thought of it, though he is still not
clear about the intricate context that theft is wrong only
because society could not exist with it and that through reci-
procity he also benefits from this condemnation. He now
considers it wrong "as such." What is as such only useful,
namely useful for society, is now enthroned as "the good."
Fear of vengeance becomes, by internalization, the "evidence"
of this good.

Conventional, non-sociological, philosophical ethics begins
at this stage of internalization. Reason as the higher self,
so it says, demands of us the glorious good as that which is
intrinsically and evidently better. But it does not explain
why it is better and why we should act contrary to our
immediate drives and impulses. Accordingly, it does not recognize the relative though unrealizable right of psychological
drives, but simply condemns them. From this conflict of the
two factors, one of which must win, though the other too can
adduce reasons for its justification, there ensues for traditional ethics a Manichaean struggle between light and darkness.
Though appealing to reason, it is really acting irrationally.
The perceptible chain of motivation is no longer actualized,
but suppressed. The real motivation would be too rational,
prosaic and naturalistic, for it is based on personal interest.

Against Hobbes, Locke partially approved of the natural

struggle of egoisms, for instance in economic competition (as
Adam Smith also did), and he was also epistemologically the
spokesman for nature and the senses, which he does not contrast with thought, as Descartes does. Therefore he held that
in the social contract the individuals surrender only a part
of their rights to the state, namely the right to violence.
As Hobbes established absolutism, Locke establishes liberalism.
In harmonistic faith -- which we have lost today -- the welfare
of the whole society is seen as the result of the competitive
struggle of the egoisms of the individuals (which Hegel even
sees as promoting the historical purposes of the world spirit).
Locke revives the Pelagian faith in an inborn goodness of
irrepressable human nature; his view of the basic goodness
of human nature changed the European view of indigenous peoples from crude "savages) to "natural peoples" (Lafiteau) and
even excited enthusiasm for them (Rousseau); it also revolutionized the theory of education, replacing previously repressive philosophy of education with a liberal one permitting
self-development. From the same faith others (Grotius, Shaftesbury, Hutcheson, Hume, the "moral philosophers of sympathy"),
disagreeing with Hobbes, supported an original and real
"social instinct." As a consequence, moral actions were no
longer seen as stemming from refined egoism, but as having
their own root in genuine altruism. But a distinction must
be made between altruism for the neighbor and consideration
for society as a whole. The two can collide: if the goal is
the "greatest happiness for the greatest number" (Bentham's
utilitarianism), then the happiness of the individual is
restricted. Romanticism rejects the entire contractual ethics:
one must not start atomistically from the individual, society
always exists before him, it bears and shapes him.

Communal morality is first "group morality": outside the
group "hunting conditions" prevail between individuals and
from group to group. "The law of nations" (Grotius) seeks to
mitigate this; universalism seeks to transform a "closed
society" into an "open society" and thus to progress to more
humanitarian solidarity (Bergson).

2. Ethics of the Individual. To protect the individual,
communal morality must restrict him. It restricts him by its
very nature, but often more than necessary, and so it deprives
him of a part of his self-realization. Therefore the counter-
action is a revolt of the individual. Titanism demands self-
fulfilment only for the "strong natures." Anarchy demands
greater scope for all; it believes in a natural concord of
men without coercion, for they are basically well-intentioned.
Since society cannot submit to the denial of its claims,
periods of enthusiasm for the individual usually fade away,
as happened in the Renaissance and in Storm-and-Stress and its

aftermath, except in the closed circle of libertinistic sects
and in the free territories of philosophy and the arts. Un-
inhibited fulfilment of egoistic drives remains restricted to
the "cold-blooded" criminal, who risks his own destruction for
one great moment of freedom, and to the privileged few whose
economic and political power permits them to place themselves
above the law.

The prevalent laws, says Plato's Sophist Thrasymachus,
were established by those in power. Yet even the subjects
believe they apply "by nature." However, since this is only
an illusion, one may without scruple follow one's own will
to action and violate the law. In that case, violence does
not oppose law as such, but violence meets violence. A somewhat later dialogue character of Plato's, Callicles, argues
differently. For him it becomes simultaneously clear that
what the individual is attacking is often not morality as such
but only democratic equality. For him the law does not stem
from the strong, it stems from the many weak men who join
together to protect themselves from the few strong men and
constrain and intimidate them since childhood by arbitrary
restrictions. They call it evil that the stronger rules over
the weaker and that he has greater wealth than others. Actually that is just the law of nature as can be seen among the
animals and in the behavior of states toward one another.

Nietzsche's _Genealogy of Morals_ still shows a certain
affinity with this: he too unmasks morality as something
historical, as a social "symptom," and for him too the prevalent morality, which he calls Platonic-Christian, is an invention of the weak. In order to more easily bear the yoke of
their masters, weak men require of themselves submission and
patience and they preach justice and equality to the strong.
Full of "_ressentiment_," in a great "revolution" which is more
than a reversal, they deprecate the values of the masters and
represent as true values only those advantageous to themselves.
The secret of European history is that this "slave morality"
has won. The mighty themselves became confused about their
inherited "morality of the masters" (_Herrenmoral_), they then
submitted to the suggestion that the morality of the oppressed
is the true morality and so were unwittingly dethroned. Their
ruler-instincts declined. And men actually became equal. The
pseudo morality of the herd, which now became general, was a
"counterattack against the strivings of nature to produce a
higher type of man." One lives less dangerously with it, but
on a smaller scale. The worm-man crawls, the tame man feels
that he is the meaning of history.

In contrast to Callicles, the ethos of Nietzsche's masters
is not one only of power and force. They stand for values of
nobility and majesty, and for a heightened power and producti-

ivity of life. What Nietzsche defends is not amorality, but
a different morality.

According to Nietzsche, in the Platonic-Christian revolution, not only do false values replace true ones, but lower
values replace higher ones. An older reproach against such
communal morality accused it of comprising only an ethical
minimum. It forbids theft, but does not bind to generosity.
Where is the positive side of morality that makes it worth
defending, asks Herder, beyond the restriction of the most
elementary evil? The intent of such objections is not to
eliminate morality in order to make room for the tyrannical
individual. In its proper place, for the coarsest matters,
communal morality does have a function. But it is only "lower
morality" (Fichte) and it should therefore not be considered
absolute, for then it would occupy the place that belongs to
"higher morality." As the goal of the first is to make communal life possible, so the goal of the second is the self-
realization of the individual, or perhaps better, of the person. Only in Humboldt does the intensification of life envis-
aged here pale down ot a mere inner development through education.

The liberated individual of the new ethics that is struggling for a break-through can in particular cases come into
conflict with the general code of morality, but this is not
emphasized as it is in Callicles. He may also be in complete
harmony with communal morality and not take a stand essentially
outside it. The relation between the two moralities is not
that of alternatives, but of two strata. In the "higher morality" the individual, with his intensified autonomy, announces
that he does not merely support existing law, nor approve it
merely after the fact as a general norm already pre-recognized
by philosophy (whereby the individual at the moment of becoming
independent immediately surrenders his independence again), but
he creates a new, still unexampled good out of his own self. A
good that is no longer general, but still is a good! Sartre
later modified this to mean that there are no pre-formed, exemplary "essences" of the good, that we are the "creators" of
our good, and he redefined existentialism in terms of this
antithesis. But in this way individual ethics is shifted, as
already in Heidegger and Ernst Jünger,into an empty "decision-
ism"that locates the good in the free decision of the individual, whereas originally not this was meant, but only that the
individual should be free to find his own law.

It was the individual pantheistic and monadological conviction of the Age of Goethe that the divine pours itself out
into the fullness of "particularity" (Hamann). As the Age of
Goethe accepts no uniform ideal of cultures and forms as standards to measure itself by, but with its great sense of history

admires precisely the unique and constantly different, so in
etihics it does not impose one ideal upon action. Old religious ideas reappear here in secular form. For St. Paul, the
strong man who has the spirit is responsible only to God not
to the law. "Love God and do what you will" (Augustine): you
cannot go wrong; indeed even if you do, God remains with you.
That is revived when, for Storm-and-Stress, each person may,
not only in his style of writing, set up an ontogenetic mode
of behavior based on his true reality (not on arbitrary whim).
If communal morality seeks to drive wickedness out of the
individual by binding him to general rules, here his goodness
becomes evident only by liberation from such rules. "The first
rule of life is: know yourself. Become aware of the form that
is in you and express it" (Herder). As in Kant's view the
genius does not create by artistic rules, but rather these
rules are abstracted from his work after the fact, so it is for
Jacobi with moral rules: "The preservation and elevation of
his particular nature is the object of the absolute drive of
the individual." Every individual is, according to Fichte
(and Ranke later said something similar of the nations) a
"thought in the mind of God"; each is designed by a respectively different primal image. "Each one is supposed to be what
only he is supposed to be and can be...only he and absolutely
no one else." For Schleiermacher, each man in his own way
represents all of humanity. The community is not threatened
by the differences between its members: it becomes still more
capable of life. "The only law is: express your particularity,
your uniqueness; know yourself and be yourself." One must
not (in a variation of Heraclitus) follow the same commandment twice (Kierkegaard). Remaining timelessly the same blinds
us to the demands of the constantly changing "present" (Grise-
bach).

The concept "individual law" coined by Schleiermacher was
later taken up by Georg Simmel. Out of the root of every life,
which is more than a mere empirical accident, arises, for
Simmel, a respective image of the highest possibility of its
being, a norm of its own. Although individual, it is no less
severely binding than a general norm, indeed it is more so,
because here the excuse that the general rule must be modified
to fit the particular case is not admissable. Individual behavior can and should be understood only by this norm, which
is concommitant with a life. If it is judged externally by a
general law applied from the outside, this is juridical rather
than ethical. Based on individual law, the phenomenally identical modes of behavior of different men have different meanings. As partial aspects of the entirety of completely different lives, they cannot be compared. Simmel claimed to have
discovered the presence of individual norms in art also, for

instance in Rembrandt, where form is not stolidly pre-existent
but a factor of life itself in its diverse manifestations. He
even tried to bring it into harmony with Kant's "categorical
imperative," which in its formality allows room for the uniqueness of persons and situations. This is very questionable
because, for Kant, we act ethically precisely from the level
at which, as rational beings, we are all the same. Kant still
represented the quantitative individualism which led to the
"human rights" of the French Revolution, not the qualitative
individualism which led to the personality cult of the nineteenth century.

  3. Value ethics. Consideration for one's fellowman and
for the development of one's personality, even taken together,
do not exhaust the scope of morality. Even things require a
certain behavior of us. The worker has a duty toward his work.
Institutions make their claim on us: after the company has
been founded to earn money, the businessman then works "for
the company" as if it were itself the purpose -- this change
has often been described. Marx blamed the gaining of autonomy
by the capitalist system as a whole for the alienation of
modern man. Gehlen defended institutions: they unburden, give
security, and elevate the individual above himself.

  Above all, we stand under the "axiological determination"
of what have, since Nietzsche, been called "values." Let us
use as example a value such as order or truth. Such a value
sends an appeal to us not to violate it, to be "truthful" or,
on a higher level, to investigate it more thoroughly. In all
this we serve neither our neighbor nor ourselves, or if so,
only indirectly. We respond to the purely objective demand of
a value. The rank of a "moral stance" is not measured only by
its benefit to others. Greed remains negative even when no
one is harmed by it. Value ethics is irreducible to social
ethics, though the content of some values does coincide with
the demands of social and individual ethics. The three forms
of ethics are not so much different fields of content as
different motivations.

  For Kant, the "moral law" exists only in the form of the
imperative: "Thou shalt." A contentual determination of the
will independently of it would, according to him, in bad disjunction, be heteronomous determination by nature. He seeks
to derive the content of ethics from its form; that is Kant's
"formalism." Max Scheler opposes it, but not with a material
ethics, as his con ept of the "material value ethic" might
suggest: every philosophical ethics is, as philosophy, formal.
He opposes it with a non-formalistic ethics of material -- he
could better have said, contentual -- values. The context of
moral foundation runs, as Scheler correctly saw, in precisely
the opposite direction from Kant's formal justification: the

moral obligation is based on the values. As in Husserl's anti-
psychologism the logical laws first express conditions of being and only therefore and secondarily also become "laws of
thought," so for Scheler the values are an ideal area of being,
and their normative force for us follows from this and obliges
us to "realize" them in good actions. Scheler thus reaches
back before Kant to the Aristotelian-Scholastic doctrine of
virtue. The organ of "value-perception," rehabilitated again
by Franz Brentano is feeling ("emotional intuitionism").
Following the example of natural science, all science at that
time was required to be "value-free" (a term made famous by
Max Weber). But "nature" is accompanied by "values," under
which South German neo-Kantianism includes more than ethical
values. Knowledge of value does not create the value (Rickert),
however knowledge must not be blind to the objective color and
level of value (Scheler). Envy implies inferiority; if one
wanted to ignore this, one would fail to grasp its quality.
Along with the "cognitive" part of the moral judgment there
must be the factor of acceptance or rejection (Hare).

A distinction must be made between what could be ideally,
and really. Every positive value should also be real. But no
imperative of realization by every individual follows from
this. The virtue that one man strives for and that gives him
his moral merit, another man, as seen above, has as his natural
disposition. Thus he experiences no imperative. Natural graces
are unattainable by any effort: a friendship that one must
foster is never as precious as a spontaneous one. By definition
it is impossible to want to be a "beautiful soul"; either one
is so, or one is not. Nothing can bring back lost innocence.
One man in his situation may achieve what lies out of reach
for another in his. A mortally ill man is not expected to
save the lives of others (Broad's "principle of execution").
Only what can be willed is concretely imperative. Thus wherever one turns, a value, no matter how clearly seen and esteemed,
does not automatically impose a duty. There is also a merely
"categorical optative of the ideal" (Fries), a horizon-setting
obligation to the unattainable, a "remote goal" as opposed to
an "immediate goal" (Ernst Bloch); logically, of course, the
remote goal should be effective in the immediate one.

But even when we experience the good as making a demand
upon us, it still needs, in addition to knowledge and justification, inner appropriation and existential affirmation (Brood's
principles of "dijudication" and "approbation"). Socrates
defined virtue as knowledge. Euripedes in his Medea objected
to this, that passion can win against better knowledge ("I
see the better course and I approve it, but I follow the worse
one," Ovid). To which Socrates replied: then it simply was
not yet real knowledge based on solid reasons, and we must

continue to seek it. Future better knowledge will be virtue.
Reason, Spinoza later demands, must itself become feeling. For
religious men such as St. Paul, reason always remains impotent
without grace: the devil can ensnare it.

But even if virtue does not inevitably follow foom knowledge, vice versa knowledge must precede virtue; in this Scheler and N. Hartmann agree with Socrates. For both, it was
already a primary moral task to overcome the narrowness of the
value-horizon, to train and differentiate value-perception. We
should not overlook the abundance of the ethically significant,
we should participate in it with our understanding, make ourselves receptive for many new values. That also has an effect
on our judgment of men and events (though that is not the reason it is required). Then our choice is no longer governed
by chance and by habit; we decide it in full freedom and
responsibility, though the broader perspective makes it more
difficult. Philosophical ethics as knowledge of values thus
becomes an ingredient of moral existence itself. Opponents,
however, did object that such comprehensive empathy was more
appropriate to the intellectual historian, who seeks to be
fair to all value-attitudes that have arisen in history, than
to the moral philosopher, and they accused value ethics of
aestheticism.

Every value has a corresponding disvalue, and indeed the
distance between them is generally about equal. Since there
are, measured from the level of indifference, higher and lower
values, it follows that for high values the corresponding disvalue lies only slightly below the line of indifference, but
for the low values it lies far below it, since almost the
whole scale extending downwards from them is negative. The
higher the value, the less bad its disvalue, and vice versa.
For the high values our value reaction lies on the positive
side, for they are seldom realized: heroism deserves admiration; lack of heroism, on the contrary, no contempt. Its
fulfilment is meritorious and arouses approval. For the low
values, on the other hand, the value reaction is on the negative side, for the fulfilment of these values is expected of
everyone: honesty is not particularly noticed, but dishonesty
arouses contempt. Non-fulfilment is a crime -- the more serious, the lower the value is -- and it is disapproved. The high
values, generosity, fidelity, love (3 Moses 19, 18) are enjoined
by commandments: we should realize them, but still they cannot
be demanded bindingly of anyone. The low values are subject
to prohibitions: we are not to violate them, and whoever does,
is prosecuted.

The low values, according to N. Hartmann, whose views are
being described here, are also "strong," the high values are
"weak." For the higher values can only be built on the founda-

tion of the low ones. The meaning of existence is not fulfilled in health and bare life, but these are preconditions
for it. If the low values are threatened, then all the higher
ones concurrently. Therefore a more unconditional fulfilment
of the lower values is expected, and their violation is a more
drastic breach of ethics. In serious cases the law, with its
penalties, will concern itself with violations (there are
several theories about the function of law: atonement, vengeance, education, deterrance).

Since demands requiring general observance can be connected
only with the low values, morality has the tendency to limit
itself to them, and this is the cause for scorn of "mere morality." A complete ethics also includes the more difficult demands. Whoever sins against them does not commit a crime and
is not prosecuted by law, but he does incur guilt which can
burden the conscience no less and for which the atonement consists not in punishment but in repentence and inner conversion
(the Biblical teschuba).

Scheler attempted to give criteria for the value level and
to derive rules of preference from them. Ethical choice
(Aristotle's prohairesis, most impressivley illustrated by
Kierkegaard's "Either-Or") in complex cases can be made not
between good and evil, but between higher and lower. Since
even the low value is still a value, guilt can be involved in
its neglect, no matter how justified it may be. This is all
the more so when values are of the same level. Not only "the
good" exists, but a plurality of supreme values, antinomies
of value such as that between justice and love, purity and
profusion (Hartmann). Here the "conflict of duties," which
philosophy has generally ignored or denied but drama (Aeschylus)
has depicted, reached its peak. Every decision for the one
value made necessary by the life situation is wrong to the
other value, and thus inescapably tragic. In ethics the books
never seem to balance quite right. Ethics can neither free us
of the subjective decision nor take away sadness at the possibilities that were not called to life.

Furthermore, intrinsic values have to be distinguished from
values which serve as means. But even intrinsic values can be
turned into means. Kant's demand was that a person should
never be used as a means. Virtues can be put in the service
of crime: but then, are they still virtues? Does the good
purpose justify the means that, considered as such, are bad?

Different peoples live in different moral systems, each
of which is considered "natural" and accepted dogmatically.
From this the Sophists' conclusion was ethical relationism.
Others conclude: one of the existing moral systems could still
be true; or, then it would still have to be discovered; or
"natural law" is behind positive law, which is never quite

adequate (here "positive law" recalls the Sophistic expression "established law"). The historically later nineteenth
century wanted to replace normative ethics, which always sets
a certain morality as absolute, with a descriptive "moral
science" (Guyau), which accepts the multiplicity of languages,
religions, etc. The question about the criteria of "ethical
progress," however, remains. The old Teutons had no respect
for the human life of others as such, but the ten commandments
did. That the moral systems are many does not mean that they
are equally right.

The heritage of "moral science" still survives in value
ethics. Hartmann describes ancient, Christian and modern
views in succession, and thus uses history as a principle of
classification. Bollnow distinguishes sociologically between
aristocratic and bourgeois virtues. But value ethics differs
from moral science in not concluding from pluralism to relativism. The realm of values is great, human value-perception
in general narrow. Depending on nation and age, it cuts
sectors out of it. By wandering about historically in this
way, it grasps and realizes values which are different yet
always genuine, eternal and absolute. It was left to our
tolerant age to encompass them with equal justice. But this
excessively Platonic theory has not gone uncontested. It merely combines an aggregate of ten incompatible elements. It sees
the historical standpoints as conditions for knowledge, not
for the formation of values.

According to Bollnow only a "high ethos" as it is formed
by a clerical, political or intellectual elite has historicalness: purity, humility and self-denial are Christian; indus-
triousness and thrift are bourgeois; a harmonious personality
is a humanistic virtue. At the base of these peaks is a relatively constant stratum of "simple morality": consideration,
comradeship, reliability, fairness. But this leads back to
communal ethics. To have shown its own limits was precisely
one of the special merits of value ethics.

CHAPTER 15

AESTHETICS

The Aesthetic Judgment

As we saw in ethics, knowing and doing the good is not
enough without the addition of inner factors; this applies
analogously and much more cogently to the field of aesthetics.
Contrary to his teacher Socrates, who demanded of all action
that it be able to "give reasons' for itself, the young Plato
already in Ion saw that the poet stands under a different law:
he practices his art, not by virtue of knowledge, but through
a "divine gift" (theia moira). But this early insight became
a counterweight to the predominant rationalism only since the
seventeenth century. There is, it was discovered, a faculty
in us which does not judge by rational criteria but still is
more than arbitrary whim and in its way discovers the right
thing. In the manner of Quintilian, Balthasar Gracian speaks
of "taste" (also tact, sensitivity) which no one can teach or
learn and according to which the man of the world does what
is suitable in every situation in life. Pascal contrasts the
"geometrical mind" with "mental sensitivity." No proof is
given why one loves a person; it is based on something indefinable. Similarly in the eighteenth century Shaftesbury
knows of a "moral sense" as an instinct for right order and
proportion, and Mendelssohn, Sulzer and others discover "feeling" as a source of judgments not rationally motivated yet
nonetheless valid. All these concepts are more comprehensive
than just aesthetics; they are also ethical; but they consolidate principally as aesthetic terms. Beauty is "pleasing
without any concept" is a statement late in Kant's Critique of
Practical Reason, which originally was to have had the title
"Critique of Good Taste." Leibniz had striven for a synthesis
with rationalism. He ascribed the "indefinable something"
("je ne sais quoi": the 'non so che" already of Italian
Baroque aesthetics) by which we praise or reject a work of art
without being able to explain why, to the fact that we unconsciously count the harmonies of which it is composed and which
ultimately consist of mathematical ratios (cf. the "aesthetics
of information" of Max Bense, etc.).
As on the part of the recipients, "taste" cannot state its
reasons rationally, neither can, on the part of creativity,
"genius," which is the complementary term introduced by Baroque
aesthetics and re-transmitted to the continent by the English

pre-Romantics. For if no recognizable and eternally demonstrable standards of beauty exist and make a work of art beautiful, it follows that the artist need no longer bind himself to traditional rules, such as the "laws of tragedy." There are, then, no obligatory classical patterns in the arts and no genre-models that must be observed. On the contrary, "imagination" must "creatively" invent something "original" (Young) and "characteristic" (Goethe). It is not a question of being a "second" Pindar or Anacreon -- and this inserted into the quarrel of the "ancients" and the "moderns" the question as to which of the two was greater. No such repetition can and should take place. Art, like every product of culture, must always grow out of the new historical situation. Therefore Shakespeare is greater than the Frenchmen who imitate Seneca.

Art, understood since antiquity as imitation, now becomes the spontaneous "expression" of an internal experience, though it does not encompass it completely: "Every form, even the most sensitive, contains some untruth" (Goethe). Pseudo-Longinus' writing On the Sublime had called the elevated style "the echo of a great soul." Subjectivity is depicted in the work but also first discovers itself and gains profile and intensity in it (this then applies analogously to the observer). Yet this subjectivity aims to be more than merely private. It serves as the spokesman of deeper human values for a nation and an epoch. Therefore it does not create arbitrarily. The principles of its creativity remain unconscious because they bring to light something belonging to the general climate in which it lives. They are always extracted from the work after the fact (Lessing, Kant). Formulations that the age finds for this process are: not the poet, "it" (the secularized "divine intellect" that works mystically from the depths of the soul itself) must be writing within the poet. But then he does not imitate nature in the sense of created reality (natura naturata), he follows the example of nature as a creative principle (natura naturans). He must create out of feeling, not out of understanding. As soon as the spontaneity of inspiration subsides and awareness and will seek to "make" the poem, the quality also declines -- as Coleridge shows with his "Palace of Kublai Khan." Valéry emphatically opposed this theory and today poets again want to be "scholarly poets."

As the eighteenth century expected the artist to create original works out of the preconditions of his time and his person, so complementarily "historical distance" can increase the scholar's ability to understand earlier styles in their particularity by including those historical preconditions in his judgment. The multiplicity of styles does not prove their relativity; there is a plurality of absolutes. As the old poetic handbooks, with their canonical instructions for the

poet, have been invalidated by creativity, so for the reader by
the emergence of the empathetic "sense of history": these are
the two wings of the "historical revolution."

The aesthetics of the eighteenth century, placing taste and
genius above reason -- and therefore temporarily becoming an
avantgardist discipline -- articulated more than merely an
aesthetic principle. In the model that goes back to the Greeks,
the objective pole of reason and the universal norm it perceives are predominant over the initial subjective pole.
Reason is the detector-organ of a universal pre-existent truth,
which the subject must submit to, even in his actions. Only
after withdrawal of the norm does the subject, which can no
longer be disregarded, discover itself in its concrete uniqueness and gain strength as the ultimate authority. Subjectivity,
independent and professing its office as judge and creator,
is constituted of "feeling." Personality becomes the responsi-
bly determinative intellectual force, and the transcendent origin. It draws its criteria, which are proper to it and yet more
than empirical and accidental, out of itself and precisely out
of its particularity. The Renaissance had only lived individuality; the seventeenth and eighteenth centuries establish it
in its philosophical rank and invent the language for the
qualitative individualism of modern times.

But the exemplary, protagonistic nature of modern aesthetics
would be but inadequately described by the fact that it has
discovered a new subject-centered form of knowing truth. This
is a secondary feature that is based on something more primary.
If antiquity derived art from knowledge and imitation, the
concept of art since the Renaissance, which became possible
only then and against the background of the idea of God contained in Genesis, is radically different from this. Here the
artist has as his theme not only the world created by God,
which he can stylize toward the ideal or give personal colora-
tion. Like a "second God" he himself engages in "world creation," places in his work an autonomous world, of independent
meaning and equal rank with the world itself. As modern science no longer aims to depict the world, which it knows is
transcendent to itself, and instead constructs its own system
of symbols of immanent consistency, so now the work of art is
an independent sphere, which borrows elements from reality but
composes them according to a completely different law. The
genius does not merely invent new plots and forms; that is
only his artistic vehicle. Decisive is competition with
already existent reality, the establishment of what has never
been before, a _materia nova_. Art now becomes the sister of
modern technology with its production of "artificial" materials,
its world which is cast back into the melting pot and recon-
structed better by reason. Kant's epistemology and Fichte's

metaphysics of the self are already translations of this modern
aesthetics (and could therefore be translated back into aesthetics by the artist-generation of the Romantics). But this
creationistic principle of art reached the awareness of the
general public only when Expressionism made it absolute.

Formal and Contentual Aesthetics

After the decline of normative aesthetics, psychological
aesthetics came into being. Hartley, Hutcheson, Home, Burke
and Schaftesbury analyzed the subjective experience of beauty
and sought to formulate its laws. The continuation of their
work in the nineteenth century constituted "formal aesthetics"
in contrast with the "contentual aesthetics" of Schelling,
Hegel and Schopenhauer. For formal aesthetics, artistic
pleasure is based on spacial articulations and rhythms; it
depends on the organization of the elements and their relation
to the whole (Herbart, R. Zimmermann). Fechner then established "experimental aesthetics," which also seeks to be a
naturalistic aesthetics "from below." His method included
presenting the simplest acoustic and geometric structures,
such as wavey lines and differently located circles, to his
test persons. His discoveries include: unity is pleasing,
uniformity displeasing; what impresses one as beautiful must
deviate from strict mathematical regularity (as already in
Polycletus' canon); in a complex structure such as a melody
the tones and beats are not merely accumulated, but they
potentiate one another (the principle of "aesthetic intensification"; cf. also Wundt's "creative resultants"). Even
primitive man observes the same basic laws as we -- rhythm,
symmetry, suspense. Evidently, then, there are in the aesthetic sphere universally valid "natural laws" as well as those
conditioned by history and style.

In ancient Greece, the Pythagoreans had reduced music to
mathematics (Kepler's "world harmony" still stands in this
tradition). For Polycletus, the body, for Vitruvius a building
is beautiful through numerical proportion. On the other hand,
Plotinus, in his treatise On the Beautiful, stated that beauty
consists not in symmetry, but in what "radiates from it." Analogously, in the modern era formal aesthetics (represented by
Külpe and Lipps) met with opposition (from Croce, Dilthey,
Dessoir) on account of its elementariness, for it cannot really
explain the whole of the parts, and its unhistoricalness, for
it does not take the diametric changes in the sense of style
seriously enough, but mainly because form at higher stages no
longer acts as mere form but as the expression of mind and
soul, e.g., the Gothic pillar that rises to heaven as a symbol
of the longing for transcendence. "Style is essentially a way

of seeing things" (Flaubert).

At the beginning of our century two schools of aesthetics (both rejecting positivistic biographism and causalistic investigation of influences) stood in opposition to one another: Wölfflin's form-historical method, which derived the changes of style from "self-movement of form": a linear, tectonic or closed form is followed by a picturesque, atectonic or open one; and Dilthey's idea-historical method, for which art is the "organ of the understanding of life" and world-views speak through styles (as also in Schiller and Hegel). Dilthey's student, Nohl, wrote about the "world-views of painting" and spoke of the "silent intellectual work of the eye." Later Wölfflin himself admitted: form-history must be seen together with intellectual and religious history. Mannerism is not only an immanently aesthetic answer to the previous schools of painting, but a gesture of the counter-reformation (Dvorak).

Childish and uneducated interest in the work of art remains limited to the material. For the man of the Enlightenment it is only the enunciation and illustration for ideas. He sees art as justified not by its beauty and our admiration, but only because it broadens our understanding of reality. More mature aesthetic judgment, however, is interested in the form. But interest exclusively in the form results in an aestheticism that also does injustice to the work. Extreme formalism even demands that the painter should choose as irrelevant a subject as possible -- a wooden shoe -- so that attention will be drawn exclusively to his method and ability. But artistry which has nothing to say and merely displays brilliant virtuosity is vacuous. On the other hand, even the most significant statement of content is aesthetically deficient if the form is crude or merely conventional and indifferent. Merely depictive and narrative or intellectual art errs in the other direction as much as that which is only artistic. Content and form (Gehalt and Gestalt -- Walzel) must go together, must both be captivating; and here too an "aesthetic intensification" occurs: the combination becomes a new thing containing much more than existed in the separate components of content and form. Very instructively, Johannes Pfeiffer contrasts a well-written but shallow poem by Liliencron and a deeply felt poem by Morgenstern in which the "language was uncooperative," with a poem of Goethe's which combines the advantages of both and is the better poem by objective aesthetic criteria.

But the separation of the two elements exists only in the mind, not in reality. Whereas in science one can always formulate the content differently, perhaps better, and translate it into every language without any loss, it is a criterion of art that what it says is indissolubly fused with the manner of its saying: it exists and is accessible only through its mode of

expression. The artist himself does not first have an idea
and then make it visible in a structure, but even the content
is manifested to him only through the structure. Every altera-
tion of the significant form alters the signified content.
This calls to mind the archaic conception of language which
believed in the essential relationship of word and thing.

Through its content, art is more than decoration and play;
it has a moral significance, though not in the narrow sense
of the word. Shaftesbury brought this point to the fore again
against an ornamentalistic conception, of which there are still
traces in Kant. By its balanced fusion of form and content,
art saves man from the division of the two factors in himself,
the "material drive" and the "formal drive." Along with moral
training, he needs an "aesthetic education" which restores his
totality and teaches him how to live from his whole nature
(Schiller).

The Aesthetic Object (Reality and Image)

Every reality can move us aesthetically, as long as we
actualize it not in its obtrusive realness, but only in the
phenomenality of its appearance. Such aesthetic stepping-back
from banal-brutal and burdensome reality presupposes a suspension of the immediate daily seriousness of life, and succeeds
most easily -- but not only -- in non-practical situations.
Practicality implies reality. It is hard for art to abstract
from the concrete, actual means and purposes of our work.
Things remote from full reality and having no direct connection
with life produce a stronger aesthetic effect; for instance,
not what our daily cares are concerned with, but what only
passes us by, including myth, truth lost and no longer believed
and therefore sentimentally distanced, or what lies in the distant past, or far away in space: "the promised land in the
aura of legendary distance" (George). Sicily, where Theocritus
had localized the pastoral landscape, was located too crassly
close for the Roman Vergil and he therefore had to transplant
it to far-off Arcadia: only so did it regain its enchantment
of unreality. But even in everyday life it can happen that
suddenly a thing strikes us from the point of view of its form,
we forget its utility and are rapt in its phenomenality, and
we then need an internal jolt to emerge to reality again, with
all its demands.

Basing himself on Home's distinction in 1762 between emotions that flow into desire and those that remain dammed up,
Kant defines aesthetic pleasure as "disinterested" (at least
in the sense of selfishly purposeful m terial interest). Therefore the aesthetic judgment is for him also "indifferent as to

the existence of its object": since we only look at beauty
and otherwise expect nothing of it, it can also be merely
remembered or imaginary, or indeed an illusion, while on the
other hand "the agreeable" (das Angenehme) presupposes reality,
for the unreal cannot be agreeable. Aesthetically, Kant says,
we can enjoy the sunset although it does not really "set." No
scholar has ever established how logical truth and aesthetic
truth are connected. Starting from Kant, Schopenhauer also
characterizes the aesthetic attitude as a state in which the
will is silent. But it is always silent only temporarily,
for we are creatures of the will. Therefore aesthetic experience always occurs, to use Richard Hamann's formulation, "during
a pause." To behave aesthetically even in a serious situation
where we have to be engaged in real effort is hypertrophied
"aestheticism."

"Autonomous" art (as opposed to "useful" art) stands outside practical connections. While for "natural beauty" we
have to produce the aesthetic attitude by a de-realization of
the object, "artistic beauty" invites us to it spontaneously.
Therefore, reality-depictive art, such as painting, sculpture,
or drama, which produces the "appearance" of reality, uses
"isolating factors" (Richard Hamann) to make certain that we
are not deceived by the appearances and mistake them for true
reality. External factors that to this are the frame, stand,
or stage, but also a greater concentration and stylization of
content than otherwise occurs, which therefore stands off from
everyday connections. (In contrast Baroque and Surrealism tend
to have elements of reality cross over into art, or vice versa,
e.g., the Emperor Leopold I of Austria as an actor playing
himself, or "collages." The aesthetic experience is "honest"
(Schiller): it does not seek to deceive us, or if so, only
for seconds and then it itself destroys the illusion (Konrad
Lange). If art does seek to be mistaken for reality, then it
abandons the "aesthetic play-situation," like the play-goer
who forgot that the play was only an illusion and shouted to
the stage: "Run away, Desdemona, he wants to kill you!"

Because we innately realize what is depicted to be an
autonomous, self-contained and "meaningful structure" of art
(Roman Ingarden), and a vehicle of a truth incomparably its
own, art arouses in us only reality-free "simulated feelings"
(E Hartmann). We therefore observe on the stage with great
calmness scenes that would horrify us in real life; e.g.,
Medea murdering her children (Plutarch). To experience the
fate of others as reflected in the mirror of art without undergoing it ourself is a vicarious release from the narrow limits
of our own existence.

Aesthetic Truth

Aesthetic and theoretical behavior have a common root in
contemplation which serves neither of them for future action
but is a purpose in itself. But theory is sober in its attitude toward the object and toward truth, or if it does show
enthusiasm, it is a "cool enthusiasm"; the aesthetic experience, however is pleasureful (Burke, Sulzer, etc.). Moved and
touched by its object, it returns to it again and again, even
when the object is already known, to enjoy it in these feelings.
Theory aims at reality itself, while aesthetics only draws an
image from it. Theory is a work of knowledge: it makes new
concepts, analyzes, gets at the bottom of things; aesthetics
persists in the contemplation of what appears and therefore
at first impression seems shallow. "The true word is ugly,
the beautiful word is false" (Toateking).

Art too goes beyond the normal facts, but in a different
direction. Its subject-centeredness and emotionality, by
which it sees nature "through a temperament" (Zola), serve not
only for self-expression. What we contribute of ourselves --
here modern aesthetics and epistemology agree -- also reveals
something about the object, it manifests what otherwise was
hidden, it fathoms below the surface to more essential things.
For normally nature is hidden from us in pre-interpretations,
at least practical ones. To free it of these interpretations,
art must place it within new frames of reference, must show
it from an unaccustomed distance. Despite any political implications in Brecht, "alienation" is a law of all art. Art
effects an "interruption," a "disturbance" of the familiar
context; it represents what is taken for granted as something
quite different than it seemed (in this it resembles metaphysics). This transformation of things serves to reveal their
true selves; the only apparent subjectivity serves objectivity.
As Marx seeks to redeem things from their economic falsification into merely marketable items, and phenomenology from their
physicalistic falsification into quantities, so art always
redeems them from their everyday falsification of being taken
for granted. Poetry makes "the stone stoney again" (Russian
formalists). Thus long before the origin of theory, art reminds
man again of his autochthonous capacity to look at things apart
from any purpose, and anthropologically this is one of its
functions. It lets objects which have paled into mere orientation points arise again in their oppositeness and self-consti-
tution. Thus it also liberates our own mutilated sensory life
and becomes an instrument of general sensitization. Furthermore, unveiling an original depth of the world, it appeals to
the depth in us: "You must change your life" (Rilke). To this
extent art contains a revolutionary element in esoteric disguise,

while "banality is counterreformation" (Isaak Babel).

Something similar was meant when it was said that art does not imitate what is but what ought to be (Aristotle); it depicts "ideas" -- today it could not be said in these terms. Like rhetoric it speaks of things that it knows nothing about from within. But very soon this Platonic idea became a weapon against the Platonic view of art (Panofsky). According to Plotinus the artist has the idea of things more purely in his soul than it is realized in the things. He knows nature better than it knows itself and may therefore correct its defects (as Novalis believed that the historian ought not to see an epoch as it was, but as it wanted to be). For Plotinus the artist is creative, like the living divine principle in nature itself. Art is one step closer to metaphysics than reality. Perhaps the fact that Plotinus no longer saw about him a realistically inclined art, as Plato did, but religious art, may have contributed to Plotinus' changed opinion. When Kant says that our reason prescribes its laws to nature, then he has merely transformed Plotinus' aesthetics into epistemology (which therefore could be translated back into aesthetics by the Romantics).

Two revivers of aesthetic Plotinism were Hegel (art as the "sensory manifestation of the idea") and Schopenhauer ("Genius understands nature before it is done speaking and expresses clearly what it only stammers"). But Baumgarten expresses corrected Plotinism; as distinguished from philosophical or mathematical truth, historical or poetic truth deals with individual things which the poet must represent as determinately as possible. The perfection of sensory cognition is different from that of abstract knowledge. A further objection is that there is also an atypical beauty (the boyish woman).

If the standard of art is the truth perceived in it, then its truth can be defended against Plato. Yet, in agreement with Plato, higher truth will be found not in art but in philosophy. Out of the beauty that appears in dark matter shines, according to Plotinus, a poetically purer one that is not directly visible, therefore one must ultimately flee art too if one flees matter. For Hegel, art corresponds in the philosophy of history, to a concrete sensory early stage of humanity. The inner subjectivity is already better expressed by the Christian religion and finally by philosophy. Reflection surpasses art, which now ceases to be the highest need of the mind. Art thus belongs in principle to the past -- even though it is just at that time reaching its peak in subjective, Romantic art. Hegel's philosophism, as was already seen, fails to see the proper rank of historically contained truth; and likewise it fails to see the truth contained in art. Hegel wants to discard them both in favor of the concept. But according to

Schelling it is precisely art that in its concreteness, preserves the unity and totality of the absolute;   therefore
philosophy will "flow back again into the ocean of poetry."
Amid modern scepticism toward the power and range of philosophy and science, the truth of art remains unshaken precisely
because it is undogmatic and makes less pretensions to cogency
and therefore presents itself much more incontrovertibly (Benn).
Philosophers (Guardini, Heidegger, Bollnow, Adorno) interpret
metaphysical poets such as Hölderlin and Rilke.

As in religion and metaphysics, Marx sees only ideology
in all previous art: as a false awareness it puts a veneer
on a bad existence and aims to reconcile men with it. He
therefore faces the problem as to why this super-structure
still has something to say even after the collapse of its social
foundations; e.g., Homer after the fall of feudalism. Why do
we condemn the foundations and yet can still be delighted by
the art which is based on them. Within Marxism, even Ernst
Bloch avoids this problem by stating that all ideology contains a trans-ideological surplus. If art white-washes the
present, that is only secondarily and it can do this only
because it is primarily the non-contemporaneous "pre-view" of
a future situation, anticipation of a better world (cf. Benjamin:
"anticipated freedom"). Because it transcends the attained
level by symbols of perfection, its "heritage" is still worth
preserving in a more perfect state. It wrests from things
themselves their unconscious Utopian secret: this constitutes
for Bloch the justification of all non-imitative art, from the
primitives to the Blue Rider, and of all non-objective art
(even the ornament), which is much more than merely subjective
expression. Does Bloch's conception of Utopia stem from this
theory of art?

Even for Adorno art is more than a superstructure; as
contradiction and resistance to the prevailing practice, it
provides a critical alternative. After philosophy has been
infiltrated by science, art still retains its impetus and becomes the last refuge from the Enlightenment. As it protests
against the "diabolical world" of reified reality, its nega-
tion contains the codified symbol of a humane life without
coercion -- though it is impotent against inflexible conditions.
By this antithesis it holds a mirror before the false world.
Therefore Adorno defends Kafka against Lukács who claims that
art ought to reflect all the trends of the time, because he
unmasks the existing order as a disorder. Enlightened at last
by his arrest in 1956, Lukács also admitted Kafka's realism.

Aesthetic Autonomy

    1. Art and religion.   Artistic actions and works at first

have magical and religious meaning, but at a very early date
antagonism arises between religion and art (Jacob Burckhardt
speaks of this in his doctrine of the "three potencies"), not
only because extra-religious art, as well as theory, seems
worldly and sinful to pious zealots, and only a form of distraction (the Iconoclasts, Savonarola, Kierkegaard, Tolstoy),
but because within religious art the tendency of artists is
to perfect their creation as much as possible by immanent
criteria of beauty. The symbols religion needs, which for it
have the function of making supra-terrestrial reality transparent, are transformed under the artist's hand into aesthetic gems that glitter with their own value. The Athenians
built the Parthenon no longer as only a temple, but as an
ornament of their city (agalma tes poleos). The picture of a
saint ends up being just a perfect painting. Thus the religious valuation is repressed by the aesthetic one (just as on a
profane level Aristotle reproaches the rhetoricians that too
splendid a manner of speaking hides the idea). The devotee's
attention is divided; the picture, instead of arousing devotion, arouses a sense of beauty (Schleiermacher). Kierkegaard
compares the painter of Christ to a murderer. The aesthetiza-
tion of religion is its death just as are its ethicization and
intellectualization. Therefore early icons often have something undecorated and unfinished about them ("He prays," people
say, "before a red stone"): not because of artistic incapaci-
ty, but because they find precisely this suitable, because it
is more open to transcendence and arouses the feeling for the
invisible sacredness all the more. (Analogously, for Ernst
Bloch, the primitive and fragmentary is also more inquisitive
and open to the future.) In Franciscan churches the window
over the main doorway is intentionally crooked and asymmetrical:
what is less pleasing to men is more pleasing to God.

At a time when the exclusiveness of faith was receding,
Lowth and Herder discovered the Bible as a historical and literary document, and they treasured it precisely as such. And
vice versa, the next generation (Creuzer) already sought the
unfalsified primal religion among the Pelasgians, the Scyths
and in the Orient rather than in Homer, who already rationalizes the myths with his poetic eloquence.

As religion reveals something numinous behind the profane,
all great art reveals something deeper and more mysterious
behind everyday reality. At least the sublime (das Erhabene),
which is often contrasted with beauty, is as it were a numinosity in the aesthetic field. But the religious man is exposed
to his God in "fear and trembling," whereas we can withdraw
from the aesthetic spell at any time. It makes us serious but
it also delights us. We are deeply moved by it, but this emotion is muted and filtered by contemplative distance compared

with the religious one. There is some similarity with the
relationship of religion to the theoretical. The aesthetic
and the theoretical attitudes infiltrate into the religious
one and finally replace it; but because of its emotionality
the aesthetic attitude is closer to the religious one. Because
of this relatively close affinity, religion at times when it
has been dethroned by Enlightenment changes into "artistic
religion": for instance in Wagner or when Rilke's poems become
prayers. But this is just as much a rearguard action of
religion as it is a misunderstanding of art.

2. <u>Art and practice.</u> Art originally has a practical application as well as a religious meaning. It is "practical art":
house, utensil, and clothing are "beautiful," and even the
magic of ornament and incantation fulfills the practical purpose of conjuration. Likewise the "work song" (Karl Büchner):
Democritus was wrong when he called music an excessive and therefore late art. Even when no longer itself a part of practice,
art still usually fulfills some tasks of life: literature is
used for instruction, a portrait for social representation.
Because art is not a "pure culture of beauty," Max Dessoir
called for a "general science of art" along with aesthetics.
It would deal with the extra-aesthetic functions of art. And
he pointed out that even historically the metaphysics of beauty
and artistic theory were separate and merged together only in
the Renaissance, which made beauty the subject of art.

At the end of the nineteenth century the concrete demand
was also heard: art ought not to be an isolated realm, it belongs not only in the museum and the concert hall, it should
accompany our daily life, it should -- as socialism added --
accompany the life of all men. But it does that only when
every useful object is artistic not merely by external decoration but in its utilitarian function. After ugly manufactured
products had displaced what was left of artistic craftsmanship,
this gave rise to the "practical arts" (<u>Kunstgewerbe</u>) as a
separate branch of activity.

This was preceded by Semper, who, against the independent
aesthetic understanding of art, held with a naturalistic accent
that the work of art is determined by material, technique, and
purpose. The Greek amphora becomes beautiful to the beholder
only when he knows that it was buried with sand in the cellar
and that the wine was shut off with a layer of oil against the
air: therefore the small base and the narrow neck. Semper also
traced stylistic change to changes of technology and purpose.
But then Riegl answered with his concept of "artistic will,"
which can also change for spiritual reasons even though the
external factors remain the same. In addition Semper was forgetting what Montesquieu and Spencer (after many others) had
known, namely that though the beautiful and the useful go quite

a way together, purpose must not be obtrusive if it is to be beautiful: to actualize the beautiful, one must be able to forget the purpose (a trellis-tree is not as beautiful as a tree in nature).

It is an ever recurrent tendency of art to seek freedom from practical tasks, and to want to be autonomous "art for art's sake": it was so among the Greeks and again in the West since Giotto. Only by dissociation from practical, existential seriousness does the aesthetic come out fully in its own nature. Thus lyrics since 1770 become song-like, because they no longer have a social function (Kommerell). But with this apex, the decline already begins. The artist who paints directly for the museum and the poet's poet who writes for other poets are threatened by the danger of emptiness, irrelevance and mere artistry. As always the lack of challenge has bad results. Now it is being rediscovered that the non-art-internal purpose increases artistic quality, that the cathedral is all the more beautiful because it seeks to be not only beautiful but also a house of God. The way of art, says Winckelmann, leads from necessity, via the beautiful, to the excessive. He is the founder of the modern concept of style, for which styles are not available for choice, as in ancient rhetoric, but every style is historically bound. For Winckelmann and subsequently for Herder, the three styles are at the same time three stylistic epochs: the early style seeks the sublime and the fantastic, in the middle is the aesthetic stage, and finally in the age of mere "taste," art is crushed between routine, sensationalism, and artistic nonsense.

The liberation of art from the practical has been paralleled since the Renaissance by a liberation from morality. The aesthetic judgment, which perhaps also always has moral accents, is distorted by moral rigorism. Because a connection exists between melodies and laws (Damon, and also the Chinese knew this) Plato wanted to forbid effeminate and excessively emotional melodies in his state; he banished the poets, for whoever is a witness of incest and murder on the stage will commit these things himself. Aristotle, in opposition to this, saved tragedy with a theory which shows signs of Hellenic anti-emotionalism: art detours the emotions into irreality and so by compensation causes a catharsis. We do not imitate what we see; on the contrary, we are purified of it. Instead of acting out what we see, we settle for observing it (there is also a catharsis in artistic creativity: Werther, said Goethe, died for him; in general, self-expression very often is helpful in regaining emotional balance). But this is a moral refutation of a moral objection. By intrinsically aesthetic observation it has often been seen that negative characters are often more individual, stronger, freer and therefore more attractive than

positive ones. Dante's <u>Inferno</u> is more colorful than his
<u>Paradiso</u>; Milton's Satan more impressive than his God the
Father; Schiller read Pitaval and spoke of "the sublime
criminal." Therefore, but also to provocatively prove the
autonomy of art, which need bow to no claim from the outside,
Boccaccio, Heinse, Baudelaire (<u>The Flowers of Evil</u>: "you walk
over the dead, beauty..."), Wilde, Huysmans resorted to
"aesthetic immoralism."

When art gains autonomy, there is also a social consequence.
The artist who makes necessary objects is still a craftsman. He
has a firm place in the social structure. Once the Renaissance
discovered art as a field of values by itself, the artists now
wanted to be a distinct and respected class; but the "artist-
class" survives for only a brief transitional moment. For as
long as artistic value was anchored in a utilitarian one, it
was enough to fulfill the existing stylistic norms; an original nuance could be added to crown the work. But as soon as
utilitarian value becomes secondary as a mere external condition or is eliminated completely, originality rises more and
more as the only criterion of rank. A personal style of handwriting, originally achieved naturally, is now sought exagger-
atedly. The artist must be a genius, his work must be extraordinary, otherwise it does not count. But then the artists
are no longer a class, but lonesome individuals who stand outside the social framework. Society needs no priests of beauty.
It can, in individual cases, admire the artist as a great man
in his field and heap him with commissions and honors. But if
he does not suit the taste of the times or if he is not one
of the great, then society does not bother with him and he is
left only with his "following."

Pre-given subjects and stylistic traditions make it easier
for the artist. To have to create everything oneself because
only one's own invention counts, requires of him not only
additional strength, but it also brings him into the danger of
arbitrary and subjective invention. Art becomes "experiment."
It then lacks necessity, the "gesture of unconditionality"
(Jaspers), just as it is produced by a few individuals, often
with shattered lives or close to madness (Hölderlin, Nietzsche,
van Gogh).

Even autonomous art, removed from immediate practice, can
indirectly regain a social function by <u>engagement</u> or as propaganda. Enlightenment, progress, socialism, revolution expect
art to work for them, attacking capitalism and war, and glori-
fying a new and better age. Many artists willingly follow
this demand made on art by a non-artistic world which seeks to
use art only as an instrument for its own purposes, because
they too are moved by the impulses of the time, because it
provides them with material, delivers them from isolation as

artists and gives them a place in a greater value-context and
social whole. But the political bias is like every purpose
and end; there must be a dialectical polarity between it and
aesthetics. The bias can give art a basis and a direction,
but it can never replace the aesthetic, and if it becomes
dominant, then art dies.

CHAPTER 16

THE PHILOSOPHY OF LANGUAGE

The Sign and its Meaning

A vocal sound used as a word is a bearer of meaning. It is
a sign that refers to something beyond itself. And not in such
a way that one element of a natural whole becomes a sign of
another (<u>Anzeichen</u> "indication": Husserl; "index" Morris) in
the manner that smoke indicates fire, a footprint in the sand
a person. Rather, by its meaning the sign represents what it
means. In language man builds a representational system for
the world. Since the function of words is to stand for something else, we normally do not pay attention to them as such,
but we are carried mentally by them to what they represent.
Because the connection between signs and meaning is normally
determinate within a language-community, it is possible to say
objectively what one does not mean subjectively: with language
the possibility of lying also arises.

A magical understanding of language believes in an inner
connection between the thing and the word, which therefore
attracts the thing's presence when spoken. To avoid this effect, primitive man invents new, artificial words, and therefore knows the category of artificial linguistic creation,
except that he still clings to the idea that there are "true"
words. But even on a non-magical level, the belief in a relationship between thing and word recurs in the (partly still
Stoic) theory of similarity: according to it the "correctness"
(<u>orthotes</u>) of words consists in their depiction of what they
signify, as a whole or by individual sounds (cf. Plato's <u>Craty-</u>
<u>los</u>). Language instructs us about things. Words that exist
"by nature" (<u>physei</u>) are, however, restricted to a few onoma-
topoeic words (Morris' "icons") and even for them sound-imita-
tion is only a partial component.

The Sophists and Democritus first proposed the convention-
theory: words correspond to things only by convention (<u>thesei</u>);
they are created by man as "instruments" for the purpose of
communication and can also be made in any different way he
chooses. Even if confidence in their similarity with the object was the basis of their creation, it does not exist objectively, as is evident from the multiplicity of languages, of
which none is "more right" than the others. There can be no
such thing as a God-approved, perfect natural language (<u>lingua</u>
<u>adamica</u>, as it was later called). As epistemology discovers

that perception does not depict the object, but communicates
it to us by virtue of a fixed coordination, so linguistic
theory discovers something analogous about the word (for which
however the coordination has been established by men). Since
a fixed coordination is enough for understanding, again and
agains formerly "motivated" words (i.e., words whose motivation is based not on similarity to the object, but on composi-
tion from known elements) are polished into "unmotivated" ones
("progressive signification" of language).

Frequently the sign is called a "symbol" of what it designates. But this ought to be avoided because "symbol" has a
more specific meaning. Just as there are depictive signs in
addition to the merely conventional, arbitrary ones, so on the
other hand there are symbols which do not merely reproduce a
thing that exists by itself and is observable, but instead a
thing that is contained only in the representational sign itself, which therefore can be replaced by no other. The sign
"material" here gains (it would be historically more accurate
to say "retains") a value of its own, just as in a poem the
message resides in and only in a particular combination of
words.

Although the word is only a reference to the designated
thing, which is all that counts, there is such a thing as the
"responsibility of language," a "potency of the word" (Hans
Lipps): if, for example, I have given my word, then I am
bound, I can be taken at my word, and if I break it, then that
is more than if I merely change my mind. Words are themselves
realities, they can be parts of a series of actions, or they
can be actions themselves, for instance, when we thank someone or congratulate him (Austin's elocutionary act).

Proper names refer directly to one particular reality. But
words which are not names have the word content (semainomenon)
between themselves and reality, as Zeno, in contrast with
Aristotle, already saw: between the sound structure "horse"
and the real horse there is the "said" (lekton) meaning. The
sign first stands not for a thing independent of language but
for a language-bound concept. Only by means of the concept
does the spoken word apply to the single thing. All theories
according to which the word arouses an idea of a thing in us
by association or behavioristically (Morris) causes us to
react as we would react to the thing itself, surrender to
naturalism the logical aspect of language that had been correctly understood so long ago. The meaning is already a universal; it indicates generic traits, a structure. The concrete
object is subsumed under it. Therefore, it could be said that
the discovery of the concept by Socrates was only a logical
extension of what language always did with words, which he
used as a direct basis for his theory.

Three so-called semantic functions have been distinguished ("Bühler's triangle").

1. One and the same sentence can be the expression of an internal condition of the speaker. This proclamation of the emitter corresponds to a reception on the part of the hearer. But such proclamation need not be directed to a recipient hearer; it can also serve merely for the release of an emotion, which thus reaches its culmination and then is gradually brought under control again.

2. The sentence can be an appeal addressed to a particular person, an imperative causing a desired reaction on his part. If the first function could be called a "symptom," expressive, lyrical, monologual, then this one is a signal, impressive, dialogual, dramatic.

3. In addition to these two functions, there is finally a symbolic, epic performance, the portrayal and communication of an objective state of things. It is generally still linked with practice, so that the total content will have to be complemented from the situation of the speaker and will involve expression and appeal. For Wittgenstein it is part of a "language game" whose rules one must know in order to understand it. But it can also be cultivated for situation-remote depiction, for the information of people who are not within the perceptive situation, and who have all the prerequisites to understand the language, and emancipate themselves from the other functions. To suggest complex subject-matter not only to the person who already knows it but to articulate and prove it for the uninitiated is an art that was developed late in human history and still has to be learned individually.

Even short of such autonomy, there is a descriptive aspect contained in all human language. One may, like the late Morris, want to introduce an "interpretant" who first gives the sign its meaning by linking it with the thing, which is therefore logically constitutive for signification. But such behavioristic attempts (including Wittgenstein's) to reduce depiction to "mere practice" are doomed to failure. Expression and appeal exist even in the animal kingdom, while depiction is restricted to man, to whom Susanne Langer thus attributes primevally not a communicative but a symbolic attitude: man is <u>animal symbolicum</u>. At the University of Bremen languages and literatures are linked together in one professional field called "Communication and Aesthetics." This designation stems from a sociologistic and linguistic misconception which, blind to a legitimate function of language, no longer sees its fundamental achievement, symbolication, which makes the other achievement possible, and out of ideological prejudice no longer wants to see it.

Because man can establish signs to represent meanings,

expression and appeal play an even greater role for him than
for other species. The category "sign with a meaning" is
established genetically in the child from the point of view
of the understanding though historically it may have been
established as follows: the originally spontaneous expressive
reflex is understood significatively by others, and has a
retroactive effect upon the initiator, who now in order to
be understood, always makes use of the same sign. Thus the
natural sign is intellectualized, becomes a signal and finally
a depiction. But after this original development, the result,
though it originated at a point in time, nonetheless constitutes the logical foundation of language.

Sentence and Meaning

We speak not only words, but also sentences. In addition
to the semantic dimension, through which a sign refers to extra-
linguistic reality, and the pragmatic dimension, by which it
serves its user as expression or appeal, there is in Ch. Morris'
classification of the complete semiosis (sign activity) also
the syntactic dimension, the relationship to other signs (as
well as finally to the entire context or "universe of meaning").
Words are not isolated units; they tend naturally to associate with other words and to form larger unities. The combination is produced: 1) by the location of the word in the sentence; 2) by inflection, which is so-to-speak a social organ
of the words; 3) by so-called form-words (function-words,
clausal words), which in the more developed "analytical" languages show the relationships of the words with one another
increasingly through independent units of meaning, allowing
inflection to recede or disappear completely. They have also
been called "syntactic" words to distinguish them from the
semantic ones, and "synsemantica" (Brentano) or "syncategore-
matica" (Husserl) to distinguish them from the autosemantic
name-words. Posidonius already composed a separate work on
these syndesmoi (conjunctions), in which he proved against
Aristotle that they too have an object of meaning. However
in the case of a concept such as "and" this is abstract and
purely logical.
A sentence is more than the sum of the words that comprise
it. It is a higher structural whole in which the words have
functions. Words signify, a sentence has meaning (Frege).
Words name single objects or logical entities, a sentence
renders a statement of fact (not "the blue sky" but "The sky is
blue": Meinong).For too long linguistics was falsely oriented
toward the single word. The word with its signification exists
only to help constitute the meaning of sentences. In fact,
in a real sentence the understanding of the meaning of words,

though we must already know them lexically beforehand, is
always included in and supported by the understanding of the
sentence: each has a reciprocal priority. Understanding does
not result through a Husserlian recourse to the underlying
structure. To mean the truth goes beyond the idea of an individual thing. Analogously, epistemological theories used to
connect knowledge with a respective single object (as correlative of the word); knowledge of such objects is however
correspondingly only a partial and auxiliary achievement of
reason, whose strength and task are perhaps to understand and
construct contexts of meaning. Ontology must use the sentence
instead of the word as its model and point of departure
(Tugendhat). By reason we live not in a world of things and
their relations, which we observe and conceptualize, but of
mentally constituted "intellectual facts" (Searle), in which
we are also included by our actions.

Under the influence of language Aristotle constructed both
his metaphysics of the thing as bearer of its qualities (the
subject, "hypostasis," has accidents) and a corresponding
system of logic (the logical "judgment" -- so-called since the
Stoics -- is the reduction of the declarative sentence to its
barest outline, in which a predicate, "kategroumenon," is
assigned to a subject, "hypokeimenon," "underlying," a synonym
for hypostasis). Therefore both can be called apophantic.
The translation of the terms into "subject" and "predicate"
stems from Boethius. Therefore in logic the abbreviations:
S is P. But the concept of the copula for the interposed "is"
was discovered by Abelard. In Aristotle it was not only a
connecting element but it made the statement one about being
and non-being. This was rediscovered by the elementaristic
logic of the nineteenth century, which psychologized the truth-
reference of the judgment and would have preferred to omit it
completely.

The Middle Ages transferred the terms that were current
in logic to grammar: since they had been derived from the sentence in the first place it was easy to apply them to it again.
The logical subject now becomes the grammatical one. Down to
this day it has retained its original content and meaning in
both of these sciences. Not so in general metaphysics, where
as a concept parallel with that of substance it undergoes a
change of meaning with the decline of Aristotelianism and now
becomes a designation for the human knowing subject (because
from an epistemological point-of-view it is considered to be
the "underlying" stratum of reality). But the grammatical
meaning of "predicate" no longer is: what is said, but the
verb alone (represented logically only in the abridgement of
the copula). For that which in logic is called "predicate"
it uses the "object," a term first used in the Middle Ages

and likewise originally metaphysical. The parallelism of logic
and grammar hampered and restricted both disciplines and has
therefore been given up in the twentieth century. Classical
French grammar still considered the more logical possibility
of expression to be the better one. Steinthal, on the other
hand, held that words are not concepts, sentences are not
judgments!

According to the sensualistic theory we understand words
because by association they evoke in us the images and ideas
of the designated objects. This visualism, which is false
even for concrete words, is inapplicable to abstract words,
numbers, prepositions and conjunctions, and it is totally
inadequate to account for the complex mental meaning of a
sentence. Franz Brentano spoke of "signitive" intentions which
must rely more on the word than on the accompanying ideas. The
Würzburg school of psychology then also described experimen-
tally the non-representational pure "awareness of meaning."
As understanding cannot be equated with the evoking of mental
images, so speech is not merely a depiction of such images.
Even a descriptive sentence such as "He killed him with a
drawn sword" proves by the linguistic-discursive transposition
of the real sequence ("He drew the sword and killed him") the
independence of the meaning structure from the visible reality.
In literature too the "aesthetic side of language" (Th. A.
Meyer) is not based on mental images, as Lessing still believed
despite his polemics against Haller. As language deconcretizes
and intellectualizes the mental images, it relieves us of their
concrete sensory obtrusiveness and pushes them to a sober, perceptible distance for experience. This makes them more adapt-
able and disposable. On the thread of words we can more
easily combine and further construct them (e.g., from the
experience "warm" we can form the abstract noun "warmth").
The other side of the coin is the loss of immediacy; the deaf
and dumb experience things more concretely. Living in a world
of words and their meanings we escape from objective control
by the things themselves. Husserl therefore called for precisely the performance of "meaningful acts" as an antidote to the
excessive confidence in language which is a natural tendency of
the philosophical mind.

Parole and Langue

Ferdinand de Saussure brought the single word into another,
higher whole than the sentence. The psychologically and naturalistically determined linguistics of his time understood
language on the one hand as the subjective capacity to speak,
the ability to create or to learn a language (langage or
faculté du langage), and on the other hand as real speaking,

the act of speaking and its result (<u>parole ou discours,</u> cf.
today Chomsky: "competence" and "performance"). In contrast, de
Saussure draws attention to the language as such as the
objective system of rules of a linguistic community, which
must be studied logically (<u>langue</u>, cf. English: language and
speech, Latin <u>lingua</u> and <u>sermo</u>). Real speaking is only actu-
alizing application both of the faculty of speech and of this
objective structure of the rules of language, which is prior
to it. As de Saussure is anti-psychological, so he is anti-
historical. Along with diachronistic investigation of the
development of language, the predominant practice prior to
him, de Saussure established an ahistorical synchronistic
analysis of the language system -- which today is called
structural analysis.

Humboldt had said that every individual word already presupposes the entirety of the language as it lives in the mind,
the "inner form of the language," out of which a language
gradually and organically develops. As in the game of chess,
de Saussure explains, one does not understand the squares and
pieces by their external form but only by the rules of the
game which assign them their function, so also the elements
of language can be understood only by the context, as "terms"
in the system. Every sign obtains its meaning from its differential delimitation from neighboring signs, from its dia-
critical position (phonological opposition, such as <u>ride-
guide</u>, semantic opposition such as <u>red-violet</u>). Thus the signs
condition one another mutually; each has a valency in relation to the others. The theory of meaning, <u>semasiology</u>, must
be added to the theory of words <u>onomasiology</u>, which deals with
externals. Along with the syntactic relationships of a word
in the sentence (e.g., of the subject to the predicate)
there exist paratactic relationships to competing terms.

Even historically therefore linguistics cannot, as mainly
J. Trier thereafter showed with examples, follow the changes
of a single word atomistically, but only in conjunction with
the changes of all the words with which it forms an area of
meaning, then the entire milieu is set in motion. Even
different stages of development of a whole language can be
compared by synchronic cross-sections.

Structuralism, which distinguished below the level of the
word the smaller linguistic units of the <u>phoneme</u> (unit of
sound) and the <u>morpheme</u> (unit of meaning), later built upon
de Saussure's findings. Everything that can be said arises
from constant recombinations of a few thousand morphemes.
In every real language two levels of organization combine:
the lexical and the syntactic. Syntax contains the most
general structural schemata of possible morpheme-sequences
this side of particular meanings. In speech these schemata

become action-patterns (cf. Allesch's "impulse figures"),
which act as steering mechanisms giving classificational and
selectional commands. Under the impulse of a controlling idea
some combinations are rejected, others are sought and performed.
This structuralism was expanded by Chomsky when he discovered
not only beneath single sentences but entire groups of sentences a further "deep structure," a taxonomy of the taxonomies,
from which the various formulations result through rules of
transformation (generative grammar). To the extent that such
rules can be formalized, linguistics becomes a "mathematical-
ized science of man."

Language and Reason

1. Language as an a priori. In addition to linguistic
philosophy, there is a field of knowledge called "sigmatics"
(Klaus), which deals with the function of linguistic and other
signs for knowledge. The Greeks still believed in a direct
correlation between the structure of language and that of the
world. From the way language apprehends things by its grammar,
Aristotle concludes how they are. But only in Scholasticism
did this become language-immanent thinking that hoped to gain
knowledge without examining the facts but merely by connecting
concepts or by explicating knowledge already contained in the
concepts. Against this conceptualism, Occam demanded direct
access to the world, knowledge of being prior to its pre-
interpretation by language, through the language-free reason
of the individual, which uses words (or possibly conventional
signs it has itself invented) only as a second step toward
communication (just as among the Greeks mythos became logos:
Lohmann).
But knowledge, as Hamann and Herder discovered, cannot
cast aside its dependence on language by a mere decision of
the will. Words are not extrinsic garments for our knowledge.
Without us knowing or desiring it, they always predetermine
knowledge down to its ultimate structures. When the mind tries
to free itself from them as opposite structures, they hold it
firmly from behind and lead it in the direction they designate.
"Reason is language" (Hamann). Before the individual even
begins to acquire knowledge, language has already discovered
and articulated the world, penetrated it and given it an overall structure with modes of comprehension and delimitations
of objects. The individual's knowledge never starts from
nothing; it owes its own strength and its semasiological
equipment to the preliminary work done by language itself. The
apparently natural, initial direct contact with uncontaminated
reality intended at the Occamistic level really takes place in
the medium of and along the lines of the linguistic preconcep-

tion of the world.

If, as Kant says, we pour all experience into the forms of our understainding as such, then we discover that besides this a priori, perhaps more elementary than it, and even perhaps instead of it, the "post-natal social a priori" (Schmidt-Rohr) of language is at work. It too contains the formative order, the "conditions of possibliity" of knowledge, such as Herder in his "meta-critique" opposed to Kant. The former language/world correlation thus returns at an unreflected level -- no longer ontological but transcendental. Language does not imitate, it produces. However the two forms of the transcendental constitution of objects, Kant's Copernican revolution and that of Herder and Humboldt, fuse together relatively late in history, namely in Ernst Cassirer. Objectified creations of the mind such as language, and not only it, are likewise forms of comprehsnsion through which, according to Cassirer, the mind symbolizes reality, which is unknown as such.

When our mind spins language out of itself, as Humboldt expounds on the idea, it spins itself into it. When it sets language between itself and the world, language serves it (1) on the one hand, as an organ through which it first gains objectivity: "The transformation of the world into a property of the mind" is possible only through language. It is thus more than only a means of information and communication. It is also more than a product of our work (ergon), rather it develops an efficacy of its own (energeia). As language does this toward the world, so also (2) on the other hand, toward the subject. As language finds forms for things, so in a double movement it simultaneously communicates these forms to our mind, which thus is shaped by the encounter with the world conducted by language. Reason and language, man and language are equally primary and mutually constitutive (Herder's "circle"). If our categorical structure remains, for Kant, eternally fixed, for Humboldt it is just as man-made as the world of objects. And like objects it is through language, which communicates world and man in such a way that both become what they are together and through one another. Constituted by man, language reciprocally causes man's particular constitution (cf. Abelard: "The word is generated by the intellect and generates the intellect"). What we have shaped -- Humboldt's principle applies to all objective culture -- in turn shapes us.

Only through the "linguistic middle stratum," as Weisgerber once clarified Humboldt do we have our "worded" world. We see Orion as a constellation, because our culture -- differently from other cultures -- has formed the concept of Orion. A goal of language education is liberation from "naive language-realism." It should make us realize what we owe to language

as an effortless heritage, but it should also give us critical
distance and mental freedom and destroy the illusion that
language is absolute.

2. The historicalness of the a priori. However, not language but languages exist. And each language analyzes, combines and valuates reality differently. If language contains,
as has been said, an "unconscious ontology," a "pre-philosophy,"
then there are as many such ontologies as there are languages.
(Famous is the different division of the color-spectrum, e.g.,
the Greek chloros corresponds neither to our green nor to
yellow.) The differences of languages, Humboldt writes, is
"not one of sounds and signs, but a difference of world-view."
Instead of philosophies, which present only a conceptually
diluted form of truth rather than the truth itself, young
people ought therefore, according to Humboldt, to study languages: they are "the world history of the thoughts and feelings
of mankind."

But since, as seen above, the "world-view" of language is
also transmitted to our mind a priori and presents the world
differently depending on which language we grew up in, it
follows that there is not only -- if at all -- an ahistorical
Kantian a priori of a timeless logical subject of knowledge
that is the same for all men. Even the a priori turns out
to be subject to the historical vicissitudes of everything
human. The dependence of knowledge on the prior achievement
of language, which always places it within a horizon of meaning, involves historical dependency down into its transcendental layer. This discovery was, however, again relativized by
Bruno Snell and others, and recently by Chomsky's thesis of an
innate "linguistic competence" of man as man as an underlying
capacity at the root of the various systems of the individual
languages.

As early as 1759, the Berlin Academy selected as topic
for a prize-essay contest: "To what extent do languages influence opinions,and opinions languages?" A nation has a richer
vocabulary for the things that are of practical interest to
it, but even modes of understanding are reflected in language,
just as vice versa, according to Stenzel, Snell, Lohmann,
their language predisposed the Greeks to become discoverers
of philosophy (though once discovered it can then be reproduced
in other languages). The difference of language-intrinsic
interpretations of the world can be better illustrated by com-
paring the languages of two advanced cultures. Primitive languages contain more information based on observation than on
mental constructs. The various nuances of a thing are expressed by new words for each one (a separate word for the
arrow made of wood or reed, in its quiver, on the string, in
the air, on target; the famous 5744 Arabic words for "camel";

no word for "arm" but only "my arm," "your arm," etc.). This
makes primitive languages colorful and rich, but clumsy. Only
the more abstract languages of the advanced cultures form
unified concepts, and distinguish qualities and relationships
by separate words, whereas formerly they were regarded as modi-
fications of the thing itself. These handy, recurrent general
components make it much easier to reconstitute the respective
particular situation. By studying the syntax of primitive
languages, we can trace the development of philosophical and
scientific categories (Cassirer). Whorf's description of the
Hopi language is famous: in it wave and flame are, because of
their brief duration, verbs, the subject is not the doer of
the action, etc. Humboldt however delimits the resultant
"linguistic determinism," because for him the action is not
one-directional. As for Whorf, language acts upon the mind,
but the mind also acts upon language.

Today languages are compared sociologically as well as
ethnologically. Deficient language behavior and the related
deficient cognitive performance by members of the lower class
are based, according to B. Bernstein, among others not on a
lack of intelligence, but on a more restricted linguistic code
(a particular, context-bound structure of meaning) compared
with the more elaborate code (a differentiated and context-
independent system of meaning) of the middle class.

3. Language as the promotor and impeder of thought. The
word is, according to Humboldt, not merely an interchangeable
external husk of a thought that would also come about without
it, but its "constitutive organ." Thought attains its organization and clarity only through the spoken word. Humboldt too
knows that "languages are not means of depicting an already
known truth but of discovering a previously unknown one." This
applies generally to the genesis of language: without the word
there is no concept; the word adds to this "significant (idea),
something of itself" (cf. de Saussure: the word and the concept are to one another as the front and the back of a leaf).
It also applies to the one who discovers words ready-made, and
therefore even apart from communication, speech is "a necessary
condition of the individual's thought in secluded loneliness."
The word objectifies the idea, gives it definition, organizes
and clarifies complex realities, as can easily be seen by comparison with the more primitive mental level of the deaf-and-
dumb and of children.

Humboldt thus revives an idea of Leibniz's: as we can count
more rapidly with numbers than with counted things, as we can
close financial deals more quickly with checks than with real
money, so words are, in Leibniz's metaphor, the "paper-money of
reason": instead of operating with realities we use a handier
abbreviated system of representation and can therefore think

more easily. The abstractness of language, which was spoken
of above, also facilitates understanding. Just as only a few
numbers make up the mathematical system, and all words can be
written with only a few letters, so Leibniz contemplated an
"alphabet of thought," a mathematics-like artificial language
of "universal characteristics" which would allot one sign to
each existing basic truth. On the pattern of Raimund Lull's
Ars magna, starting with these signs and linking them according to valid general rules by an "art of combination" which
is also an "art of discovery," i.e., not by "intuitive" objective thought, but "blindly," only by formal operations,
we would arrive at "all possible" contents of thought and so
attain a "universal knowledge" (mathesis universalis). The
symbols of the objects are the way of finding new objects.

Like Leibniz we find the solution in the opposite direction from Humboldt. The interpretative nature of language was
originally discovered not from the positive side, not in Hum-
boldtian confidence in its power of world-discovery, but in
nominalistic critique of its false interpretations. Language
is like myth; some praise its depth, others regard it only as
error. The construction of new systems of signs, of precision-
instrument types of language as used in the specialized sciences
(an "ortho-lingua" in which every term would be defined: Lo-
renzen) and of formalized calculator languages is an attempt
to avoid the errors of the natural languages and to use an
aprioristic model of language to penetrate beyond the phenomenal appearance of the world as modern science does in general (Apel). Language research is joined by formal semantics.

Bacon called words "idols of the market place." The people's low level of knowledge has crystalized in them. When
in language "the wind blows," according to Spencer this implies
an animistic personification of nature that we no longer believe in. Similarly Mauthner: language substantializes, while
our science functionalizes. We have noun, adjective and verb,
Mauthner says, not because substances, qualities and activities
exist but because language must break the complex down into
elements and so it creates these classes of words, "three
images of the world" which we adopt in our language whether
or not they are adequate.

This already takes us to the neo-positivistic critique of
language and the "linguistic revolution" of "semantic philosophy. Whitehead and Russell first asked by what "logical
syntax" (as Carnap later called it) signs are connected in
philosophy and science. According to Wittgenstein "logical
semantics" must expose the understanding of being contained in
colloquial speech (cf. Ayer, and Ordinary Language Philosophy,
or Descriptive Analytic Philosophy). This can show that the
sentences which metaphysics believes to have discovered by

thought, are really only the tautological development of language-immanent definitions.

The late Wittgenstein then abandoned the criterion of correspondence between word and world. Language became for him a behavioristic factor in the context of action (cf. Pierce, Bloomfield, Watson, Bridgman's operationalism). A word, or a mere cry, is understood by the total contextual situation for man and thing in which it was spoken, and by the prevalent rules: under other rules the same word may have another meaning. "The meaning of a word is its use in the language." (Carnap, in later years, despite his logical positivism, held similar ideas.) Under what conditions a word can be used at all and correctly is determined not by logic but by its appropriateness to the situation and by habit. The formula "Meaning equals usage" was first refuted by Searle.

Semiotics (a term invented by Locke), "the universal theory of signs" not only deals with language but also contributes to it. The sign is, according to Morris, for the human sciences what the atom is for physics and the cell for biology. All three semiotic dimensions (semantic, syntactic and pragmatic) contribute equally to its definition. For a term like "Pegasus" or artistic signs, the "denotative" reference to reality is omitted but the designative function that every sign must have is still there. The cognitive factor of meaning and the non-cognitive factors by which the sign stands in a context of action overlap.

CHAPTER 17

THE PHILOSOPHY OF HISTORY

Its Questions

Traditions, once they are taken for granted, lead men to believe that things have always been as they are and will always remain so into infinity. Knowledge that times differ qualitatively generally leads to an evaluative comparison of the present with the past and the future. The first philosophies of history are evaluations of epochs: times are divided into better and worse, the movement of history between them into a rise and a decline. Combinations of the types provide numerous possible curves of movement. The present can be interpreted by its position on these historical curves.

When the writing of history begins, it is usually motivated by unreflected historical and metaphysical convictions. These are often prescribed to the historian by his profession: for the courtier the military and political deeds of the ruler, which he preserves for his glory, are what moves history. Implicit, "hidden philosophies of history," or later would-be positivistic historical science -- documented for instance by whether the monograph on an author begins with a biography or with a history of the literary genres he used -- are, according to Rothacker, who therefore tried to distil them from the history books, more relevant and therefore more conclusive than the overt philosophy of history of the philosophers.

A philosophy of history often originates from a radical change or crisis: when history breaks out of the familiar channels, men become aware of it. Everyone believed in "eternal Rome"; now Rome is destroyed by the Goths: that is the experience behind Augustine's City of God. The Enlightenment replaced a life under the guidance of traditions by rational formation of the world: this first made tradition visible to men of the time as a historical reality. Enlightenment philosophy of history likewise determines its own standpoint as that of steeply rising and consciously sought "progress" (so in Comte still, but in Hegel perfection has already been reached). It is now more than the contemplation of things that happen without our participation; before the French Revolution and in Marx it is the background and stimulus for planned changing of history. The history of philosophy here motivates the men of action themselves.

In the Orient and in classical antiquity, the philosophy

of history (here in the sense of the ontology of historical
being itself, and not of the logic of the understanding of
history) starts with a multiplicity of independent bodies of
history. In the Hebrew prophecies and in Christianity, on
the contrary, it assumes the unity of human history, and its
line of movement rises or declines or moves toward a goal.
But not every end of history has the rank of a goal: mankind
could end in an Orwellian "1984." Yet only a goal can give
meaning to the course of history. The philosophy of history
asks: does history have a typical sequence or laws analogous
to those in nature? What is the scope of human freedom? Are
the causes and determining factors in history ideal (Romanticism,
Hebel) or material (Morgan, Marx) in nature, or do great individuals "lay their hand on millennia" (Nietzsche)?

Without excessive speculation on older philosophy of history, historical science itself is demanding an "analytic
history," a "meta-history," which seeks the hidden driving
forces and constant factors underneath the waves of manifest
events, and which would be to historical science as physiology is to clinical medicine. "Structural history" seeks to
decipher in the manifold events the constant code of invaria-
bles and the logical architecture of development, which are
binding on the actor of history: he must always choose among
a limited number of possibilities, can only combine elements
according to the rules he knows. Neither his individuality,
which is only apparently a history-changing ultimate, nor the
sequence of time, in which something supra-temporal merely
undergoes variations, is therefore the determining factor; it
lies rather in an unconscious mechanism of the mind and in
objective structural laws. If then process can be observed:
crop-growers favor polytheism, nomads monotheism; every absolutism has a bureaucracy and a standing army. Other questions
are: Which circumstances lead to gradual evolution? How is
culture transferred to another area? The view of the Greeks
who sought underlying constants and recurring patterns behind
the process of history across space and time (Polybius'
"circulation of constitutions") and who were therefore accused
of misconstruing history, thus comes into vogue again. But it
can be called "meta-"history only in contrast to narrowly
factual history. Thucydides as historian himself recognizes
the striving for power as an unchanging political determinant.
While Marx reproached the historians of his time with hiding
the economic causes and not seeing class struggles -- the true
secret history of Rome is that of land ownership -- this error
has long since been corrected (Rostovtzev, etc.) not only in
materialistic" historical studies with their strong emphasis
on economics.

The "Historical Threshold"

In the course of the last six generations the scope of
history has been broadened immensely:
a) spacially. Christianity linked all history with the
main strand of Judeo-Christian salvation-history: Bossuet
has the first Chinese Emperor be a son of Noah. Even in Hegel
the "Oriental world" is only a precursor of the Greco-Roman
one. Only after the decline of this "Europocentrism" (Spencer)
did the history of other lands become an equally important subject in its own right.
b) The time limitation, first to the 3000 years since the
Greeks and the Bible, then to the 6000 years since the early
advanced cultures, has also been abandoned. Even the incorrectly so-called "pre-history," although its methods of investigation are different, counts equally as a part of history. Likewise so-called primitive men: they are not "children of nature"
(Naturvölker). Among them too historical developments are in
process. "Ubiquism," which holds that the same institutions
came into existence spontaneously at different points of the
earth, has been replaced by "diffusionism," which explains
history by wanderings. History is wherever men are.
c) In one's own cultural circle only events and changes
are noticed, and these are often in politics (which also
arouses the most general interest). Therefore until now political history has unjustifiably usurped the concept of history
in general. Only from a larger temporal distance or in view
of an alien cultural sphere do cultural conditions, though
stable for a longer time, lose the nature of preconditions
that are taken for granted and become visible as independent
historical content. For Egyptologists the state is only one
domain, and not even the most interesting, along with religion,
society, economics, technology. Kant and Hegel (the latter
contrary to his own cultural-historical conception of a progress of the mind from art through religion to philosophy)
believed in the historical preeminence of the state. Cultural
history, established by Montesquieu and Voltaire, led a marginal existence at best in Germany (Burckhardt, Lamprecht, Breysig, Spengler) and often was pushed aside into the specialized
disciplines (economics, ethnology). At any rate these disciplines became independent in the course of the nineteenth
century and it became clear that not only men, as individuals
or as nations, have a history, though it may still seem so in
the history of states. The "objective spirit" created by men
(an entire field such as language, a style such as Baroque,
a literary genre such as drama) also has a history.
The next discovery was a "concensus" (Comte) of all areas
of a culture in a period over and above the specialized his-

tories, the "spirit of the age," and the "unity of style"
(Nietzsche) and the comprehensive and cohesive "value-orientation" of entire cultures (Ruth Benedict, cf. Spengler).
Therefore epochs and cultures prove to be historical subjects,
as is also the state.   Every cultural sphere, every individual achievement always moves within the "framework" (Rothacker)
of its great assumptions. As it impresses them upon new material and thus transforms them it is also delimited by them and
relieved of toil: education by constant styles of behavior and
by traditional inclinations does not run counter to freedom
and productivity and is therefore not felt as a restraint.

The primacy of the state for historical writing was still
defended by E. Meyer when asked why only "events" -- which
are there only to "sink away" (Hofmannsthal) -- cross the
"historical threshold" and become history (Simmel, based on
Droysen), answered: through their effects: climate and race,
economics, language, religion, whose renewal also renews the
arts (as under Echnaton) and which according to Max Weber
constantly radiates into the economy (Calvinism brings about
capitalism). Indeed according to Hegel philosophy is at the
"heart of world history": The "self-movement of the idea"
draws historical movement after it. Thus history should study
not only what has exerted influence, but also what is of value
even if it never had results (for example a newly excavated
Greek statue). Furthermore, history sets a premium on novelty,
even when it is of negative value, on the first break-through,
even when it is still awkwardly groping its way. Outstanding
late Impressionists were hardly noticed any more after the
appearance of the first Expressionists.

For all these reasons political history-writing has right-
fully lost its primacy, and for good. "Universal cultural
history" excels as a counterweight, but because of the frag-
mentation of cultural history into numerous disciplines it is
still struggling to get beyond popular and ideologically bound
beginnings.

Human Historicalness

According to an old view, only man has a history, while
in nature everything repeats itself. But that is based on an
optical illusion. Biological species, minerals, solar systems
do remain the same for millennia, but they too are non-recur-
ring; they originate, they pass away and never return. C.F.
von Weizsäcker rightly has called attention to the historicalness of nature, he however incorrectly has man differ from it
only by his awareness of his history. The difference lies
much more fundamentally in the fact that man is by nature not
determined, not controlled by instinct, not destined for one

particular way of life, that he is to a far greater extent internally open and variable than the rest of nature. This formal variability changes into a factual one: first, through his command of history: in freedom he invents technology, economics, social structures, artistic styles, etc., and ever new types of employment; secondly, through his dependence on history: with great pliancy he adapts these forms that were created before him and transmitted to him by tradition. Awareness of history is added to these two historical aspects of the first and second degree only secondarily as a third degree of historicalness.

Formerly the multiplicity of cultures was merely noted, though the Sophists concluded from it that culture was based on human convention (thesis): objective plurality is an indication of subjective productivity. Because the Sophists thought in terms of cultural philosophy, they discovered that man is anchored in history, which fact escapes the political historian who deals with particular events. History is the quintessence of what is created by man -- though often because of objective "factual necessity" it is unintentional and even subconscious. Historicalness results from the real constitution of its bearer. Objective history exists, because man is the historical being. What we contemplate in history is an explication of ourselves.

Man is historical in two ways. First, Sartre's formulation that he is "compelled to freedom" is valid both ethically and culturally. Even the most elementary activities, without which he would not survive, are in his case mutable and historically conditioned in their respective modality. Above this condominium of necessity and freedom there then rises the realm of "free freedom," in which he also decides on whether activities and entire spheres of culture will exist.

Command of history is as a rule mobilized to more intensive degrees only by external provocation. Otherwise it moves only in small steps and does not become self-aware. Its zero-point is reached under conditions which merely preserve and transmit a way of life that was discovered by earlier men. Schelling speaks of a "time of complete historical immobility," in which men uniformly repeat what their fathers already did; this is really a "timeless time." Romanticism praised historical inactivity, represented by the so-called Pelasgans (Levi-Strauss' "cold societies") in writers from Creuzer to Bachofen and Klages, as an organic inclusion of man in the cosmic cycle, while Spengler despised both its precultural vegetating and its postcultural serfdom.

But Schelling also knows that historical change and unprogressive circular modes of existence are not merely two alternate phases of history. Even creative times and men behave

reiteratively in broad areas of life in which the inherited
patterns prove adequate and do not need modification. We thus
live constantly on two pyramidally stratified levels of historicalness (which in turn are based on a natural level in us).
Often an antagonism exists between the two tendencies, stabil-
ization and innovation. Sometimes innovation is only a narrow
sector within a stable culture (art is one area especially
subject to stylistic change), sometimes it extends to broader
and more elementary areas of life. According to Pareto, it is
always elites that make history, while the majority does not
give up the accepted form (or accepts the new form late and
holds firmly to it, when at the centers of progress another
new one has been predominant for a long time: "submerged cultural good"). Historical creativity however presupposes, on
the objective side, that something new can be created; if
the possibilities are exhausted, then a culture enters a petri-
fied stage. According to Gehlen and others, mankind as a whole
is now entering post-history.

Even stagnent early conditions also display an infinite
variety; they are not, as Romanticism believed, "natural culture" -- no such thing exists. Though they usually interpret
themselves as natural, they too were derived from human convention and therefore cannot logically stand at the "beginning" and are likewise historical in the sense of dependence
on history and determination by former discoveries. The
following sentence has universal validity: "I am as much
history as nature" (Dilthey).

The power to influence history, when it becomes conscious,
is usually felt with pride, and vice versa dependence on
history as a humiliation, indeed as one of the worst humilia-
tions along with the Copernican, Darwinistic and Freudian
revolutions: one's own customs and valuations which had been
considered absolute and eternal are "only historical,"
accidental, conditioned by chance, and like all earthly reality,
subject to change! It may have been this emotional block
which for the longest time restrained human self-understanding
from allowing historical determination its ultimate depth.
Man thus was divided into two halves: supra-temporal, extra-
historical, and always remaining the same in his internal zone,
he is drawn into history only in the outer zone, per accidens.
It is only the external, indifferent frame for the essential
in him. The same applies to spheres of culture: even the state,
in this view, has, either an immutable nature, which stays the
same despite all transformations of historical states, or it
is a norm by which every real state is measured. Collingwood
has proven how much the "substantialism" of the ancient historians limits their understanding: for Livy, Rome is from the
start what it remains till the end, and for Tacitus the char-

acter of old Tiberius does not change but his latent qualities
merely become visible. Development is, as in Aristotle, only
an unfolding not a transformation.

Christianity, however, sees man as different depending on
whether he lives under the law or under grace, before or after
Christ. His historical position determines his innermost being.
Even Dante condemns the greatest men of antiquity to hell
(with two exceptions) because they were pagans. Every individual must arrive at his own understanding of being from the
whole of history, which is not only past but "soteriologically
relevant," and must live by it; he becomes what he is in part
through memory and expectation. Without valuation, without
limitation to certain periods of time, this historical anthropology reappears in the Age of Goethe's "historical revolution"
-- in Meinecke's view, the second great German achievement
after the Reformation. History here becomes a radical destiny:
man does not in his innermost being stand outside of it; he
not only has a history, he is history, is completely penetrated
by it. Only in the framework of culture, nation and epoch, from
within, is our knowledge accurate. Even feelings such as joy
and love are only partially "natural," they are lived differently at different times, and concepts such as reason and
virtue are thought differently. Here too what seemed to be
supra-historical turns out to be temporal and individual.

The Three Types of Philosophy of History

1. <u>The Cyclic Theory</u>. According to the Oriental and Greco-
Roman cyclic theory, history consists of numerous disparate
bodies of history in successive or parallel existence, each of
which describes a circle analogous to the path of sun and moon
in nature or maturity and decline in living things: they are
renewed or they make room for one another. In contrast with
the Judeo-Christion conception of a unified general history
of mankind, Spengler, who revived that theory in this century
-- but for whom the actors of history are no longer only
nations and states but the comprehensive eight great "cultures"
-- considers "mankind an empty word." For Hegel nations and
cultures are acts of a single drama, in which the earlier ones
prepare the ground for the later ones; according to Spengler,
on the contrary, one would have to count the years of every
culture by its own time instead of entering them on a consecu-
tive universal time-scale external to them (just as in physics
his contemporary Einstein ascribed such a time of their own
to the heavenly bodies, because time is always relative to a
motion). Cultures are fundamentally so alien to one another,
in Spengler's view, that they neither receive anything from
one another (except only in the Merovingian Period and in

syncretistic late periods, whereas they otherwise recast everything according to their own law), nor can they even understand
one another (but he is wrong in this). It can happen that a
less developed culture uses the "language" of a more mature,
mightier one, but its true spiritual tone has to be deciphered
behind this "pseudo-morphosis."

Just as it has no unity, history, for Spengler, also has
no goal, neither intra-culturally nor as a whole. It does
reach peaks, but these always are situated in the center of
a circle not at the end of any line. History runs its course
in "noble unpurposefulness." On the same basic canvas, after
the collapse of the nineteenth century's faith in progress,
after the loss of hope in the future in the twenties of this
century when the typologies of the human and social sciences
came into being, the respectively individual existence was
rendered absolute by Heidegger, and the world became an inescapable labyrinth for Kafka. All typical stations of a
culture's course of about a thousand years, including its death,
are predesignated like those of an organism (this is not the
case for Toynbee, who grants history more spontaneity). As
soon as its creative possibilities have faded, it enters into
the merely civilized stage of petrifaction, in which it stag-
nates for further centuries or -- for political vital energy
also declines when the imagination is crippled --   it is
undermined from within and destroyed from the outside. Civilization is the last phase of every culture (while for Alfred
Weber the process of culture and civilization are two independent concurrent processes). Spengler ventures to predict the
next phase of a culture -- as Polybius had already done in
antiquity -- by comparison with other cultures (but historical
prediction is not necessarily limited to the cyclic theory, it
can also merely extrapolate the "trend" of the present into
the future: Marx, Nietzsche).

Every cyclic theory is based on formal correspondences of
the phenomena and stages, i.e., categorical "simultaneities"
between one historical era and the next. They can all be
functionally right and serve for greater familiarization with
an unfamiliar reality or for "mutual clarification," but substantially they are false because they disregard specificity.
Patrology and Scholasticism worked with correspondences:
figures of the Old Testament and of Greco-Roman antiquity "pre-
figure" those of the New Testament and the Christian Era, and
even in the "third kingdom" this typology will be repeated
again, according to Joachim de Floris. The Romantics drew a
parallel between Homer and the Nibelungenlied. For Mommsen,
Mithridates is a "Sultan," Rohde discovered "bacchantes"
even among primitives. Historically individualized terms thus
become typical: there is now also a Middle Ages and a Baroque

Period in antiquity (Leo, Burckhardt, Lamprecht's twelve "socio-psychic" stages of development even in China, according to Breysig).

Spengler on the one hand stresses that every culture has a different main premiss which establishes a universal morphological relationship of all its particular phenomena down to its military technology and its economic system (cf. the value-orientation of a total "configuration" in American cultural anthropology). Spengler thus individualizes cultures. This is his modern component which is not derived from antiquity. But as he is a master at discovering formal correspondences in different areas within a culture, so on the other hand also in establishing them between one culture and another. He excels in correspondences such as equating Descartes with Pythagoras, Polygnotus with Rembrandt, Napoleon with Alexander (more correct would be with Caesar -- while Alexander would more closely resemble a Condottiere) and the First World War not with Actium, but with the early period of the Roman Empire. Spengler refines the pattern still more by the distinction. taken from biology, of homology (morphological equivalency of organs such as the lungs of land animals and the swim-bladders of fish) and analogy (functional equivalency of lungs and gills). "The Dionysian movements and the Renaissance are homologous" (because a religious interiorization takes place in both).

2. <u>Unified Teleological History</u>. The Greeks think synchronically, Jews and Christian diachronically. If there is only one God and he is the director of history, then there is also: 1) only one common universal history of mankind. Thus, for the prophets of the Old Testament monolinearism follows from monotheism. While the Greeks previously dated their history by the Olympic Games, and the Romans "since the founding of the city," etc., Eusebius, on the basis of this monolinear assumption, later established a uniform dating system for "world history" (which however has become for us only a formal scaffolding without religious connotation and is satirized by Spengler. 2) In any one line of history no person and no event reoccurs as in the cycles. Every point is unique. The creation of the world, the deluge, the Messiah, "typical" events in the Oriental models, are singularized in the Bible. Only secondarily, in order to reconcile the three worlds of antiquity, Judaism and Christianity, is a typology of the preparatory and fulfilling parallels resorted to. 3) God, directing history, according to the prophets, follows a plan: history will culminate in the Messianic kingdom. It is thus not only a line, but a direction. It moves toward a goal. This is not contradicted when Augustine borrows from the cyclic theory the simile of the ages of life, for which actually the high point is the middle, at the time of greatest vital energy:

not old age is the goal that mankind ends in, but the "sabbath of sabbaths" that comes after death. 4) The fact that history has a goal implies the idea of a future in every way different from the present. The future as the locus of something completely new and different is here discovered for the very first time. Christianity believes in a certain perfection of earthly things upon the appearance of Christ and expects their ultimate redemption only in the kingdom of heaven; chiliasm and later Joachim de Floris, as well as his Anabaptist successors, also hold firm to the promise of an earthly higher future. The missionary strength of Christianity down to our day among peoples who did not yet have the idea of a future renewal is based on this understanding of its eschatology and not on its ethics.

5) The common goal not only provides history with an additional and more tangible unity, but it also makes it more meaningful as a whole. The meaning that it gives to history is the main reason why the meaning-thirsty soul of men is captivated by the prophetic Christian philosophy of history and has caused many to consider it the philosophy of history in the strict sense of the word, compared with the cyclic theory and its nature analogies. But on the other hand, its sense of history is based only on faith, and scientifically speaking it is a mental construct; a Greek would never have gotten this idea, not from a lack of deep thinking, but because of his cool critical mind (at all times, even today, there exist numerous speculative or paranoic meta-histories which decipher world events as compensatory keys to knowledge for ignorant men; the educated man avoids them and pities their adherents). Christianity can more easily preach of a sense of history because of the three cardinal points on which it hinges all of history: the creation of the world, the Incarnation of Christ, and the Last Judgment. The first and the last one lie outside real history and it does not need to bother about what lies between the three points since this contributes nothing to mankind's road to salvation. There is a wide gap between the historical theology of the events of salvation and a philosophy of history based on real history.

The modern theory of progress is based on the prophets and Christianity insofar as it has history move toward a goal. But the goal of the two religions consists in making everything new at one stroke by divine transformation; the goal of the theory of progress is the immanent teleology of the world itself, which can and should be realized by man in successive approximations. In the Judeo-Christian tradition the goal is already fixed (in fact the initial Paradise merely returns), while in progressive theory it is infinite, open, creatively enrichable. In Judeo-Christianity the goal consists in the "end of history," which as a whole is only an interlude, in fact a punishment for sin; in the progress theory, history is, on the contrary, affirmed and brought into motion and productivity through the goal it sets. Therefore faith in progress is not merely the "secularization" of Christian faith in the end of the world (Blumenberg).

A distinction must be made between the metaphysics of inevitable progress and the will to progress or a program of progress. Antiquity (Xenophanes, Epicurus) recorded accomplished improvement (against theories of decline: Hesiod, the Cynics, the Stoics), but did not extend its line into the future. Progress does not always take place in all areas synchronically (the "Middle Ages of electricity"; the "cultural lag" of the ethnologists). According to Rousseau, progress in one field, science and the arts, has a destructive effect in another respect, namely, the original goodness of heart, and it is therefore progress only from a relative point of view; in a more essential sense it is a step backwards. "Art is known to flourish in certain periods totally out of proportion to the general development of society and the material foundation" (Marx): it flourishes at an undeveloped level. Alfred Weber holds that of the three fields, culture, civilization and society, progress can occur only in the last two (but is there no progress in justice and freedom, and are they not a part of culture?).

While Christian philosophy of history is universal in its claim, it limits itself in fact to God's action in Judeo-Christian history. The rest of history, which is irrelevant to salvation is only grouped around this line of reference. Similarly Hegel: he mentions only nations which contributed to progress in freedom and spiritualization; all others, including these in their historically unprogressive epochs, for instance, the modern Greeks, are only "lazy existence." On the other hand, the ancient historians generally have only their own circle of history in mind (a pattern which is broken by Herodotus, of course). The cyclic theory becomes universal only under (Stoic and) Christian influence. But then it is more impartial than salvation history, and really includes all of mankind, at least in its intention, according independence to each branch of it and omitting none. The price of this completeness is, however, that the resulting universal history is merely additive. Mankind is for it no longer one substantially, but only accidentally, without a common goal or destiny.

Both theories, the cyclic and the monolinear are reconciled by factual history. The Neolithic transition from food hunters and gatherers to productive shepherds and settled farmers took place almost everywhere and was therefore an event of mankind

as a whole. This great change led to the origin of the individual advanced cultures, which were relatively cut off from one
another and for which the cyclic theory proves to be right.
Within it Jaspers (after von Lasaulx and Th. Lessing) distinguishes between the interiorizing "pivotal period" which however is limited to a few advanced cultures and despite relative simultaneity takes place only internally in each of them.
A planetary event is then only the "industrial revolution"
which has been going on since the eighteenth century. Mankind is gradually becoming a unified subject only through it.
While the Neolithic revolution did produce a similar economic
level, it left the nations separate. In this sense "world
history" begins no earlier than with our own century. The
cyclic theory thus is a close-up view, while monolinearism
holds true on a macroscopic scale.

    3. The "Own Value" Theory. As long as man has not dis-
covered himself as a responsible factor of history, he may
still believe in predetermined lines of history planned by God
or as laws of reality, to which he is bound and which he merely
fulfills. But as soon as he begins, with the Enlightenment,
to exert control over history, he no longer wants his movements
to be restricted by predesignated, determinative compulsions --
as little as the artist accepts aesthetic prescriptions or the
man of action ethical rules. It is not by chance that the
same period that witnessed the French Revolution in politics,
also broke with the old philosophies of history which contradict the newly awakened sense of freedom and of power over
history.

    As a countercurrent to the historical conception of Chris-
tianity and to the theory of incessant human progress, the Age
of Goethe returned to a succession of multiple unrelated
bodies of history. And even within these it posits neither
rise nor decline -- disagreeing on this point with the cyclic
theory -- nor an internal progress, just as it accepts no
supreme ideal established by reason for men to realize (nor
a golden age from which we have declined). The plurality of
everything historical is not merely recognized but approved,
for the human power to create history is revealed precisely
and only in it. This third type of philosophy of history,
which originated in the Age of Goethe, has been called the
"own value" theory (Eigenwerttheorie: Thyssen): according
to young Herder who is fighting a two-front battle against
both the theory of progress and Rousseau, both the various
cultures and the early and late periods within them have a
value of their own which cannot be measured by a universally
binding teleological idea. The value of cultures and epochs
lies precisely in their individuality, in their living form
with its numerous variations. As the Age of Goethe believed

in a plurality of historical systems without a cyclic theory,
it also believed in their individuality without any monolinear
theory.

Everything that comes into existence organically is, for
the Age of Goethe, meaningful where it stands. In Christianity
and progress theory the "meaning" of history means that its
total course is a meaningful occurrence. But now the intrinsic meaningfulness of each particular historical fact was
discovered, after it had actually been hidden by the meaning
of all history. From this point of view of the total meaning,
the respective achievement is seen -- or rather, construed --
as merely a component contributing to that higher meaning, or
even merely as a step toward the higher final condition.
Against such (still Hegelian) mediatization and devaluation
of the epochs of history, Ranke said that every one of them
is "immediate to God" (this does not imply as it has been mis-
understood, the thesis of equivalence). Even if history as a
whole were meaningless, there could be immanent and sporadic
meaning in individual lives, actions and structures. According to young Herder the only meaning of the process of history
is that, though every creation is necessarily one-sided and
limited, history makes new (not higher) creations possible,
and so develops mankind's inner wealth, its ability to discover ever new forms.

Rationalism had approached history critically from the
ideal forms of the individual cultural fields invented by
reason. In order to make way for a better condition, it wanted
to smash history. The Age of Goethe, however, because it surrenders an ideal norm in favor of the new and different forms
that have to be created in each concrete situation, approaches
history first, to learn from it and admire it: something is
revealed in it that reason alone could not discover. A turning to history now serves to compensate for one's own fragmen-
tariness (Humboldt). The rationalistic century that was
emancipating itself from its own past and as such was unhistorical (J. Ritter) preserved at least a knowledge of history
though no longer as a living tradition or a binding ideal.
"Dialogual" history, much acclaimed today, combines the motivations of both the Enlightenment and the Age of Goethe. Because
it does not measure historical material by a norm alien to it,
because in dealing with it, it suspends its own value-beliefs
(formerly applied naively to everything in history) the historical science that stemmed from the Age of Goethe, secondly,
penetrates to a deeper understanding than ever before. Its
approach to individual life, which cannot be dissolved into
concepts nor explained by circumstances is empathetic and intrinsic. Dilthey (with some justification) contrasted history
as understandable with nature as explainable.

It has often been claimed that the capacity of universal
historical understanding gained at that time had a laming
effect because it ranged a numerous series of equivalent
possibilities and so made one's own appear as just one among
many others. Historism is, so the objection goes, relativism.
But the many possibilities are not indifferently subject to
decisionistic choice -- and thus again are removed from history. Each of them is subject to specific, historically
changing vital preconditions and can be transferred to other
preconditions only by force and at the price of being ungenuine.   Instead the new preconditions should produce their own
new cultural forms, with their own intrinsic necessity. Milton
and Klopstock still wrote on the model of Homer's and Virgil's
"epics"; only later was it seen that the epic is not an eternal paradigm, but the product of an early age, in which we no
longer live. When the sense of history teaches that every
form must be seen together with its conditions, with its vital
basis, it does away with the normative and contributes on the
contrary to facilitating the production of suitable, individual
expression for a changed situation (Dilthey, cf. Sartre). Thus
only the semi-historical isolation of the forms is confusing.
Historicalness that is reflected upon and taken seriously
restores creativity.

Factors and Laws of History

Though history is not bound by pre-established curves, it
does not proceed in total freedom. Its changing course is
determined by constant factors. The dispute is still continuing as to whether spiritual or material factors play a greater
role. Comte and Buckle hold that progress in knowledge draws
other progress after it; Morgan sees technical progress as
primary. For Spengler, opposing basic conceptions of space
and time shape all areas of a culture; for Max Weber religion
determines even economics. Hegel assumes an intermediate
position: on the one hand, history is based on a dialectic
of ideas, on the other hand "world-historical individuals" act
only according to their own "interests and passions; but a
"cunning of reason" has so arranged it that with their "particular" desire, although they neither know nor desire it, they
are "marionettes of the World Spirit" and always bring about
the next stage of the great process. Out of this all too
ingenious interconnection Marx retains only the interests --
for him, economic ones -- as decisive even for the "super-
structure" (but he expressly notices that the Old High German
vowel-shift could not be explained either by them or by "historical materialism"!). An older naturalistic theory that goes
back to the Greek doctors and was renewed by Montesquieu is

that of the influence of climate. Taine had milieu, race and
point-in-time act together. Nietzsche revived Thucydides'
theory of the striving for power (for him, not only in a political sense) as the active principle of history. Today the
trend is to accept an "interdependence of factors."

The more monocausally one thinks the more readily one will
come to accept historical laws. Taine wishes to deduce such
laws from psychology, Wundt from "folk-psychology" (as Comte
in his "social physics" sought to deduce them from social laws).
Laws for specialized fields can be established more easily
than for history as a whole (for instance, in every economic
development, first land, then capital is predominant: Roscher).
The more factors are multiplied, mixed and delimited, the more
caution is required with respect to laws. Laws can be completely formal (Hegel's dialectical triad, or the generation theory
of the 1920's in the history of ideas). But they can be recorded purely externally without statement of the causes; for
instance history moves from East to West (Varro, Hegel).

Reflection on the philosophy of history first brings about
a transcendental turn. The perspective of the individual who
overestimates the scope of his freedom and thinks he is free
because he wants to be free is corrected by the historical
perspective, which proves to him how much he is conditioned
by elementary, supra-personal forces. What is experienced by
the individual psychologically and ethically as his decision
is revealed from this perspective as already predetermined.
The individual is not at all what matters: if Napoleon had
fallen at Marengo, then his historical achievements would have
been attained by other persons; we are free, as the Stoics
said, only to choose whether to accept our destiny or to
struggle futilely against it (Schiller). Such knowledge may
be fatalistically crippling, but it can also become an incen-
tive to complete the mission oneself, to accelerate the arrival
of what must come. Many sects wanted through certain practices
to "conjure Christ," i.e., to create the preconditions for him
to return soon.

What history offers us is, however, generally only oppor-
tunities: which ones we seize, what we make of them, whether
Latin becomes a vulgar soldiers' jargon or the subtle instrument of Scholastic distinctions, how and at what level we fill
in the framework, all that is within our own decision. Often
something new comes into being unexpectedly: the eighteenth
century with its Rococo and its scepticism was already a period
of decline, yet looking back from today it was a new beginning.
What in retrospect may seem like a necessary line of history
was in prospect still open and required initiative, talent,
good luck.

CHAPTER 18

PHILOSOPHICAL ANTHROPOLOGY

Basic Anthropina: Unspecialization, Creativity, Awareness, Freedom, Individuality

The animal's behavior is determined by biologically inherited instincts typical of the species. Through instinct
and through its organs the animal is specialized for a particular mode of life in a particular environment (Umwelt: Uexküll), and thus it is a finished being. By contrast, man is
(1) unspecialized in both respects, by a "diminution of the
instincts" and by organs that have remained "archaic" (Bolk's
"fetalization" by "retardation"). Compared with the animal
he at first seems to be unperfected, as it were unfinished
at creation. By his "anthropine gap" he is the "indeterminate
animal" (Nietzsche), an "open question" (Plessner). Of the
twenty-three anthropina (human properties) which we shall
distinguish, this is the fundamental one.

But unspecialization looks like a gap in a "defective
creature" (Mängelwesen: Gehlen) only if the animal is set up
as the standard. Looked at from the point of view of man as
a whole, it proves, on the contrary, to be a positive factor,
namely the necessary correlative to (2) creativity. Man can
and must be unspecialized because he has received both the
mission and the power to shape the course of his life himself.
If he were already determinate in everything, then he would
have no further openness to finish creating himself. Even the
most elementary action for survival -- not to mention for the
"good life" -- is not imparted on him by the species, as is
the case with the animal, but is invented and developed in
history. "Nature wanted man to produce completely by himself
whatever goes beyond the mechanical arrangement of his existence" (Kant). He is the homo hominans (man-making man) who
must always himself make the homo hominatus (man-made man).
He completes his own creation; he produces himself. Creativity,
often falsely ascribed only to genius and otherwise dealt with
only in the marginal sphere of aesthetics, is the second basic
anthropological category.

It is not true, as naturalism (as early as Protagoras)
would depict it, that man was first afflicted with defects and
then, to compensate for these, became intelligent. Unspecialization and creativity are, rather, from the first, a mutually
attuned structure (Herder). If anything, the opposite is true,

because the brain developed, specialized organs and instincts receded.

The dualistic concept of man makes him a composite of two heterogeneous, alien, indeed hostile (Plato's Phaido) "substances" (Descartes) linked together only in an extrinsic combination: on the one side, the soul or reason; on the other, the indifferent "animal" body. Even Scheler who gave the impetus for modern philosophical anthropology, was unable to free himself from Schopenhauer's spirit/drive dichotomy. Within this framework it remains only a matter of emphasis whether "the truly human" is located -- as in the Platonic-Christian tradition -- in the spiritual half, or naturalistically in the material half (economics, drive to power, sexual drive). However, the anthropologies of the 5th century B.C., of Herder and Goethe, and of the present age seek to understand man as a unity in which even his animality is specifically different from that of the beast and his body and mind are mutually oriented to one another.

Even within this unity, however, the duality is retained between "what nature makes of man" and what he "as a free-acting creature makes or can or should make of himself" (Kant). There remains a constant stratum of human nature, out of which his "history" then ensues. Therefore, since Hegel, those who consider freedom to be man's essence and who hold him to be the historically changeable and growing being reproach philosophical anthropology of mere descriptive naturalism. But this reproach is wrong, for firstly, nature, as anthropology speaks of it, is only the basis and not the whole of man; secondly, this nature, by its very constitution, includes the necessity of history. As a mere open form, it necessarily calls for its historical content. Man is an equation with variables whose concrete definition must always come from history. It is in history that his innate indeterminacy is changed into determinate decision. The dilemma, anthropology or philosophy of history, is a false one.

Nor is it true, as the metaphysics of history and Platonism would claim, that a direction is already designated for man to progress in and that he has to merely "discover" the normative idea of himself, like a truth not yet realized but already present seminally and ready to germinate. What he must do is not discover but invent it. "Artificiality is the nature of man" (Ferguson). Without pre-given "essence," man must "design" himself as what he wants to be, into a future that is completely his responsibility; he must "produce" himself: this applies not only to the individual (Fichte, Sartre) but, even primarily, to man as a species (Marx).

Man not only lives, he leads his life (Plessner). He not only reacts, he acts (Gehlen). He is not, he chooses himself

(Sartre). All this implies, compared with other life, (3) awareness and (4) freedom.

Furthermore, since -- as seen above -- his species as such contains an emptiness, because it assigns him the task of determining his own mode of being and discovering his own way of being a man, he must -- nations and epochs as well as individuals must -- in order to arrive at complete reality, go beyond his species and what is pre-formed in it, and add something to it qualitatively. The creative being is also the (5) most individualized. Self-realization necessarily leads to individualization.

Today structuralism is, after the pattern of linguistics, seeking to discover, as it were, the phonemes of culture. According to structuralism, even cultural changes are regular and predictable re-combinations of common elements, immutable basic patterns that were present from the first. The true lever of self-creative history is, accordingly, a generative social grammar acting upwards from the meta-level and guiding us subconsciously. Like historical "evolution," the creative, intuitive individual as the subject of history would thus prove to be a false invention of the eighteenth century. The true science of man originates only with "the end of man" (Foucault, Sebag, cf. Levi-Strauss). The individual as center and beginning was a myth. Structuralism, with its revival of Platonic and naturalistic tendencies, is as much contrary to philosophical anthropology as to philosophy of history. The end of the individual, which it signifies for scientific thinking, is, however, only a symptom of the real end of the individual which we face. For Sartre, to stop at the structures is a scandal: man becomes himself precisely by always being more than the structures that condition him.

Knowledge in the Total Human Context

Since antiquity, man's knowing reason has been considered his distinctive feature. But this is to give priority to something secondary. Man has the strongest and most versatile knowledge only because he is creative, just as analogously the type of perception in the animal is correlative with static structures of behavior. In each case, the two things must be seen jointly as a single structure. In the animal, the specialized reaction-schemata of the instincts correspond to specialized receptor-schemata. Its senses act as selective filters admitting only data relevant to its behavior. They need nothing more, for the respective sensory stimulus is enough to trigger the available and appropriate instinctive reaction. Since man, on the contrary, is not specialized in his behavior by the instincts, so he is also (6) not specialized in his

perception of the world. In order to construct his own behavior he must be more generally and thoroughly familiar with
its materials. It is, therefore, false to say that man shares
his sensory level with the animals, plus the additional faculty
of thought. Even the sensory operations in man are intelligent
and specifically human.

But it is just as false to declare man an ascetic negator,
who places a hiatus of renunciation (Scheler) between his
"drives" and the goal they seek. For this would presuppose
the existence of a direct road to the goal, which is only
interrupted by the "mind." In reality, the mind must itself
first build the road, indeed it often establishes the goal.
Man's (7) theoretical disposition is not added after the fact
by Platonic antithesis or Aristotelian superimposition on top
of a sensory-motor system analogous to that of the animals,
rather it is just as primary as his animal needs. Man's biological needs rely on his reason to achieve their own satiation.
The specifically human practicality is determined equally by
his needs and by the theoretical factor.

Precisely in order to serve this practicality, the theoretical must never stand exclusively in its service. Reason must
be (8) independent of practical necessity; it must be allowed
to develop freely according to its own inclination. Otherwise
it is re-specialized by the respective practice. Only if unspecialized can reason prepare new practice. In order to judge
what use can be made of something, knowledge must first know
it prior to and independently of the utilitarian aspect.

Psychologically, the theoretical aspect of man is expressed
as (9) an urge to explore.

This propensity has an extensive dimension: man is not
limited to one environment, but (10) "open to the world" (Scheler).
He transcends the horizon of what he already knows; he creates
new categories. In fact, nations and individuals always com-
partmentalize themselves into "secondary social worlds": here
again a certain way of life selects what is perceived, apprehends only what is relevant to it and creates for itself dogmatically one-sided interpretative symbols (Rothacker) which
retroactively greatly stylize its own attitude. But man can
always break such a closed circle; by understanding and changing such an interpretative system he can establish a new circle
of reality for himself. And so man has a history. The animal's
environment is species-wide and inescapable; the human one
is self-established and relative.

The intensive dimension: man penetrates into the interior
of things; he knows or believes that (11) he knows things as
they are, the properties and laws that are theirs "as such,"
their intrinisc nature.

This already implies: For man, things constitute not only

goals for or resistances to his own vital stream, they not only fulfill functions in a practical sequence, but they now separate from the series for the first time (12) <u>as independent, objective things.</u> They now reveal themselves to the theoretical power on the subjective side as an objective counterpart in the strict sense.

Therefore, according to Plessner, man does not, like the animal, merely orient the world naively around himself as center (though he does this too), but at the same time he reorientates himself "eccentrically" by the world; he knows his place in it and so he becomes objective to himself along with the objects of the world. "Man's position is twofold: he stands within his perspective, yet also outside it." He lives out of himself and toward himself. In the indirectness of this "mediated immediacy," in which he becomes his own double, he is a body from within and yet disposes over the external instrument of a body; he is included within situations and yet stands masterfully over them. He not only is what he is, but he plays a role: so modern philosophical anthropology and sociological role-theory overlap. Because man penetrates into the properties and possibilities of things, he also is constantly learning from them in his actions and he joins them in a reciprocal "circle of action."

Knowing means not only to reach the particular, but also to experience (13) <u>general</u>, world-articulatory <u>concepts</u>. Originally (not in time, but in logic) located in a baffling field of disoriented "stimulus flooding," man must, according to Gehlen -- language leads the way in this -- first develop his categoriality into an equivalent of what the animal already has in his receptory schemata: man uses his categories to eliminate excessive sensory congestion and make the world surveyable and accessible. But man's <u>gestalts</u>, as distinguished from the animal's, are not inflexible; he can detach elements from them analytically and construct new forms by recombining the elements (Wolfgang Köhler). Practical creativity precedes the creativity of knowledge and imagination, in which concepts are formed.

Reason knows not only what is presented to it; it (14) <u>reaches out in anticipation to new horizons</u>. It develops articulated advance-schemata of action, which are then realized in practice (Piaget). It imagines the Utopia of a still non-existent condition of the world, inhabited by a new mankind living a better life (Bloch).

The Shaping of Culture and History

Some things are created only for the moment; others acquire duration. In systems of value, norms, and purpose, in

customs, techniques and regulations, in inventions and structures, the act of creation becomes solidified into a created
thing, the human mind into "objective mind." Man, even the
most primitive, criticized as barbaric by later levels, is
(15) never without this "external apparatus" of "culture"
The word "self-domestication" has been used, but there has
never been, nor can there ever be, a "wild form" of man. Therefore philosophical anthropology today is converging toward
"cultural anthropology" (identical in name and also partially
overlapping in content with American ethnology). "Institutions," as Gehlen calls them, first give stability and direction to the behavior of a being which, as a result of instinct-
reduction, has a constitutional excess of drives and variable
motor impulses. The dismantling of traditions, however much
it may serve as a challenge, contains, when it becomes radical,
the danger of a primitivization of man.

Man lives not only in culture in general, but always in
(16) a particular culture. His basic structural plan specifies
only that he needs culture; but which culture he is surrounded
with is not prescribed by heredity, it is the result of his
own free positing or convention (Gr.: thesis) under the dual
influence of tradition and his social world. So he arrives
at an astonishing variety of ever differing customs (nomos),
and culture in a real sense is created only in this way. The
plurality of historical worlds is the objective equivalent to
man's subjective creativity: each points to the other. As
man is forming culture, he makes history. Philosophical anthropology can, therefore, be only a formal anthropology: it, so-
to-speak, draws the geometric curve on which cultures lie, but
their content of concrete particularity results not from binding universal ideas but from life, which institutes them.

However, man's freedom to shape his form historically also
contains a danger. Man can cling to poor and base forms; he
can strike upon false and destructive forms. Ethics fears
that he could violate the norms; philosophical anthropology
has the deeper fear that the norm itself could be disastrous.
Other beings merely carry out the disposition of their species
naturally, man faces a task and duty -- and therefore he can
fail. So again and again man is said to be a "misconstruction
of nature" -- a view which, along with the appeal for man to
realize his "cosmic responsibility." has become much in vogue
in our time because mankind's self-destruction, in fact the
destruction of all life, by ABC-weapons lies within the range
of possibility. Fearing that man will misuse his freedom,
many philosophical systems prevent him from even becoming aware
that he has it, while repressive social and political systems
obstruct it in fact. So, to avoid risk, these systems try to
bring the historical process to a halt. But the loss of free-

is a deadly handicap. For man learns by trial and error from
his sufferings. His mistakes can lead antithetically to improvement.

Malleability, Man as Shaped by Culture and History, animal educandum, Traditionality, Sociability

Man is the creative being, but he is also the being that
receives and is determined by previous creation; he is the
creature of his own creations. Man, in his creativity, does
not begin with nothing; his present creativity can start at
a higher and more specialized level based upon the creations
of the past. Cultural patterns objectified by man's creative
ability, acquired historically and learned later by others,
replace the animal's inherited instincts. Creativity thus
acquires a counterweight and complement, psychologically in
man's (17) malleability by the formative power of culture and
history, phenotypically manifested in his (18) actually being
shaped by culture and history. By the structures of "objective mind" man is constantly giving form to his own life. Ob-
jectivation is self-construction. This process is an unending
one. Renewing the forms, man renews himself in a regular
cycle of the subjective mind at work historically within him.

Capable of knowledge, man is also (19) in need of learning
(animal educandum). This is reflected biologically, as Portmann showed, in the rhythm of growth. In man the childhood-
phase is absolutely lengthened, expanded forward through
adolescence and even backward by the "extra-uterine year."
(This is counter-balanced by his living longer than most other
animals.) He must stay young for a long time, because he must
stay impressionable as long as possible, i.e., he must be in
a position to acquire and appropriate cultural achievements
and customs from his social environment (though neither trait
need be either cause or effect in this meaningful coordination).
Even the helplessness of the newborn, already observed by the
ancients, turns out to be only the obverse side of malleability, the positive formability of an organic system not constructed by nature in the womb, but shaped in the realm of
the community and of history.

The form in which something is preserved once it has been
discovered is the tradition of a community. Each generation
receives it from the older generation and passes it down to the
next one. Man is thus (20) the traditional being, and (21) the
most social being. For though other animals live in communities,
he must rely on his community more than they do. In the animal
the parents -- despite exceptions -- rear their offspring
rather than educating them: the innate, biologically determined
behavior develops by itself. Only man first learns from the

fellows of his species how he is to look upon things and how
he is to move. Along with this socialness which conveys cultural goods he also has cooperative sociability.

But the vehicle of all sociability is (22) <u>the ability
to symbolize ideas</u>.

Although tradition stems from creative processes and so
is secondary to them, historically it seems to be primary.
Considering itself natural and necessary, and exercising extensive, rigid domination, tradition at first hardly permits
individual, innovative freedom to escape from its power; and
when it does, only by unguarded ways. Only late, among the
Greeks, and still more since the Renaissance, does <u>individu-
ality</u> -- this corollary to properties (4) and (5) -- now free
itself from the "compulsive power" (Parsons) of society and
become strong and independent. In Cynicism, Gnosticism, Ana-
baptism, Storm-and-Stress, Anarchism, Expressionism, and Surrealism, it seeks to cast off institutional bonds completely
and to rely exclusively on its own autonomy. This can never
be completely successful, but it remains religiously, artistically and politically an ancient desire of men: namely, to
liberate spontaneity from form and to be totally self-sufficient. Malleability and creativity, the already created and
the newly creative, history that makes us and history that we
make -- these are the polar forces that struggle or combine
in various historical mixtures. Man not only lives from them
both but he also faces the task of (23) <u>mastering their inter-
play</u> and interrelating them in each respective situation.

Para-anthropologies and Semi-anthropologies

Man, who is incomplete as a natural being, becomes a complete entity only in history. He does this within the various
cultures -- through particular ways of being a man. Man does
not merely live his existence. Rather, he articulates and
elevates it teleologically, establishing a self-image, an image
of man. And generally he is not aware that his image of man
is only one particular modality of human possibilities among
others: he considers it an objective ideal of man as such,
anchored in reality.

The establishment of such particular images of man is
generally also called "anthropology." Therefore philosophical
anthropology is often reproached with reifying and ontologiz-
ing the basis of possibility in man, analogously with inanimate
objects (Jaspers, after Bergson and some trends in the philosophy of history). But this reproach applies only to the contentual anthropology of particular images of man -- for which
another name should be found -- and not to the formal philosophical anthropology of the underlying human structure. Pre-

cisely the crisis of the competing and, consequently, non-
binding self-interpretations of man first moved the question
of man to a deeper philosophical stratum for the Sophists, and
for Herder and Scheler. Philosophical anthropology, like the
philosophy of history, originates in transition periods.

Ethnologists and historians have discovered that many ways
of thinking and believing, formerly considered to be supra-
historical constants by a closed cultural group, are merely
temporary values of a variable function. Yet it is still useful for "historical anthropology" (Nipperdey) to abstract such
typical structures as, for instance, "the Gothic man." Although
not absolute anthropological constants, they have a relative
constancy with respect to particular cultures and epochs. As
a "historical a priori" they always underlie the particular
events and works of a period, which otherwise fascinate the
historian. Thus they are comparatively "meta-historical,"
though the appearance of this is caused only by their prolonged
stability.

When metaphysics distinguishes man spiritually by his
"reason" (as religion does by his "immortal soul"), the result
is not, strictly speaking, philosophical anthropology but only
a particular "view of man." The same is true when the naturalistic reaction subjects man totally to the needs and drives
common to all living organisms. In each case, valuation is
what mainly occurs: one part of man is declared to be more
distinctive than the other. But this part is neither correlated
with the other nor understood in its specific type and function
from the perspective of the whole human being. Descartes did
not correct this error (though he must be credited with destroying anthropomorphisms and so making man more conscious of his
special being); nor did Schopenhauer or Scheler. These three
thinkers merely amalgamated two different images of man. But
the chances for philosophical anthropology are more favorable
in pantheism than in the metaphysics of either spiritualism or
naturalism. Yet, in principle, metaphysical anthropology is
as unsuccessful as metaphysical ethics. Philosophical anthropology is not found in the great metaphysicisns but in the
few men who had the "anthropological perspective": Protagoras,
Diogenes of Apollonia, Pico della Mirandola, Herder, Plessner,
Portmann, Rothacker, Gehlen.

Since the "anthropological turn" of the 1920's, many
science such as psychology, pedagogy, sociology, political
science and theology, have incorporated the anthropological
point-of-view, and so we speak of "psychological anthropology"
("anthropological psychology" would be better), etc. But insofar as the findings of philosophical anthroplogy are not
being applied and extended, as is being done mainly in pedagogy,
the motive for this is primarily the anti-positivistic one of

attempting to reach a "view of the whole" at least within the
respective sciences after the collapse of metaphysical total
interpretations. For these sciences to construct an image of
man from accumulated knowledge is merely a method that happens
to be in vogue. Fundamental anthropological insights are as
far from being gained thereby as in metaphysics. In metaphysics the intention is too broad for anthropology; in the
sciences the material is too specialized. To compensate for
this impediment, various human and social sciences are using
an interdisciplinary approach: for instance, along with
sociology, the two sciences which appropriated the concept of
anthropology during the anti-philosophical wave of the nineteenth century: biological anthropology (including cybernetics)
and ethnological anthropology. (In France and the Anglo-Saxon
countries, philosophical anthropology is little known, because
anthropology is there equated with ethnology.) Such interdisciplinary cooperation may eventually be either systematized
or may turn into a positive advantage Habermas' reproach
against anthropology: that it merely synthesizes the results
of other branches of science.

Properly speaking, it is not anthropology, but merely
appropriation of its ownerless name, when, for example, a
doctor discovers that medicine deals not with sicknesses but
with sick men, and creates a system of "anthropological medicine." And similarly, when historical materialism, blaming
philosophical anthropology for starting with the individual
instead of with history, society and economics (which is why,
among other things, Ernst Bloch was considered a "revisionist"
in East Germany), still approves the subjective factor in a
separate study of man (e.g., the Praxis-group in Yugoslavia,
Baczko and Schaff in Poland, Kolakowski), it might in some
cases, be more accurate to speak of personalism rather than
of anthropology. Still, the starting-point of such Marxist
schools is the genuine anthropological perspective of the
young Marx (the Paris Manuscripts) that man has become alienated from his fellowman and from himself by his own false
organization of the labor process and social product and that
the goal must be to recover "the humanity of man." With
"alienation" Marxist anthropology hits upon a key anthropological concept, except that Marxism frames it too narrowly in
content and hopes to solve the problem too easily. Alienation
is produced in men everywhere by the deep-seated opposition
between institutions and spontaneity, between the immobility
of tradition and the movement of the present; and therefore
alienation is, to a certain extent, inevitable.

Even myths contain natural self-interpretations of man,
of his specific difference and mission. Statements beginning
with the words "Only man..." are frequent: only man feels

shame and knows good and evil (<u>Genesis</u>), must work (<u>Genesis</u>
and Marx), has no natural defensive and aggressive organs
and is naked (Protagoras), has no breeding season, needs a
long period of care as a child, lives to seventy years of age
(the Sophists), has hands (Anaxagoras), walks upright and
speaks (Diogenes of Apollonia and Herder), imitates -- more
than the ape -- (Aristotle), is free to make what he wants
out of himself (Pico della Mirandola), preserves the past
(Nietzsche), aims for the future (Buber), invents Utopias
(Bloch), can commit suicide (Ehrenberg), can laugh and cry
(Plessner), asks questions (Löwith), says no (Hans Kunz),
distinguishes between a picture and the thing itself (Jonas),
celebrates holidays (Bollnow), is most capable of knowledge,
encephalizes, has no firm ecological niche (compared with the
animal), etc. All these observations, even when they claim
to be definitions, are really just components. They give too
much predominance to a single, often secondary detail. They
settle for a statement of fact; or, if they interpret, they
do so too immanently. Philosophical anthropology's appraoch
must be, starting with such an evident characteristic, to
trace it back transcendentally, asking: <u>how must a being be
made for this trait to fulfill a meaningful and necessary
function in it</u>?   Only such a deeper organizational law then
makes it possible to interrelate the partial aspects and
organize them systematically.

Kierkegaard opposed Hegel's hypostatization of philosophical concepts by affirming the specific priority and reality
of our singular existence, which does not fit into such concepts or is overlooked by them. Against science's construction
of a mathematized nature devoid of meaning, in which man becomes
alienated, and also against a naturalistic explanation of
consciousness, Husserl stressed experience as it is presented
to itself and the "world of life" of which it is a part. Thus,
Kierkegaard and Husserl, different as they are, agree in what
they oppose. The two thinkers return to the point-of-departure
left behind and extinguished in the upsurge of reason. Therefore Heidegger was able to adapt Husserl's approach so as to
equate it with a return to Kierkegaard. Along with the exis-
tentialist and the phenomenological approaches, that of philosophical anthropology is a third way to save the subject and
its immediacy among objectivities to which we can no longer
find a motivated relationship and which threaten to overwhelm
us with their immanent objective laws. But the task does not
consist just in adding the forgotten science of man to the
many other sciences or, as the case may be, in saving man from
his misinterpretations of himself. Once philosophical anthropology by retrogression unveils the constitutive point of unity
in "man's world," the various sciences can cast light on one

another. Though Kant, and even Husserl, treats only of the
constitutional operations of the extra-mundane knowing subject, while the living real subject remains, for both
philosophers, an object among other objects, the new approach
of philosophical anthropology opens up a stratum within the
"whole" man, involving action and creation as well as knowledge. This stratum is the "transcendental of transcendentals."

INDEX